# The Ridiculously Simple Guide to Google for Business

A BEGINNERS GUIDE TO GOOGLE APPS, GOOGLE ANALYTICS, AND CHROMEBOOK

SCOTT LA COUNTE

RIDICULOUSLY SIMPLE BOOKS

ANAHEIM, CALIFORNIA

www.RidiculouslySimpleBooks.com

# Table of Contents

**Disclaimer**: *Please note, while every effort has been made to ensure accuracy, this book is not endorsed by Alphabet, Inc. and should be considered unofficial.*

# INTRODUCTION

Chromebooks of the past used to be more of a novelty best suited for casual use. In 2013, Google tried to change this with the Chromebook Pixel—its first higher-end Chromebook. While most saw it as a worthy first effort, it was not largely viewed as ready for primetime.

Google discontinued its first official Chromebook in August of 2016 and announced its successor in October of 2017: The Pixelbook. Everything about the successor proved that Google had learned from previous generation Chromebooks and was ready to seriously compete with the Windows Surface and Macbook.

The hardware alone matched high-end Mac and Windows computers, but the software is where the Chromebook really shines. In addition to Google Assistant, a Siri-like tool for productivity, the computer also is amongst the first Chromebooks to be able to run Android apps—combined with a convertible touchscreen, this means you can leave your tablet at home. For a computer ranks against Windows and Mac, see Appendix A.

Google isn't alone in its attempt to make Chromebooks a serious PC/Mac competitor. There are dozens like it—each with specifications that prove it is a novelty no more. Today it is used in businesses and schools alike to create major projects.

If you've used any computer, then a Chromebook will be easy enough to use as soon as you open it up for the first time. If you really want to take advantage of all the features and be as productive as possible, then this guide will help. Let's get started!

Better comparison of how the

# [1]

# TELL ME THE BASICS AND KEEP IT RIDICULOUSLY SIMPLE

This chapter will cover:

- What's Chrome OS
- The Keyboard

## A WORD (OR PARAGRAPH OR TWO) ABOUT CHROME OS

For years, Google has taken what you could call the "Apple approach" to computers and tablets. Computers ran Chrome and tablets ran Android (e.g. iPads run iOS and MacBooks run MacOS). Like iPads and Macbooks, there were similarities between Android tablets and Chrome computers. But there were also differences.

The Pixel Slate breaks this tradition by running the same operating system (OS) that you are familiar with if you have a Chromebook. What's more, newer Chromebooks can also download Android apps. That means if there's an app you love on your phone, you can use it on your computer as well.

## THE KEYBOARD

The layout of the keyboard isn't completely different from other computers, but there are a few keys you might not be familiar with. The list below is an overview of those keys. Because there are so many different Chromebook models, this list will vary, so the following is just a reference.

| | |
|---|---|
|  | Searches all the apps installed on your computer as well as the web. This button is where the Caps Lock key normally is—to use Caps Lock, hit this button and the Alt key at the same time. |
|  | Launches the Google Assistant (Google's version of Siri). |

| | |
|---|---|
|  | Goes to the previous page in your browser history. |
|  | Reloads your current page. |
|  | This puts your current application in full screen mode; all the tabs and the launcher will be hidden. |
|  | Shows all windows in Overview mode. |
|  | Dim the screen. (F5) |
|  | Make the screen brighter. (F6) |
|  | Play/pause (F7) |
|  | Mute (F8) |
|  | Lower the volume. (F9) |
|  | Raise the volume. (F10) |
|  | Open your status area (where your account picture appears). |

# [2]

# All About Chrome OS

This chapter will cover:

- User accounts
- Settings overview

Chrome OS is a very close relative of Google's Internet browser, Google Chrome. As the owner of a Chromebook, you'll quickly see that Chrome is about to become a very big part of your life. This is a good thing; it's a fast, easy-to-use web browser with all kinds of features and seemingly unlimited potential for enhancement thanks to apps and extensions available in the Chrome Web Store. The Chrome browser means so much more than just web browsing in Chrome OS though, due to the fact that almost every app you run in Chrome OS runs inside a Chrome browser window. Don't worry if that sounds bizarre at first—you'll get the hang of it quickly and we'll walk you through everything you need to know!

The Chrome Web Store contains products that are similar enough to major desktop applications that you'll hardly be able to tell the difference. As a bonus, many of them are completely free (and if you've ever shelled out for Photoshop, we know that's going to come as a relief!).

Since most of Chromebook's functionality happens within a browser, Chromebook users can get to the majority of their Chromebook work from any computer with the free Google Chrome browser installed. Google's cloud storage system—Google Drive—is baked into Chrome OS and steadily saves your work as you go. As long as you're connected to wi-fi, if catastrophe strikes your physical Chromebook, your important files and documents are safe and sound in the cloud.

If you're scratching your head at this point, don't worry. Chromebook is easy to use, and the best way to understand it is to turn the thing on, roll up your sleeves, and dive right in. And we're going to do just that in the next chapter!

## USER ACCOUNTS

One of the best features about any Chromebook is the ability to add user accounts; unlike other computers, you can take all of your settings with you. So let's say you have a Chromebook, and log in to another Chromebook. All of your apps, settings, customizations are there waiting for you. It's almost like you are using your personal computer even though you are logged in as a guest. This also means when you get another computer in the future, it's very simple to set up. Just log in and you are done!

Having multiple accounts also makes it very easy to share a computer in your household. From the login screen, you can either add a user or log in as a guest. Anyone who has a Google account (if you have Gmail then you have one—if you don't have Gmail you might have one without knowing it, as this is what many businesses use), can set up an account on your computer. Don't worry: this won't give other users access to any of your files or personal settings.

There is only one important thing to remember with regard to user accounts: set up the device owner first! If you use another account to sign into the computer for the first time, then that's the device owner and the person who will have administrator rights that other users won't have. There's no way to transfer ownership to another user, so you would have to reset your computer if that happens.

## SETTINGS OVERVIEW

We'll discuss the settings a little further throughout this book, but there are a few settings you'll want to know about right now.

### User Accounts

If you want to disable people from being able to log in to your settings, then log in to your account, click on your user profile image (bottom right corner of the screen), then click the settings button:

From here, you'll be taken to a browser window with a list of some of the most common settings. Scroll to the bottom of the list and click the button labeled "Manage Other Users." By default, everything is toggled on; click it once to toggle it off. Hit the back button and it saves your settings automatically.

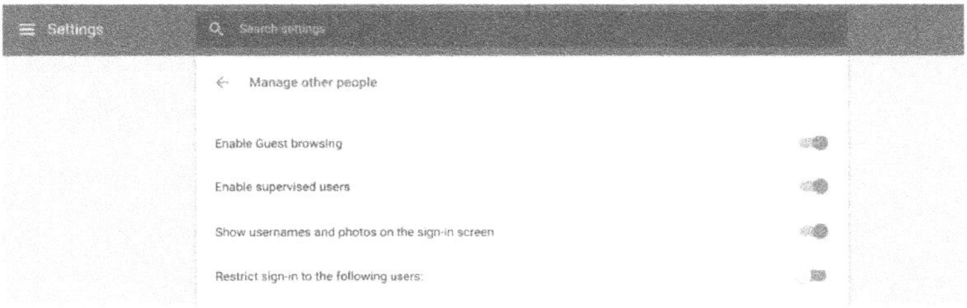


## Keyboard Settings

The location of the Alt key on a computer keyboard is what a Mac user might use as the Command key. There are several keys like this. You can either retrain your mind or you can go into the keyboard settings and change the shortcuts around a little. In the settings you can also change things like the language.

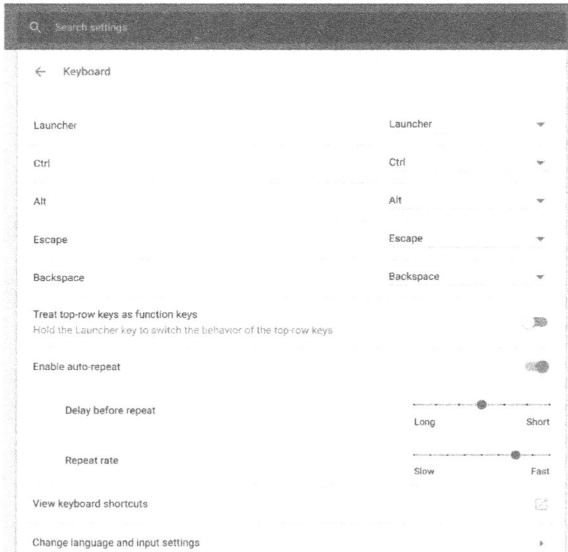


## Touchpad Settings

Mac users will be a little annoyed with scrolling on their new computer! That's because the scrolling on an Apple device is the opposite of scrolling on the Chromebook! Again, you can either retrain your mind or you can just change the setting. "Australian" is the scrolling you will want. Another setting you will probably want to change is the Touchpad speed; to some users, it might feel a little laggy. It's an easy fix. Just slide the Touchpad speed button to the right for a faster scroll.

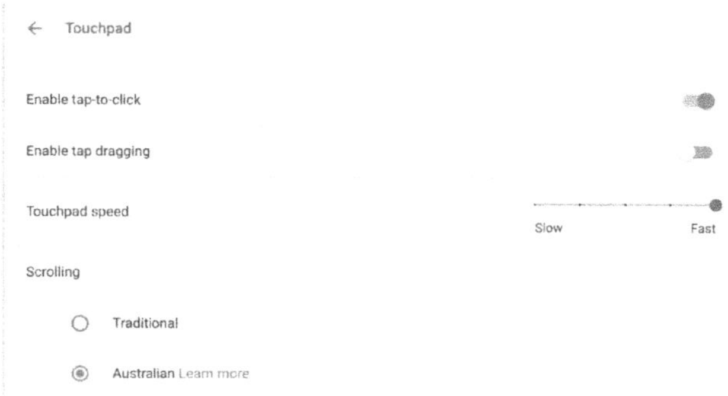
Touchpad
Enable tap-to-click
Enable tap dragging
Touchpad speed
Slow
Fast
Scrolling
Traditional
Australian Learn more

# [3] Getting Around the OS

This chapter will cover:

- The Desktop
- Launcher and Chrome Shelf
- Chrome Windows
- Files and Google Drive
- Offline Mode

Google's OS seems much like a marriage between Windows OS and Mac OS, and that's a good thing, because with very little instruction, everything will start feeling natural. In this section, you'll get a crash course in the basic features of the OS and where things are located.

## DESKTOP

Your desktop takes up the bulk of the screen. It includes a desktop wallpaper image, which can be customized, and you can also store files and shortcuts here for easy access, just like other desktops. Chances are, however, you'll probably find yourself not making much use of the Desktop space. Chrome's intuitive interface makes it easier just to store everything in your Google Drive. I've used Chrome OS for many years, and I find the desktop is usually just a place to put a pretty picture.

## THE LAUNCHER AND CHROME SHELF

The Launcher button is similar to the Start button on a Windows computer—only a bit simpler. Clicking on the Launcher button will reveal every app associated with your Google account. This apps menu does extend to the right, and you may need to use the horizontal page indicator icons at the bottom of the menu to move from screen to screen.

Next to the Apps button, you'll find your Chrome "shelf." You might be used to thinking of this area as a taskbar or dock, but in Chrome, it's called the shelf. The shelf contains shortcuts to your favorite apps and documents, and lets you know what's currently running. In the screenshot above, you can see that we're currently running the Chrome browser, gmail, the app HipChat, and the Files app, due to the small gray dot under those icons.

To the far right (where your photo is) is the Systems Tray Menu; this is where you'll see settings, apps that have updated, and battery life.

## CHROME WINDOWS

Chrome is almost entirely browser based; there are a few more traditional looking apps (like Google Hangouts), but most of the apps you see on your Chrome Shelf are more like shortcuts to a web page. I'll explain the apps that come with the Chromebook and how to get additional ones later in this book.

## FILES AND GOOGLE DRIVE

Every computer has "local" storage—which is all the stuff (files, photos, documents) that are stored directly on the computer; Windows computers have File/System Explorer; Mac Computers have Finder; and Chrome computers have Files. Chrome computers have one extra storage drive: Google Drive. Google Drive is cloud-based, which means whatever you store there will be available on the Internet (privately unless you make it public). This makes it easy to store a file that you want to use on another computer. The Files app shows you both local files (on your computer) and cloud files (stored online). If you were to connect a USB storage device like a flash drive or an external hard drive, you'd see that in Files as well.

Keep in mind that Google Drive is not unlimited storage; your Google account has 15GB of free storage. After that, it's $1.99 a month and up. It's a very inexpensive solution, and one you should consider for backing up files you store on your computer. Also, buying any new Chromebook may mean you are qualified for free storage. You can see Google's current offerings here: https://www.google.com/chromebook/offers/

## OFFLINE

The Chromebook is designed to be used online. That said, the Internet is not required. Even Google's suite of online apps (Docs, Sheets, and Slides) can be used offline. If you plan to work on a Google Doc file (or Sheets/Slides) make sure you move it into the offline folder before logging off.

# [4]

# ALL ABOUT CHROME OS

This chapter will cover:

- Anatomy of the Chrome Window
- Tabs and Windows
- Incognito
- Bookmarks
- History
- Passwords
- Autofill
- Chrome Extensions
- Web Store and Apps
- Installing and Managing Chrome Content

## THE CHROME BROWSER

The web browser that comes standard with your Chromebook is, for all intents and purposes, the very same version of Chrome that's available for Windows, OSX, and Linux computers. So if you're already using Chrome on another device, then there's very little learning curve. One thing you'll love right away is all of your bookmarks and settings will be carried over from one device to the next. There are still a few things you'll want to know about, so I'll cover them here.

You'll notice that opening Chrome doesn't automatically put the browser into full-screen mode. You can resize Chrome window two different ways—by pressing the green maximize button or by tapping the three dots in the top right corner and then tapping the full-screen button next to the zoom options.

If you're using Chrome on other devices, you'll be able to access all of your currently open pages and bookmarks by clicking "Other Devices," (click the three dots, hover over "history," and scroll to the bottom of the list). If you've accidentally closed a web page, Chrome will save it for a period of time under the "Recently Closed" menu.

## ANATOMY OF A GOOGLE CHROME WINDOW

Chrome stays out of your way, for the most part. The vast majority of a Chrome window is reserved for content—whether it's a web page, a Google Docs document, a game, or any other Chrome app.

Everything you need to manage a Chrome window is located at the top of the page. At the top right corner, you'll see the Back, Forward and Refresh buttons. These are used to navigate back or forward through your recent screen views and to reload a page. They match up with the three keys on the keyboard directly to the right of the ESC key on the top row.

In the center of the top part of the screen, you'll see the address/search bar, known as the Chrome "omnibox." Type a website's address (google.com, facebook.com) here to go directly to that site. You can also use this area as a search bar ("kittens," "DIY birdhouse," etc.).

At the right end of the omnibox, you'll see a star. Click that star to bookmark the web page (we'll go into more detail on this process in just a second).

Finally, at the far top right corner, you'll see the Chrome menu button. Here you'll find everything else you need to manage a Chrome window. We'll refer to this button pretty often throughout this guide!

## TABS AND WINDOWS

There are two viewing units to be aware of in Chrome—tabs and windows. Tabs open inside one window, as pictured below. You can open a new tab by pressing CTRL+T (remember: t for tab), by right-clicking the Chrome icon in the shelf, or by clicking 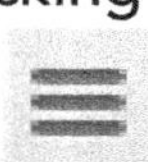 > New Tab.

Opening a page in a new window, on the other hand, opens a completely separate frame (which can then be populated with a new group of tabs, if you like). You can open new windows by pressing CTRL+N (N for new), by right-clicking the Chrome icon on the shelf, or by clicking  > New Window.

When tabs were first introduced, they streamlined the laborious process of switching between several windows while browsing the Internet. As a result, many users now associate tabs with easier workflow. However, on a Chromebook, it's often easier to switch between windows than between tabs, thanks to the Window Switch key on the top row. Pressing the Window Switch key reveals every open window, giving you the title and a visual preview of each one. Keep this in mind when you're formulating your workflow windows/tabs strategy!

## BROWSING INCOGNITO

If you're shopping for birthday presents, or doing anything else that you don't want enshrined in your search history, Incognito is the browsing mode for you. Pages you view while in an Incognito tab won't be saved in your history. Search terms won't resurface in your search history, and website cookies won't be stored on your computer. However, if you download or bookmark anything, remember that it will be retained on your system.

To open an Incognito tab in Chrome, press CTRL+SHIFT+N, right-click the Chrome icon on the shelf, or click 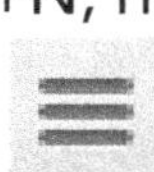 > New Window. You can tell at a glance which windows are Incognito by looking for the shadowy figure in sunglasses peeking from behind the top left corner.

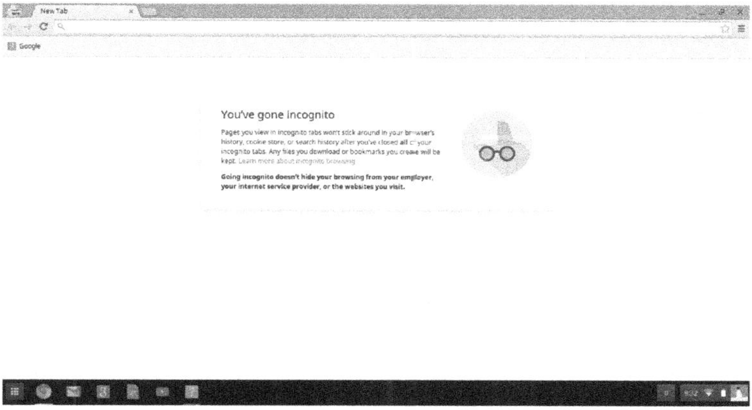


## BOOKMARKS

Bookmarks are a handy way to organize your favorite sites for fast access later on. There are a few different ways to bookmark a site. You can click the Star outline in the omnibox, as previously discussed, or you can press CTRL+D. You can also navigate to  > Bookmarks > Bookmark this page.

By default, your bookmarks are stored in the bookmarks bar, which is not visible by default. The bookmarks bar, when enabled, appears underneath the omnibox. To display the bookmarks bar, click  > Bookmarks > Show bookmarks bar, or press

CTRL+SHIFT+B. To hide it, follow the same path or use the same keyboard shortcut.

If you don't like the automatic wording for each bookmark, you can easily edit it, either when adding the bookmark or later by managing your bookmarks. To manage bookmarks, right-click the bookmark and then click Edit (or Delete, or whatever you need to do). Then click  > Bookmarks > Bookmark Manager, or press CTRL+SHIFT+O. Inside the bookmark manager, you can right-click bookmarks to edit them, as pictured below. You can also rearrange the order of your bookmarks either in the Bookmark Manager or by dragging them around on the bookmarks bar itself. The most common edit we make for bookmarks is shortening the name in order to fit as many as possible in our bookmarks bar!

Of course, you may eventually run out of room in the bookmarks bar. If this happens, a double arrow will appear at the end of the bookmark bar. Clicking the arrow will reveal the rest of your bookmarks. This may be enough for you, but if you'd like a better way of managing large numbers of bookmarks, we recommend organizing your bookmarks into folders. To do this, open the Bookmark Manager (CTRL+SHIFT+O). Click the Folders heading on the left, and then click Add folder.

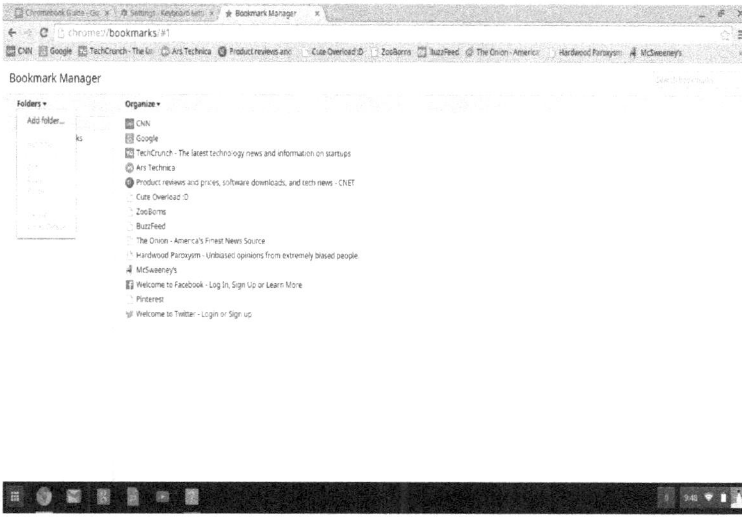


You can add as many folders as you like. Once the folders are added, you can drag your bookmarks into them in the Bookmarks Manager. You can either display your folders on the bookmarks bar or organize them in the Other Bookmarks folder, which you can get to at  > Bookmarks.

Don't forget that in Chrome OS, practically everything you look at is going to be a web page. This means that you can set up bookmarks for Google Docs documents, Google Slides presentations, games, etc. It's a great way to organize a project as well as a way to organize your favorite websites.

## RECENT AND HISTORY

Chrome stores your recently viewed pages and full browsing history to make it easy to get back to places you've already been. You can see your recently closed tabs at 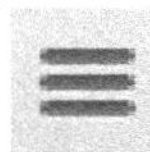 > Recent. This is a lifesaver if you accidentally close a tab!

You'll find your full browsing history at  > History or by pressing CTRL+H (H for history). To clear your history at any time, visit your History and then click Clear browsing data. You can either delete history from the past hour, day, week, month, or, as Google so poetically phrases it, the beginning of time. You can also specify what kind of history you want to delete. For example, you can delete your list of recently visited sites, but retain any passwords you've saved in Chrome.

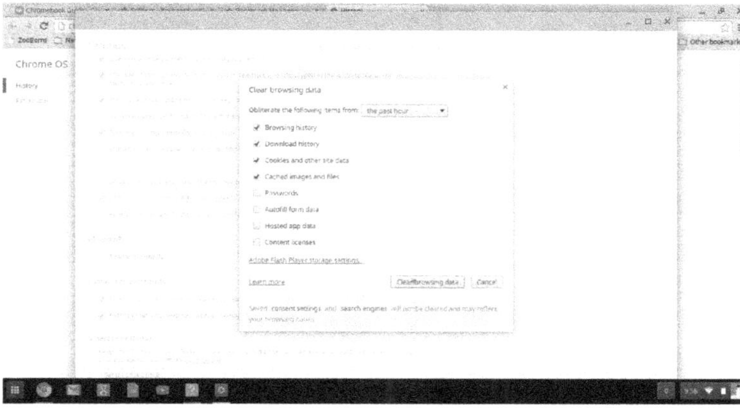


## GOOGLE CHROME AND YOUR GOOGLE ACCOUNT

When you set up a new Chromebook, your system will automatically sign you in to the Google Chrome browser. You can sign into Chrome from other computers as well, though. Signing in to Chrome will allow you to see your browsing history from other Chrome sessions on other computers, your stored passwords, your extensions, and more. To sign into Chrome, click Sign in at the top right corner of a Chrome browser window.

## STORED PASSWORDS

Google Chrome will offer to remember passwords for you whenever you enter them into a website. A popup box will ask you if you want to save the password. You can say Nope to dismiss the box once, or you can click the arrow next to Nope for the Never for this site option.

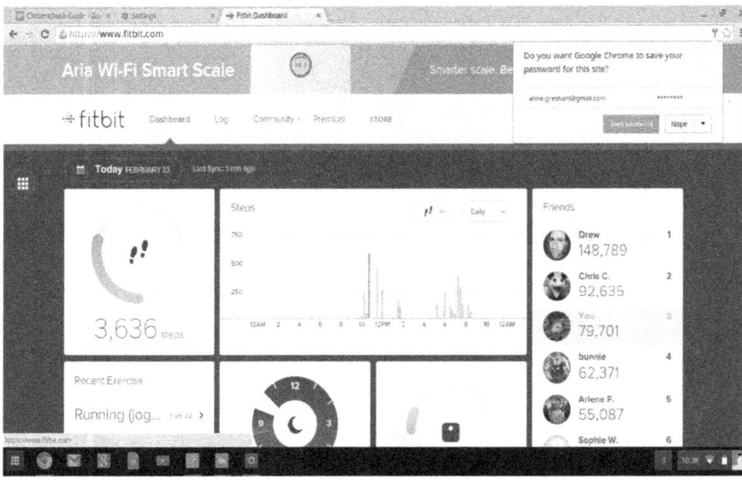


Any passwords you save on your Chromebook or Slate will actually be associated with your Google account. This means that you can use them any time you sign into Chrome, on any computer (though we recommend avoiding signing in on public computers, just to be safe).

If you need to manage your stored passwords, visit  > Settings. At the bottom of the Settings screen, click Show advanced settings. Scroll down until you see the Passwords and Forms heading. Underneath it, click Manage passwords. Here, you can edit or delete your stored passwords. You can also deselect Offer to save your web passwords if you don't want Chrome to store any passwords for you.

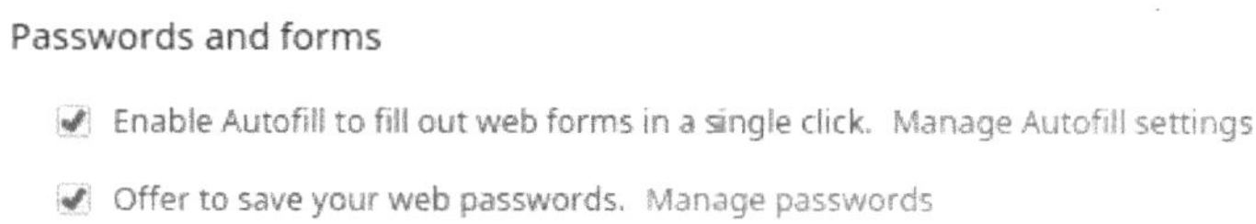


## FORM AUTOFILL

Form Autofill handles forms that you repeatedly fill in. It can remember your name, address, phone number, email address, etc. It's useful for repeated data entry, but you may occasionally need to manage your Autofill settings if you move or change your phone number. To do so, visit Settings > Passwords and forms and click Manage Autofill settings.

## CHROME EXTENSIONS

Extensions extend Chrome's functionality in all kinds of ways, and the enormous range of free extensions to choose from is a huge part of what makes Google Chrome so great. We'll share some of our favorites later in Part 5, and you can explore on your own in the Web Store, which we'll cover next.

## THE CHROME WEB STORE

You'll want to get to know the Web Store sooner rather than later, since it's where you'll find new apps and extensions for your Chromebook. Fortunately, this "Store" has an enormous free section in it, so tricking out your Chromebook won't necessarily break the bank!

You'll find the Web Store by clicking the Apps button in the lower left corner. If you're an Android user, be aware that the Chrome Web Store isn't exactly the same thing as the Google Play Store, though there's a lot of duplicated content.

There are three big categories in the Store—apps, extensions, and themes. You can choose which broad category you're interested in at the top of the Web Store navigation panel on the left.

Before jumping in, it's worth noting here a very big feature added to both the Chromebook and all new Chromebooks: The Android store!

Why is that important? All those apps that you've already downloaded on your Android tablet or phone can now be downloaded on your computer. It also turns your Chromebook into a tablet. You can download any app from the Play Store and it will install on your computer (play.google.com).

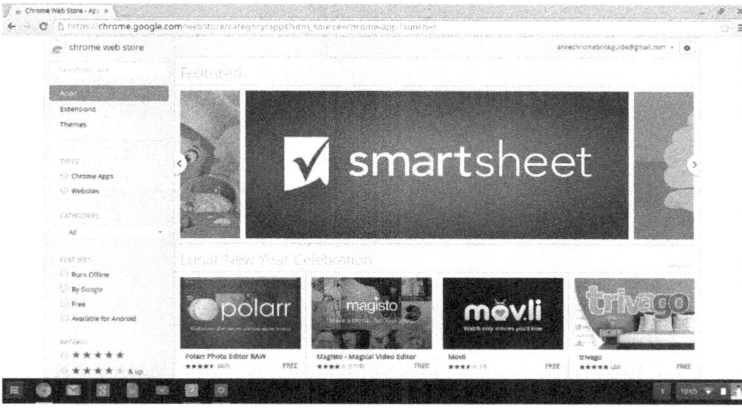


APPS

The apps section of the store contains two types of apps—Chrome apps and website apps. Website "apps" are basically bookmarks. These are websites that you can visit anywhere from any computer, generally with any browser. They're usually free. Chrome apps, on the other hand, make modifications to your Chrome browser in order to function. You will need to be running Chrome in order to use them, and they will need to be installed on the copy of Chrome you're using. This distinction is largely academic for most users. Whether an app is a web app or a Chrome app, adding it to your Chromebook will mean that it appears in your Apps button menu and that it can be pinned to your shelf.

Store apps can be browsed by category, using the dropdown menu under Categories in the left menu. You can also search by feature, like "runs offline" (meaning that the app doesn't require an Internet connection to function), by Google, Free, and Available for Android (very useful if you want to keep your Chromebook and Android smartphone or tablet closely in sync). Finally, you can also sort by the average star rating.

## EXTENSIONS

Unlike apps, extensions allow you to do more with every page you visit in Chrome. Extensions let you do more with the Chrome browser, and there are all kinds of possibilities out there. There are extensions that convert currency on webpages for you, help you pin images to your Pinterest boards, generate secure passwords, or help you manage your online privacy.

Like apps, extensions can be narrowed down by category, special features (including Free), and star rating.

## THEMES

Themes are similar to desktop wallpaper, but instead of decorating your desktop, they decorate the Chrome window itself. Themes change the appearance of an empty window, typically by showing an image or pattern, and altering the color of the outer edges of the window. In the example below, we've enabled a dark theme.

We freely admit that while apps and extensions make us salivate, we're not quite as enamored with Chrome theming. We're usually in too much of a hurry to get to our websites, content, and apps to appreciate them. Your mileage may vary, though, and it's not a bad idea to browse some of the free themes in the Store to see if any strike your fancy.

## INSTALLING NEW CHROME CONTENT

Installing a new app, extension, or theme is incredibly simple, especially if it's free. To install free content, simply click the FREE text from a search result, and then click the Add to Chrome button that appears on the content's information screen.

If an app, extension, or theme costs money, click the Buy for... button.

Then click Add. At this point, if you haven't already set up Google Wallet, you'll be prompted to do so. Google Wallet is simply Google's credit card manager. Add a payment method as prompted, and Google will save that information for later. You can add more than one payment method if you prefer. From there, confirm the purchase, and your new paid app, extension, or theme will be installed for you.

## MANAGING APPS, EXTENSIONS AND THEMES

After you've started amassing a library of apps, extensions and themes, you may occasionally need to temporarily disable or delete them. You can manage your apps by clicking the Apps button and then right-clicking the app you'd like to delete or alter.

Extensions are a little more complicated. You can find your extensions under ☰ > More Tools > Extensions, or under ☰ > History (alternately, press CTRL+H). On the History screen, click Extensions on the left. This will display a list of every installed extension on your system.

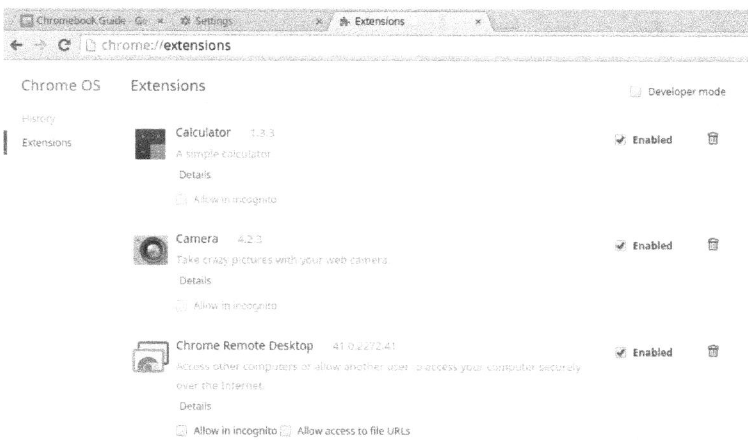


Note that you can disable extensions by deselecting the Enabled checkbox (a good temporary measure), or you can click the trashcan icon to permanently delete something.

# [5]

# There's a Pre-Installed App for That

This chapter will cover:

- Google Docs, Sheets, Slides
- Scratchpad
- Google+ Hangouts
- Gmail
- YouTube
- Calculator
- Camera
- Chrome Remote Desktop
- Photos

- Keep
- Google Maps and Google My Maps
- Google Forms
- Drawings
- Play Music, Play Books, and Play Movies
- Google Calendar
- Google Play
-

Just like any computer, your Chromebook will have apps installed right out of the box. Here is an overview and what they're good for.

GOOGLE DOCS

Google Docs, briefly, is Google's version of Microsoft Word or Apple Pages. You can edit a document just like you would in any other processor, but it's all online and synced automatically, which means it's very difficult to lose anything. You can also share documents and collaborate in real time.

Docs really shines through its connection to Google Drive. Anything you start in Google Docs is automatically saved in your Google Drive account—no need to worry about losing work through power failures, device catastrophes, or really just about any other scenario. Changes are saved as you go, and so are versions, so it's easy to revert to an earlier stage of a draft if you need to.

The main Docs menu consists of File, Edit, Insert, Format, Tools, Table, Add-ons, and Help. Each of these menu items contains a dropdown menu full of features. The full power of Docs is beyond the scope of this guide, but we'll show you some of the basics.

### Starting a New Google Doc

To start a new document, simply open Docs for the first time, or click File > New to open a new document. Notice that Google Docs > File > New will also let you start new Sheets, Slides, Drawings, or Forms projects as well.

### Saving a Google Doc

Google Docs saves everything as you go so you'll rarely need to save manually. You can find the status of your file to the right of the menu if you're concerned. Google Docs does save your work offline as well, so if you're not connected to Drive, you won't lose your work and you can verify that Chromebook has saved it for you.

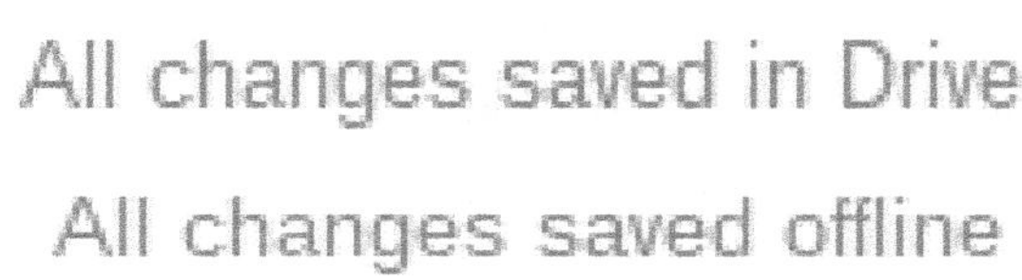

## Formatting a Google Doc

You'll find all the standard text editing options you'd expect in the top menu area, including font size, typeface, bold, italic, underline, text color, hyperlinks, and text alignment. If that doesn't cover you, though, you'll also find spacing, lists, indent control, and format clearing under More.

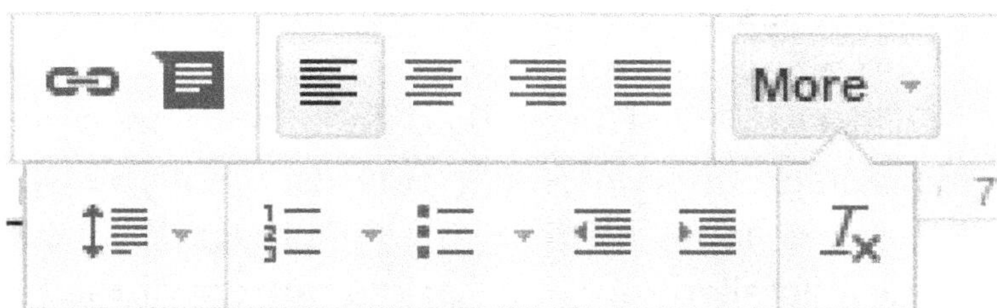


## Collaborating Using Google Docs

Google Docs is hands-down one of the easiest ways to work on a group document. To invite people to share your Doc, click the blue Share button in the top right corner (note that hovering over this button will also give you the current shared status of your Doc).

You can add existing Google contacts by entering their names, or you can invite anyone through their email address. Note that your collaborators will need to set up a free Google Account to use Google Drive. You can choose the level of access you want collaborators to have—they can edit, comment, or merely view your shared document.

You can remove them at any time by using the Share button again.

When two or more people are editing a document at the same time, you'll be able to see that person's cursor position and watch edits in real time. If you're concerned about losing work, remember that Google Docs saves version history for you, so it's easy to revert if you need to. Click File > See revision history (or press CTRL+ALT+SHIFT+G). By default, revisions are shown grouped into daily periods, but if you want to see changes made by the minute, click "Show more detailed revisions" at the bottom of the revisions panel. You can see which collaborator made each change in a group document. Of course, the slightly less elegant Undo and Redo functions are always available as well!

Revision history
Today, 4:32 PM
Anne C
March 1, 4:08 PM
Anne C
February 28, 10:25 PM
Anne C
February 28, 7:51 PM
Anne C
February 24, 10:21 PM
Anne C
February 23, 10:53 PM
Anne C
February 23, 8:18 PM
Anne C
February 22, 6:15 PM
Anne C
February 21, 8:38 PM
Anne C
Show changes
Show more detailed revisions

### Dealing with Other File Formats

Fortunately, you can edit Microsoft Office files in Google apps like Google Docs. Just open the file and edit away. Google Docs can also open files with .ODT, .DOT, .HTML, and .TXT file extensions, though there's always a chance that the original formatting may not survive the conversion entirely intact.

### Add-ons

Most of the Google productivity apps include the ability to add on functionality, typically designed by third party developers. You can search for add-ons by clicking the Add-ons menu item at the top of the screen. Click Get add-ons to start searching for the additional functions you need. For example, in Docs, you can install add-ons that reveal the document's structure in a table of contents presentation in the sidebar. There's even a Sudoku add-on for Sheets!

## GOOGLE SHEETS

Google Sheets is Google's answer to Microsoft Excel. If you're familiar with any spreadsheet program, you should feel pretty at home in Sheets. Like almost every other spreadsheet program, Google Sheets will do all the heavy lifting for you when it comes to calculations. Entering formulas in

Google Sheets is reasonably similar to Excel. Just type = at the beginning of a cell and then fill in your formula. Of course, there are some minor syntactical differences you'll need to get the hang of, but it's nothing too difficult. Sheets will help you build your formulas by giving you input examples, and you can create charts from your data and define custom sorting and filtering rules.

## GOOGLE SLIDES

Google Slides is a presentation app, like Microsoft PowerPoint. Slides includes several prepackaged presentation themes to get you started, or you can begin with a blank slate. Your completed presentation can be downloaded as a PowerPoint, PDF, image, scalable vector graphic or plain text file, making Slides presentations compatible with just about any environment. There's also a very useful "Publish to the web" feature available in the File menu that will generate a public URL that you can share with your colleagues and/or the entire world. You can also embed Slides presentations in web pages or blog posts. To do this go to File and Publish to the Web.

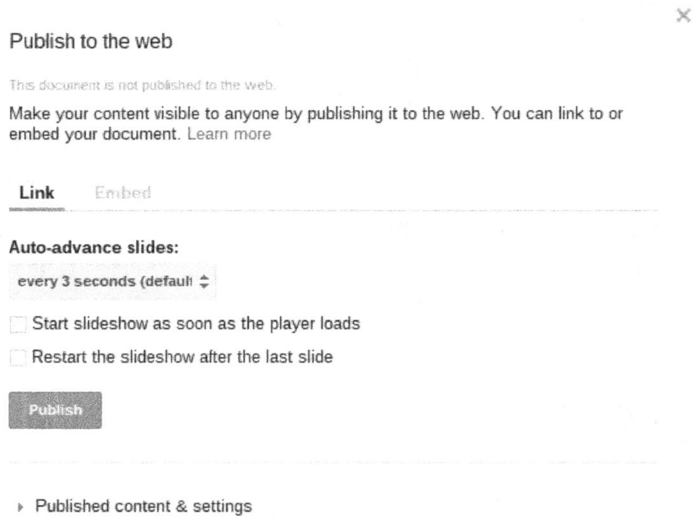


## SCRATCHPAD

Scratchpad is meant for small, simple document creation (like Notes on Mac or Notepad on Windows). Things like grocery and to-do lists that don't necessarily need advanced formatting or structure for later publishing work well with Scratchpad.

## GOOGLE+ AND HANGOUTS

Google+ began life as Google's attempt at a social network. It was their answer to Facebook and Twitter. If you are reading this wondering what is Google+ then you probably can tell they didn't quite accomplish everything they hoped. It will, in fact, be discontinued shortly.

Google+ has been out for over six years, which may surprise you. It certainly isn't Google's most widely used product, but it has grown in popularity since it came out and has evolved a lot. Sharing photos, videos, and more are made possible through the network. For businesses, the most important feature is Hangouts—a Skype-like service that lets you have group video calls and share screens.

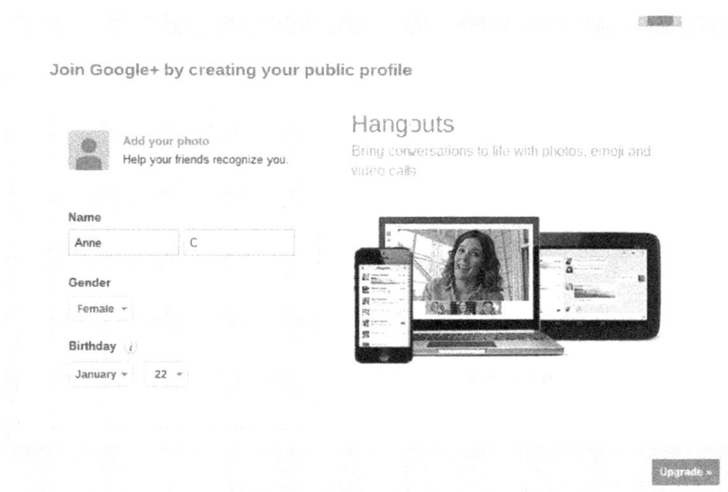


To sign up for Google+, you'll first need to enter your name, gender, and birthday. Next, Google+ will suggest people you may know, based on any existing Gmail contacts you've entered. Use the Add button to add them to your circles (in Google+ you'll organize your contacts into circles, like friends, college buddies, frenemies, etc.).

Next, Google+ will suggest some topics for you to follow that you might be interested in. Finally, you'll be able to update your profile by adding a photo and some additional personal details. Then you'll be all set to start using Google+!

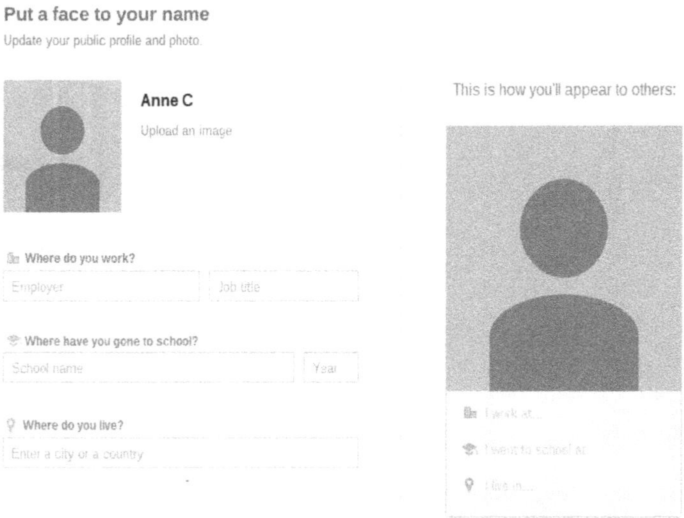

Inside the Google+ app, there are a few things to be aware of. In the top left corner, you'll see a button labeled Home. Click this button to expand the Google+ menu.

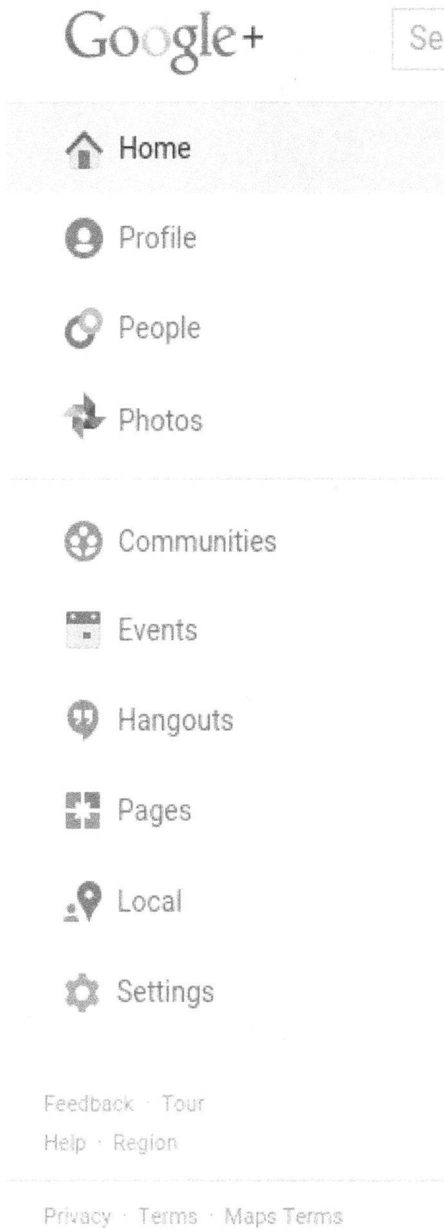
Google+
Se
Home
Profile
People
Photos
Communities
Events
Hangouts
Pages
Local
Settings
Feedback · Tour
Help · Region
Privacy · Terms · Maps Terms

This menu should be familiar to Facebook users. You'll see options to get to your profile and edit it if necessary, as well as links to the people you follow and the photos you've posted. You'll also find Communities, Events, Hangouts, Pages, Local info, and Settings.

## Posting in Google+

You can post various items in Google+, just like Facebook. You can add text, photos, links, videos, events (which you can invite your contacts to, of course), and polls.

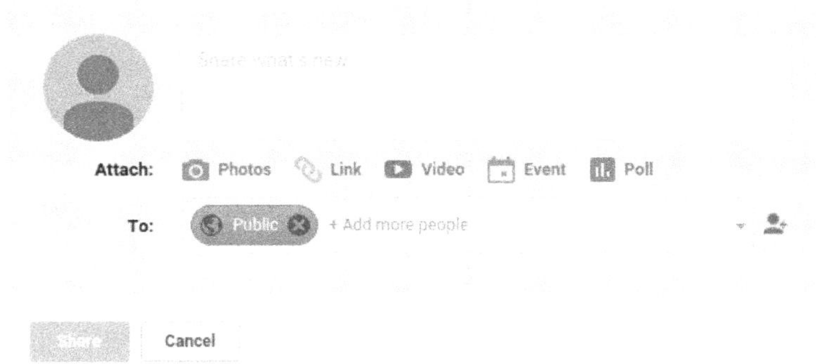


Google+ posts can be shared publicly, with certain people, or Google+ circles using the To: field in the post dialog box.

### Hangouts

Without a doubt, Hangouts is the most successful aspect of Google+. It's like everything that was great about a late 1990s chat room combined with the power of Skype-like services. A Hangout generates a URL. Participants can use that link to leave and come back to a Hangout at any time, just like a chat room.

You can start a Hangout from inside Google+ or Gmail, or you can use the dedicated Hangouts app. To start a Hangout, you'll enter friends' names (if they're contacts in Google+) or email addresses (if they're not). You can also add entire Google+ circles or make a Hangout open to the entire public. If you'd rather have a private call, though, just add a single name.

Hangouts takes advantage of your Chromebook's built-in microphone and camera, just like Skype or FaceTime. It's easy to use and, as long as you have a free wi-fi connection, completely free.

## GMAIL

Gmail is Google's proprietary email client, and we think it's the best of the bunch when it comes to web email hosts. If you've set up a new Google account for your Chromebook, then your Gmail address is your username plus @gmail.com. If you need to check your Gmail account from another computer, visit gmail.com and enter your Google Account username and password to sign in. You can open Gmail in any browser, like Internet Explorer or Firefox.

Opening the Gmail app on your Chromebook will take you straight to your Gmail inbox.

Gmail presorts your mail into three tabs—Primary, Social, and Promotions. This is a great way to tame an unruly inbox. All your Facebook notifications show up under Social, and those daily emails from that store you went to once will appear under Promotions, helping you focus on the email you most likely really want to read.

Of course, occasional mistakes will happen. If a message appears under the wrong tab, just drag it to the tab that you'd like future messages from that sender to appear under.

You'll notice the first time you open Gmail that the Chromebook Gmail app guides you through some basic setup tasks that will help you really get to know Gmail, if you don't already. You can choose a theme, import contacts, work through a tutorial, install Gmail on a mobile phone, and add a new profile image. Take some time and work through these steps—you'll be glad you did and it makes for a great introduction to Gmail.

### Sending Email in Gmail

To start a new email message, open Gmail and click the red Compose button in the left menu.

This brings up the Compose pop-up screen, which allows you to compose your email while keeping an eye on your inbox. Enter the email address of your recipient in the To field and the subject of your email in the Subject field. If you need to add a CC (Carbon Copy, which is visible to other recipients) or BCC (Blind Carbon Copy—invisible to other recipients) recipient, click the gray Cc Bcc text in the top right corner of the New Message window. Then, of course, your message goes in the big blank area. When you're finished writing, click the blue Send button in the lower left corner of the New Message window to send your email.

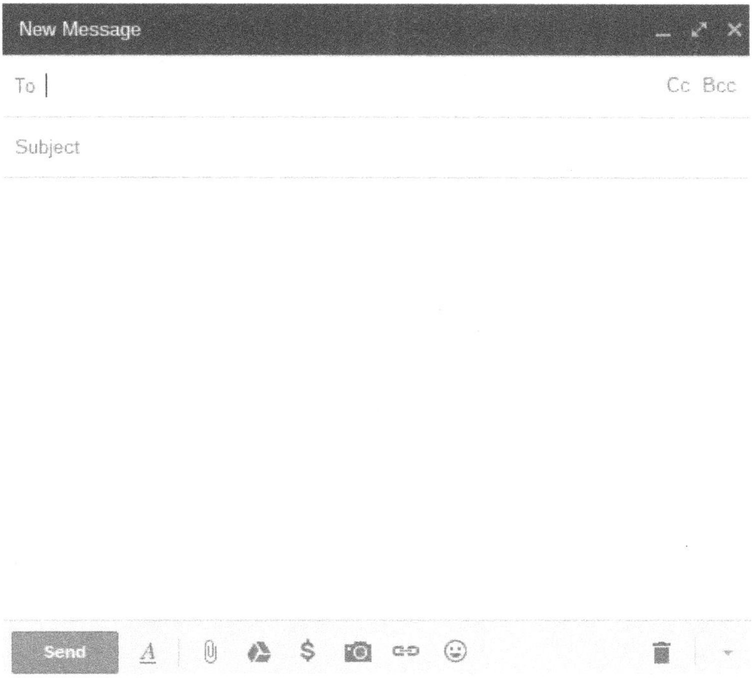


Gmail also makes it easy to format your email and add attachments and multimedia. Next to the Send button, the A icon will display options for formatting text (bold, italics, font choice, etc.). Next, the paper clip icon opens up a dialog box that lets you browse your Chromebook for files to attach to your message, like PDFs, Google Docs documents, etc. If you have a file in Drive that you'd like to insert, use the Drive icon instead of the paper clip. You can use the $ icon as a sort of Google version of PayPal, if you have a credit card or bank account set up in your Google account. The camera icon lets you add images to your email—either as attachments or inside the email itself. Next, the chain link icon lets you add links to your email. If you type a full website address, like www.google.com, Gmail will recognize the link and will send it as such Finally, you can insert Google emoticons using the smiley face icon.

Gmail saves draft messages for you automatically. If you accidentally close a message you're working on, you'll find it safe and sound in your Drafts folder on the left. However, if you decide you don't want to save a draft message, use the trashcan icon in the lower right corner of the New Message window to delete it.

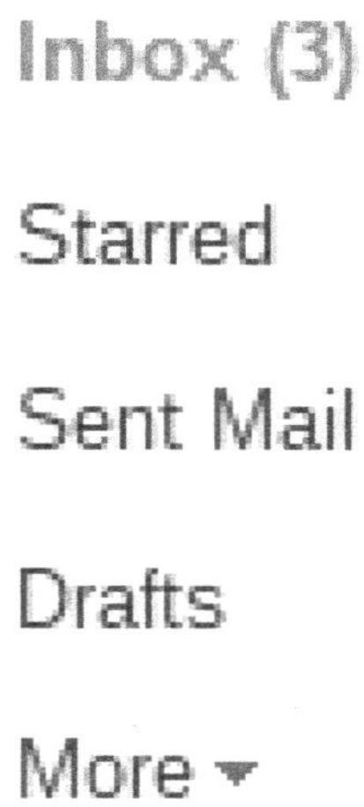


The downward arrow in the far lower right corner of the New Message window gives you a few more options for managing your message. Perhaps the most immediately useful thing here is the spell-check function, but it's good to know how to print a draft or send it to full screen as well. We'll talk about labels in just a minute.

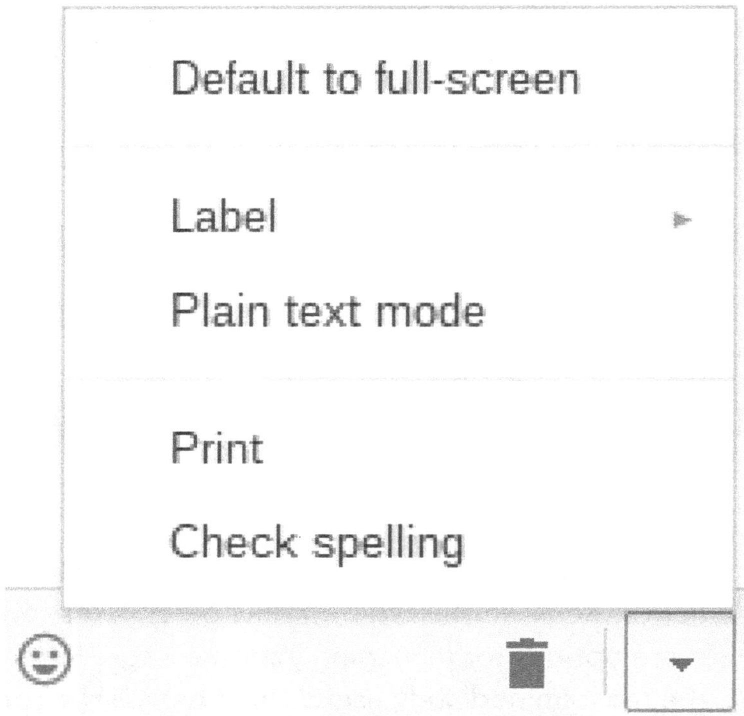


Managing Email

Gmail makes it exceptionally easy to deal with the daily barrage of incoming messages in this day and age. The toolbar pictured below appears at the top of every email, and will appear when emails are selected in the inbox or a folder.

When you're finished with a message, you can delete it, either from inside the opened message or by clicking the checkbox next to the email in your inbox, and then clicking the trashcan icon. However, Gmail makes it easy to get messages out of your inbox, thus decreasing clutter, without actually deleting them, thanks to its Archive feature. The archive button is the first icon in the Gmail toolbar. When you archive a message, it disappears from your inbox, but not from your account. You can search for it at any time using Gmail's search bar at the top of the Gmail screen.

Of course, sometimes archiving isn't quite nuanced enough, and that's where favorites and labels come in. To make an email a favorite, just click the star icon next to it. You can then get to all of your starred emails by clicking Starred in the left menu.

Labels are an easy way to categorize your email. You can add as many custom labels as you like in the left menu. Just click More in the left menu, and then click Create New Label at the bottom.

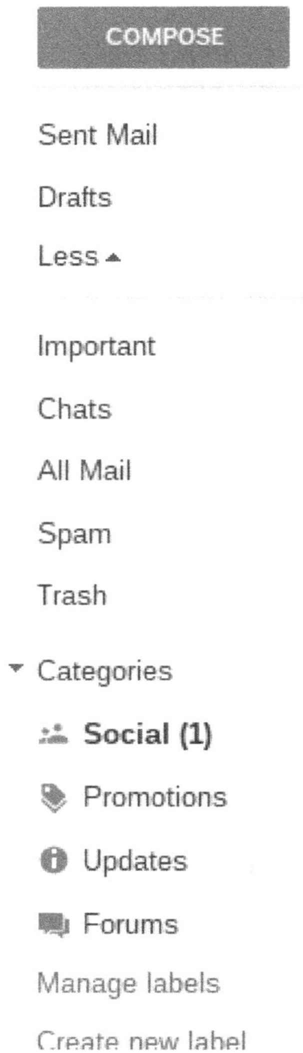


To apply a label (or labels) to a message, click the Label icon in the top toolbar. A dropdown menu will appear that gives you a list of all of your existing labels. Click on one to apply it, or type in a new label in the box to set it up and add it to the message.

## Contacts

You may have noticed that there's no dedicated contact app in Chromebook. That's because, between Gmail and Google+, there's no real need for one. Gmail is an excellent contacts manager in its own right, and Google+ adds additional contacts capabilities.

To manage contacts in Gmail, click the red Gmail text in the top left corner. A dropdown menu will appear, allowing you to switch to Contacts or Tasks view. All of your Google+ contacts will be automatically added, but you can add non-Google+ information and people as well. To manually add a new contact, click the red New Contact button.

You can then add names, pictures, emails, phone numbers, addresses—basically, as much or as little information as you want. To add a field other than the ones displayed, just click the Add button underneath all of the text entry fields. There's plenty to choose from!

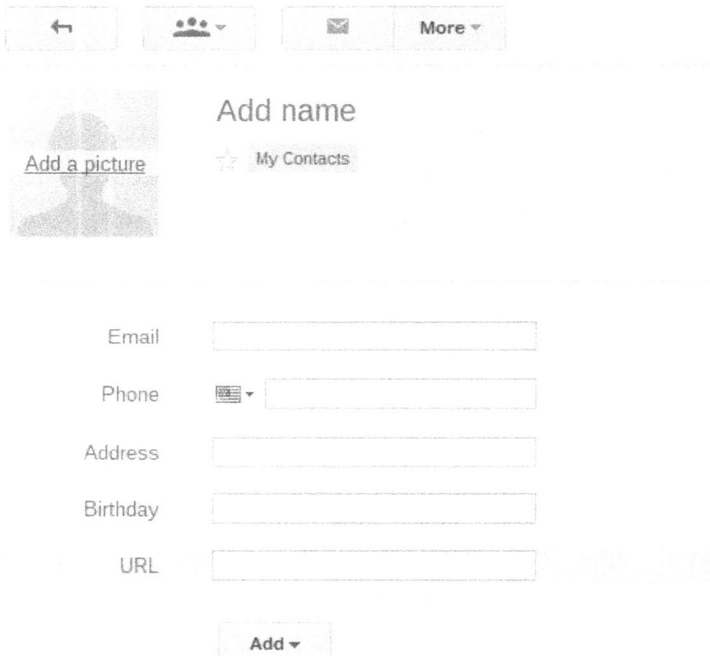


## Chat/Calls

You can start chats and initiate calls from within Gmail itself. At the very bottom of the left menu, you'll see three icons—Hangouts, Chats, and Phone Calls. Click each one to view any contacts you may have that have these features enabled.

You can start a Hangout (Google's Skype-like video calling service, covered in more depth later on in Part 3.8), text-based chat, or phone call by clicking a contact's name.

### Tasks

Much like Microsoft Outlook, Gmail includes a Task list. You can add items to your task list, add new lists altogether, and set due dates. It's a very simple task manager, but like everything else in Gmail, it's accessible from any machine with an Internet browser.

## YOUTUBE

We can't imagine the modern Internet without YouTube. YouTube is very tightly integrated with your Google account, so you're automatically signed in whenever you open the YouTube app.

### Watching Videos

Perhaps the most obvious thing you'll want to do with the YouTube app is watch streaming videos online. This is easy and extremely addictive! You can search for videos using the YouTube search bar at the top of the YouTube app page, or you can browse around the featured videos underneath.

When you've found a video you'd like to watch, simply click it in the search results list. It'll start to play. Note that many popular YouTube videos and/or videos that use copyrighted material like songs may play an ad before the video starts. Try not to be too annoyed—this is how YouTube remains free and full of hilarious parodies, remixes, and reinterpretations that make it so much fun!

There are media controls in the lower left corner of the YouTube player window where you can pause the video, control the volume, and see the elapsed and remaining time. In the lower right corner, you'll find some additional features, including (from left to right) Watch Later, Settings (where you can adjust the speed and quality of the video playback depending on your system and connection speed), Theatre Mode and Full Screen. Theatre Mode is sort of halfway between the normal

YouTube display and Full Screen—try it out to see if it's for you. Full Screen, of course, is the best way to get your computer to mimic a television.

To the right of the video player, you'll see a list of related videos. This is great if you're entertaining yourself with one of the millions of YouTube memes out there (literal music videos, inappropriate music for movies, and Sharky the Pit Bull are some of our classic favorites).

You can thumbs up or thumbs down a video, or comment on it to take advantage of YouTube's social features. Scroll down to see the comments underneath the player. We're not going to lie to you here. YouTube comments can be...rough. We ask in the name of a brighter Internet future that if you're going to participate in YouTube commentary that you 1) don't feed the trolls, and 2) don't be a troll! Trolls, for the record, are Internet users who say inflammatory and frequently extremely offensive things for the purpose of eliciting a reaction, and you're probably going to come across them if you spend much time on the site.

## Account Features

There's more to YouTube than simply browsing around and watching online videos. Using your Google account, you can create playlists of YouTube videos, subscribe to other users' channels, access a list of your recently viewed videos, and create a Watch Later list for when you just don't have time for that twenty minute documentary on urban beekeeping but are really interested. You'll find all of these options in the YouTube menu to the left of the main content area. You can click the menu button next to the YouTube logo in the top left corner to hide and reveal these extra features as needed.

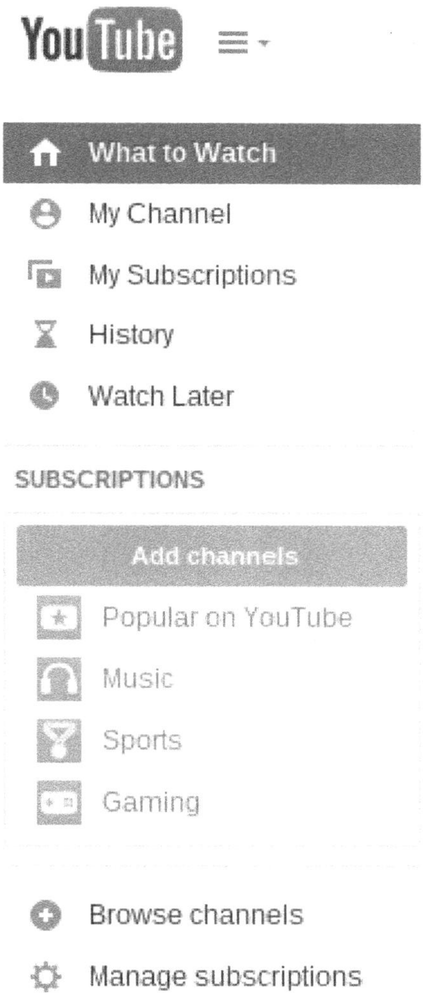
YouTube
What to Watch
My Channel
My Subscriptions
History
Watch Later
SUBSCRIPTIONS
Add channels
Popular on YouTube
Music
Sports
Gaming
Browse channels
Manage subscriptions

To subscribe to a YouTube channel, locate the channel's owner on a video page, or, if you know the owner's name, just search for it using the YouTube search bar. Then, on their profile page, click the red Subscribe button. You'll then find new content from that user under Subscriptions in the YouTube menu.

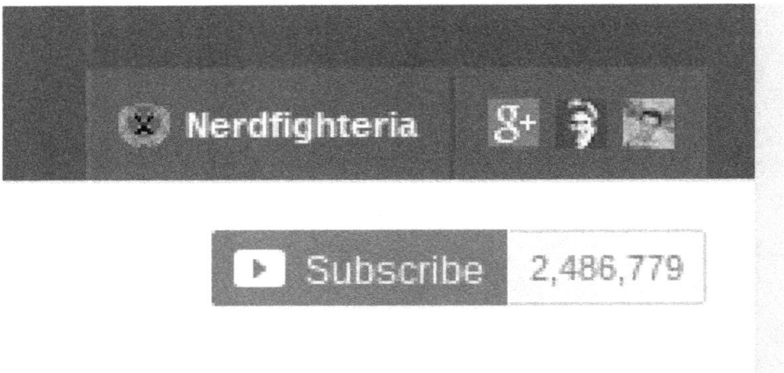


To create a playlist of YouTube videos, click Add to underneath the creators' names on the video's page. Before you can take advantage of this, though, you'll need to set up your Google+ profile and your YouTube channel page. The first time you click Add to you'll be prompted to set all of this up if you haven't already.

Uploading Videos

If you'd like to upload your own videos to YouTube, just click the Upload button in the top right corner.

You'll need to set up your Google+ profile and your YouTube channel page before you can upload, but after that you can easily upload and share your videos. Videos can be private or only shared with certain people. You can also choose to enable or disable public comments, depending on your preference.

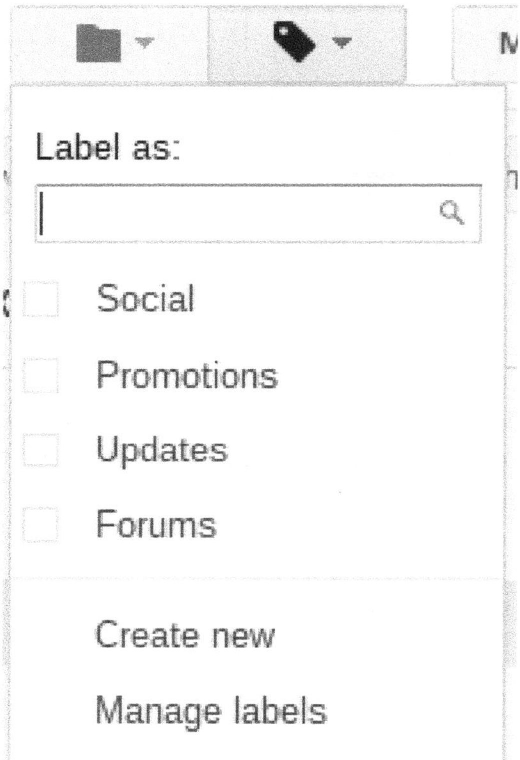


You can click on your labels in the left menu to see all messages categorized with them. You can also search for labels in the Gmail search bar.

## CALCULATOR

The Calculator app is a simple utility and a rare example of an app that doesn't open inside a Chrome window. It performs basic calculations—no more, no less. It's nice to have a calculator that appears outside of all your other Chrome tabs and windows, though, and you may want to consider pinning it to your Chromebook's shelf if you find yourself using it time and time again.

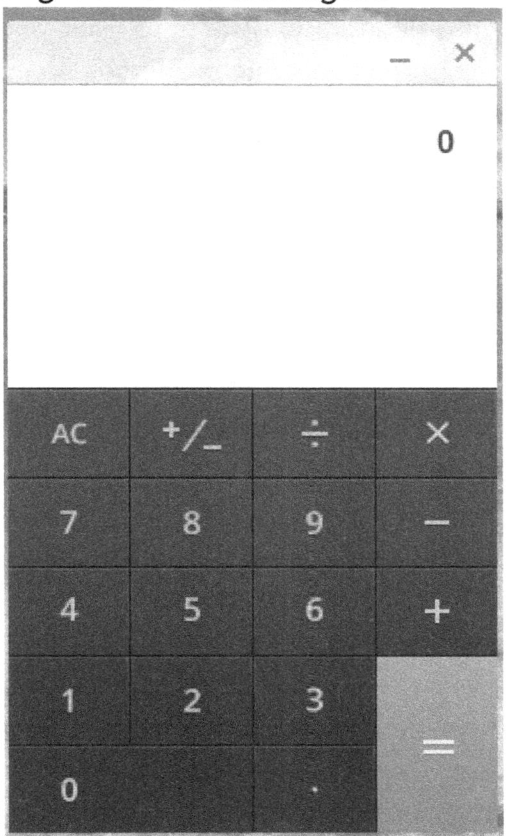

## CAMERA

Most Chromebook devices include at least a forward-facing camera, and the camera app is your go-to for Chromebook or Slate selfie purposes. The Camera app includes several filters to add fun (and sometimes funny) effects to your photos, a timer, and mirroring, which reverses an image so that it would match what you see in the mirror. It's a simple single-action app, but it's great to have when you need a quick snap for a profile pic or message.

## CHROME REMOTE DESKTOP

Chrome Remote Desktop (CRD) is similar in function to Windows Remote Desktop and Apple Remote Desktop. Basically, it allows you to view and control a different computer or device remotely. It's incredibly helpful for Instructional Technology (IT) professionals and for getting help with your system.

For Chrome Remote Desktop to work, both machines must be running the CRD app, which can be installed in Chrome in any operating system, as long as the Google Chrome browser is installed. To open a connection, the remote user needs to open the CRD app and click Share. This will generate an access code, which the remote user will give to you. Enter the access code into CRD on your Chromebook, and you'll be able to see and control the remote machine.

## GOOGLE+ PHOTOS

The Google+ Photos app is your Chromebook's photo manager. It's not entirely unlike Apple's iPhoto, but it is very tightly integrated with Google+, for better or worse. Google+ Photos helps you consolidate your photos, organize them and share them through Google+.

To get started, open the app using the Apps button. You'll need to sign up for Google+ if you haven't already done so. From there, you can import photos from your Google+ account, your Chromebook, or Google Drive by clicking the Add Photos button in the top right corner. You can then organize your photos into albums, share them through Google+, delete them, or save them to your Chromebook or your Google Drive account.

The Photos app includes the ability to rotate the photo and/or enhance it using the Enhance tool, which appears when you move your mouse over the photo. This is an automatic fix rather than a set of manual features. For serious photo editing, we recommend Pixlr Editor or another photo app from the Web Store.

## GOOGLE KEEP

Google Keep is a note-taking app that aims to compete with products like Microsoft OneNote or Evernote. You can add notes and reminders lists that will sync with the online version of Keep at keep.google.com. There's also an Android app that you can download for your smartphone or tablet.

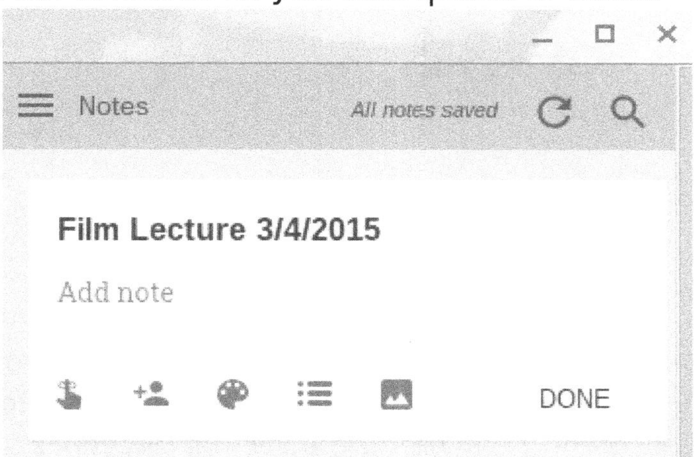


Notes in Keep can include lists and images, and you can share them with others. It's a handy way to keep yourself organized, and it's a quick note-taking app for those times when you don't need all the bells and whistles of Google Docs.

## GOOGLE MAPS AND GOOGLE MY MAPS

Google Maps is, in our opinion, the best free online maps service in the game, and it's built right into your Chromebook.

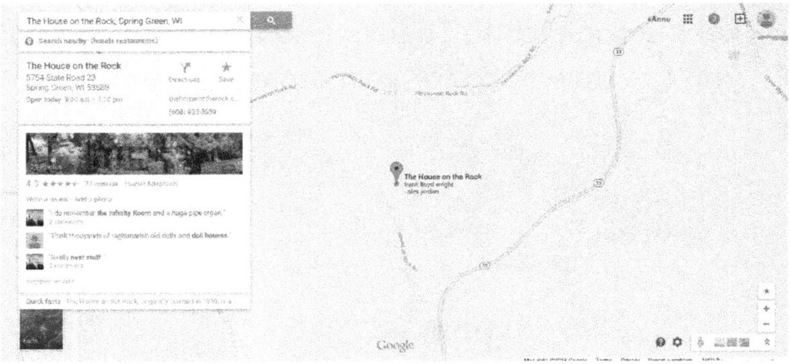


To use Google Maps, type the address, town or place name (The House on the Rock, Yellowstone National Park, etc.), into the search box in the top left corner. From there, you can get directions to that address by clicking Directions, or you can save the location for later reference. In the example above, you can see that Google Maps also pulled reviews and contact information for us, since we searched for a popular tourist destination.

In the bottom left corner, you will see a box labeled Earth. Clicking this box will toggle Google Earth—a beautiful satellite mode that will give you a photographic aerial view of your mapped area.

You can switch back to Map mode by clicking the Map square in the bottom left corner.

In the bottom right corner of the screen, you'll find a few controls for adjusting your Google Maps experience. The Target button is a shortcut to your current location. Click it to get a map of your immediate surroundings. Beneath it, the + and - buttons let you zoom in and out. You can zoom out to a planetary view if you like!

The little yellow man in the controls area is the Google Streetview operator. Drag him from this menu to a spot on the map to enter Streetview. Streetview is a great way to check out a neighborhood or to explore the world a little. The screenshot below is the view from beneath the Eiffel Tower.

Google My Maps

The Google My Maps app is somewhat confusingly named, but it's extremely useful if you ever need to share directions with a large group of people. It's basically Google Maps, but slightly remixed in such a way that users can save maps in Google Drive and import layers of data into the Maps interface. For example, you might have a spreadsheet listing addresses that you'd like to add. You can also add placemarks and give them your own description or draw lines or add Google Maps routes and directions. Once your custom map is complete, you can share it using a generated link that can be copied and pasted wherever you need it, or through email, Google+, Facebook, and Twitter. This is a very handy feature for invitations or websites.

## GOOGLE FORMS

Google Forms is a form generator that works closely with Google Sheets. If you've ever used Survey Monkey before, you should feel right at home in Forms. Your Forms questions can include multiple choice, text, checkboxes, scales, grids, dates and times, and you can make as many answers required as you like. Once your form is complete, you can invite people to fill it out through a URL or through email invitations. Responses will be automatically recorded in a Google Sheets spreadsheet for analysis (though you can turn this off if you'd prefer to keep all responses inside the Forms app for some reason).

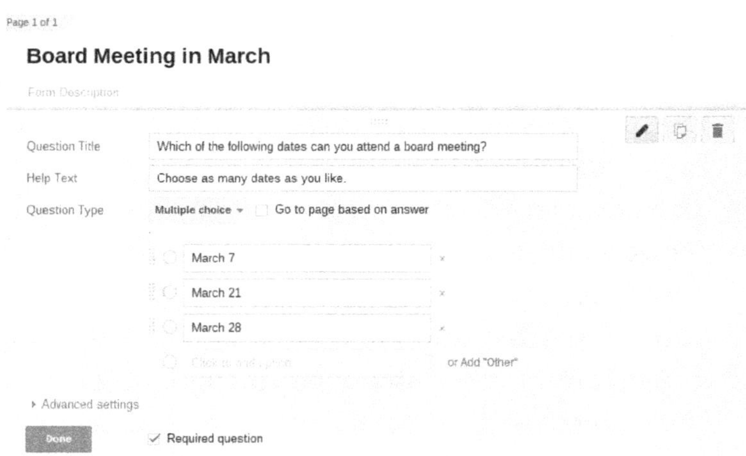

## GOOGLE DRAWINGS

The Google Drawings app allows you to create and annotate images. You can also insert text boxes, shapes, and lines. The freeform drawing tool is called Scribbles, and you'll find it under Insert > Line. Drawings shouldn't be compared to giants like Photoshop or Illustrator. Its closest relative is probably Microsoft Paint. Of course, any images you create in Drawings are saved in Drive, meaning it's very easy to insert them into other Drive apps, like Google Slides or Google Docs.

## PLAY MUSIC, PLAY BOOKS, AND PLAY MOVIES

These three media apps make it possible to enjoy music, books, and movies purchased from the Google Play Store and from elsewhere on your Chromebook.

### Play Music

The Play Music app includes an optional subscription that gives you access to millions of streaming songs without any ads. First time users generally get some sort of free trial offer, but after that it costs $9.99 a month.

If you decide to use the Standard version of Play Music, you'll then be given the option to upload your music from other sources, including iTunes. To do this, you may need to navigate to

Google Play Music from the device that has your tunes on it, which is probably not your relatively low-memory Chromebook. However, once you've uploaded your library (from anywhere), you can enjoy it streaming through Play Music on your Chromebook and on most other devices by installing the Play Music app. You can upload up to 50,000 songs free of charge.

### Play Books

Play Books is an ebook app that's half bookshelf and half bookstore. At the top of the Play Books app, you'll see two links—My Books and Shop Books. Any books you've purchased through the Shop link (or through the Google Play Store on a different computer) will appear under My Books. Buying books is identical to buying apps or extensions. If you don't already have a credit card number on file with Google, you'll be prompted to enter one. Of course, there are a number of classics and other free titles in the Play Store, so there's no need to whip out the plastic if you don't want to!

Any books you buy through Play Books will be available on your Android smartphone or tablet as well, and the Play Books app will keep everything synced up. This means that no matter what device you're using to read, your current read will open to exactly where you left off.

### Play Movies

The Play Movies app allows you to enjoy movies and television shows purchased through the Google Play Store. Just like the Play Books app, Play Movies includes a Shop link where you can find streaming video to watch.

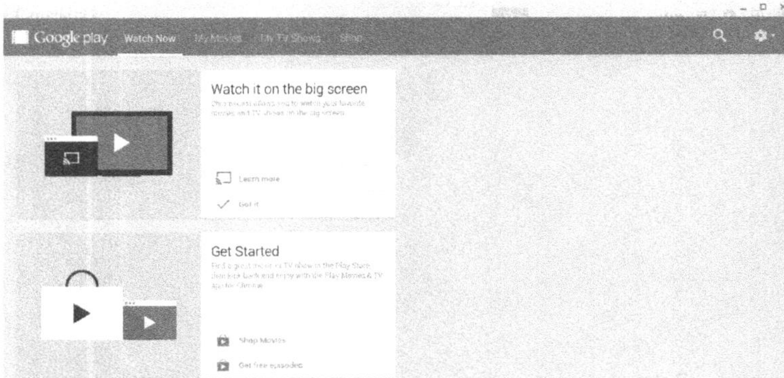


Google Play movies and television shows can be bought (you can stream them as many times as you like) or rented (you can only stream them during a certain amount of time). There are often pretty good deals on the Play Store—for example, at the time of writing, Star Trek was on offer in HD for just $4.99.

## GOOGLE CALENDAR

Google Calendar is a great calendar tool, particularly since it's so widely used and importable into a variety of other calendaring systems. It's easy to use, available through google.com/calendar on any computer with a web browser, and will notify you of upcoming events so you never miss a thing.

## Adding a New Calendar Event

To add a new event to Google Calendar, click the red Create button in the top left corner.

Enter as much or as little information about your event as you need. Keep in mind that Google Calendar has some powerful time management features to help keep you on track. It will send notifications before your event, at an interval of your choosing. You can also set recurring events by clicking the "Repeat" checkbox.

## Adding and Sharing Calendars

The Google Calendar system includes the ability to set up multiple calendars. Maybe you'd like to have one personal calendar and then a shared family calendar or a team project calendar. To add a new calendar, click the boxed downward pointing arrow to the right of the My Calendars heading in the left menu. This will take you to the New Calendar setup screen. At the bottom, you'll see options for controlling your calendar's privacy and inviting people to view and/or add to the calendar.

## Hiding Calendars

We've found that it's very easy to get enthusiastic about calendars, only to find yourself drowning in calendar entries. Fortunately, it's easy to temporarily hide calendars to help clean up your view. To hide a calendar, just click the little colored square next to its name in the My Calendars list. This won't delete anything, but it will hide all events associated with that calendar so you can focus on the events that need your attention.

# [6]

# MAKING IT YOUR OWN WITH CUSTOMIZATIONS

This chapter will cover:

- Changing the Appearance
- Device
- Searching
- People
- Date and Time
- Privacy
- Web Content
- Languages
- Downloads

- HTTPS/SSL Certificates
- Google Cloud Print
- Startup
- Accessibility
- Powerwash and Reset
- Supervised Accounts
- Troubleshooting
-

If you already have the watch, then you can skip right ahead to the next chapter. How's that for ridiculously simple?! This chapter is just for readers curious about all the different watches available.

The Apple Watch comes in several different.

In this section, we'll talk about several ways you can customize your Chromebook to suit your unique needs and personality. There are quite a few useful tweaks available for Chromebook, and we'll walk you through them all here. We'll also show you how to manage user accounts on your Chromebook, including children's accounts, and give you a few tips for troubleshooting and finding help.

To open your Chromebook settings, click the area of the screen that displays the time, wireless connection, battery, and your profile picture in the bottom right corner. Then click Settings. We're going to examine each heading that appears on this screen.

## CHANGING THE APPEARANCE

The Appearance heading in Settings covers, well, the appearance of your Chromebook. Here you can set your desktop wallpaper to a custom image by clicking Set Wallpaper. This will open up a dialog box where you can browse your Chromebook for the image file you'd like to use. You can also click the Get Themes button to be taken to the Themes area of the Chrome Web Store. Themes add a graphic layer to your Chrome window—an image or color for new tab windows and colors and designs for the menu area. There are plenty of fun themes to choose from, and if you change your mind about any of them, you can always click Reset to Default Theme to go back to Chrome's original appearance.

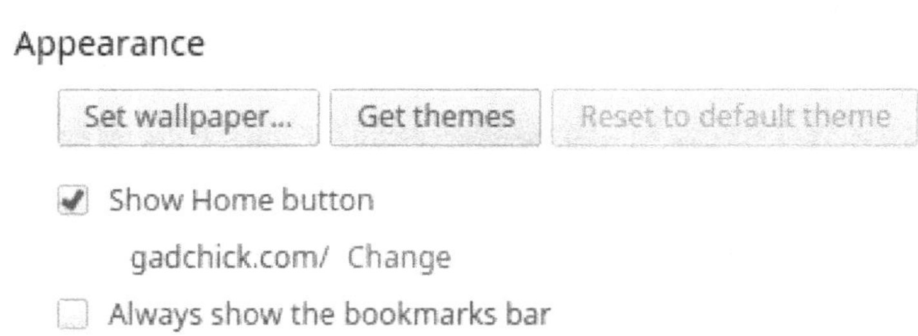

You can also set a home page here if you like. First, click Show Home button to tell Chrome to show the Home button in your Chrome browser as a special shortcut to your home page. Click Change to add a new home page. This is the page that will be displayed every time you open Chrome.

Finally, you can choose to always show the bookmarks bar in Chrome here as well.

## DEVICE

The Device heading is a pretty important Settings area, even if it's a little bit of a catchall. There are some really useful options and features tucked away here.

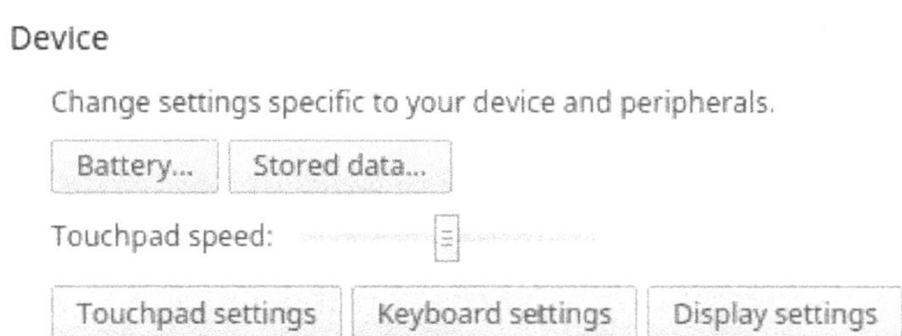


First, you can take a look at what's using your battery by clicking the Battery button. This is a great way to maximize your Chromebook's battery even further if you need to. Just close the apps that are sucking up the most juice.

The Stored Data button is also a fascinating glimpse into what Chrome is doing with every page and app you visit or use. Check out what our Chromebook has to say about weather.com.

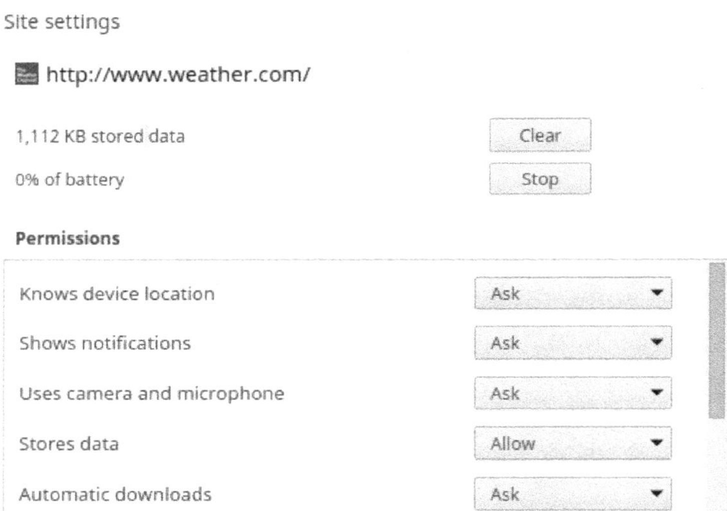


We can see how much stored data from this site is eating into our hard disc (in this case, not very much), as well as how much of the battery it's using. Right now, it's not running, so it requires 0% of our battery. Then we can see a fairly extensive list of permissions for the site, and change them as we see fit. For this example, we may want to allow this site to know our Chromebook's location so that it will always give us the weather of our current spot.

Underneath the battery and stored data information, you'll find some options for configuring your touchpad, keyboard, and display. You can adjust your touchpad's speed to match that of your fingers using the slider, and you can also change the direction the page moves when you scroll and enable or disable tap-to-click. By clicking Keyboard, you can view the shortcut display mentioned earlier in the book, and you can also change the behavior of certain keyboard keys if you like—namely Search, CTRL, and ALT.

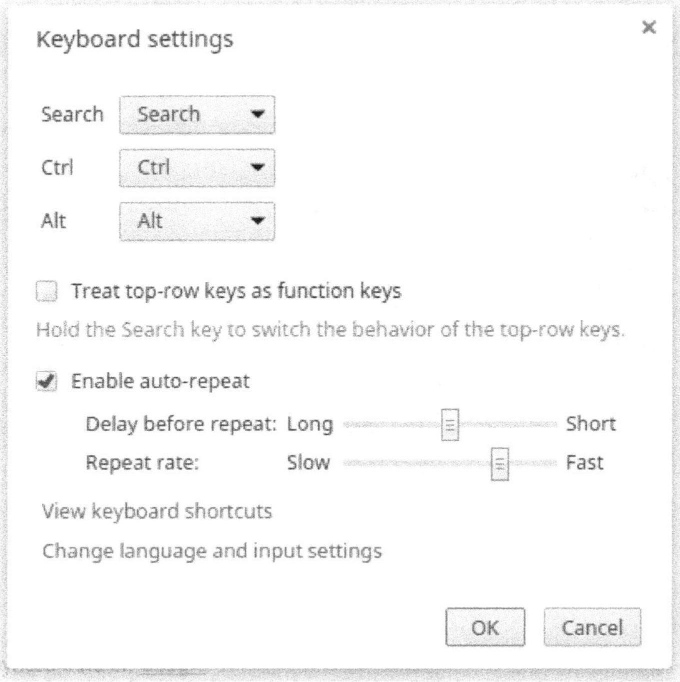


## SEARCHING

One of our favorite things about Google products is their flexibility. It would stand to reason that the proprietary Google OS based on Google's browser would limit users to the Google search engine for the Chrome omnibox, but that's not the case. In the Search heading, you can change Chrome's search engine to Yahoo!, Bing, Ask, or AOL.

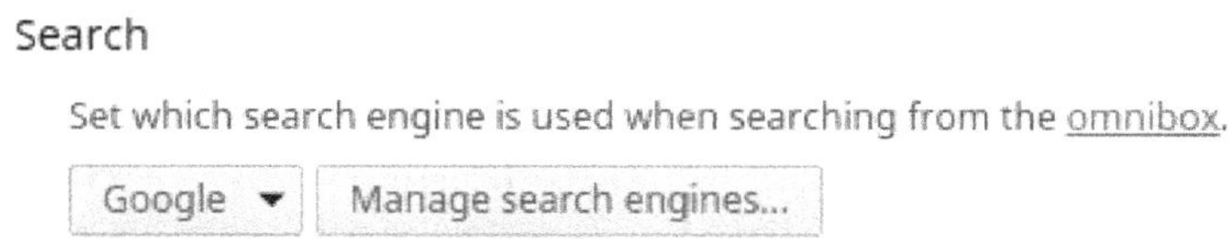


The Manage Search Engines button finds additional search engines, like YouTube search, for example. You can add these highly specific searches as your omnibox default if you'd like (though for most users we do recommend sticking with a general internet-wide search engine).

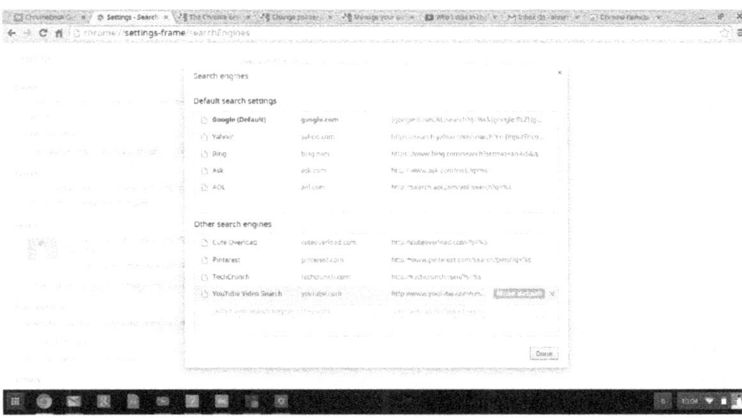


PEOPLE

Under the People heading, you can accomplish two important tasks. First, you can manage what aspects of your Chromebook sync with your Google Account by clicking Advanced Sync

Settings. By default, everything is selected, but you can adjust as needed. You can also choose how you'd like Google Chrome to encrypt your data.

The other feature under People is the ability to manage logins on your Chromebook. More than one Google user can sign in, and you can manage other users as needed. You can decide whether or not to enable a Guest account and supervised users (which we'll talk about in more detail shortly) and whether or not to restrict sign-in to certain users. You can also add users to your Chromebook here.

At this point, you'll need to click Show Advanced Settings to see the rest of the Chrome settings menu!

## DATE AND TIME

There's not much here besides the ability to change your time zone and switch your system clock to 24-hour time. Chrome will set the date and time automatically based on your time zone.

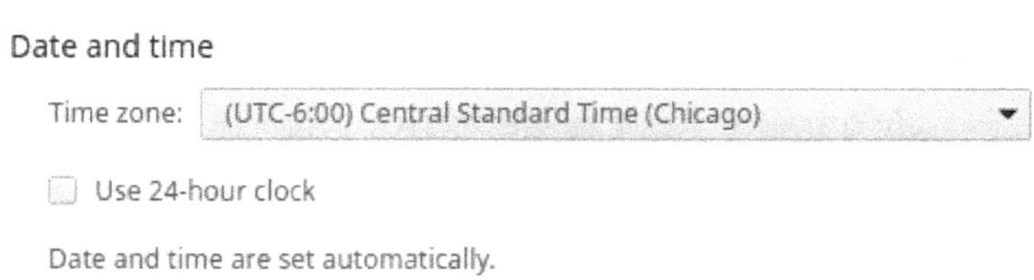

## PRIVACY

Your privacy settings give you some control over how much information your Chromebook shares with the rest of the world. Google uses quite a few prediction services in order to load pages fast and get you where you want to go, but you may not want all of them accessing your personal information, search engine terms, etc. To disable any of these services, deselect them under the Privacy heading.

The Content settings button includes several Chrome options, like pop-up blocking, location tracking, JavaScript settings, automatic downloads and more. Most of these settings include a Manage exceptions button. As you surf the web, Chrome will ask you if you'd like to make these exceptions. For example, when Chrome blocks a pop-up, it will notify you of the action and then ask if you'd like to allow pop-ups once or always for that site. You can then revoke those exceptions later if you need to in Content Settings.

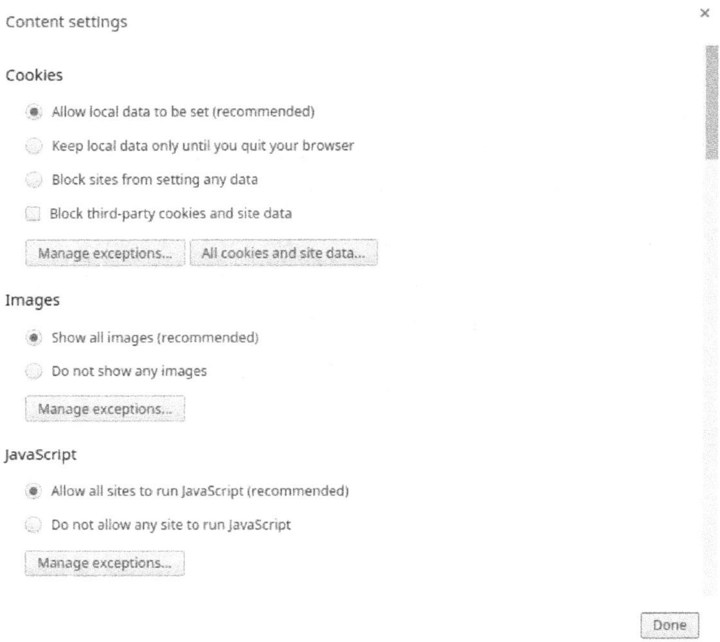


Generally we recommend leaving these settings with their defaults, as we think there's a good balance between end-user protection and convenience of use. Nevertheless, you may occasionally need to turn off the pop-up blocker or adjust another one of these settings, and it's good to know where to find them.

## WEB CONTENT

The web content settings allow you to change the default font size and page zoom for web pages. You can also choose what sort of font you'd like Chrome to display as a default.

## LANGUAGES

The Languages heading allows you to turn automatic translation offers on and off. You can also manage the languages you'd like to use with Chromebook by clicking the Language and input settings button. You can add more than one by clicking the Add button in the lower left corner. The language at the top of your list will be your default language, but adding additional languages gives you the ability to set up keyboard input options so that you can quickly switch languages as needed.

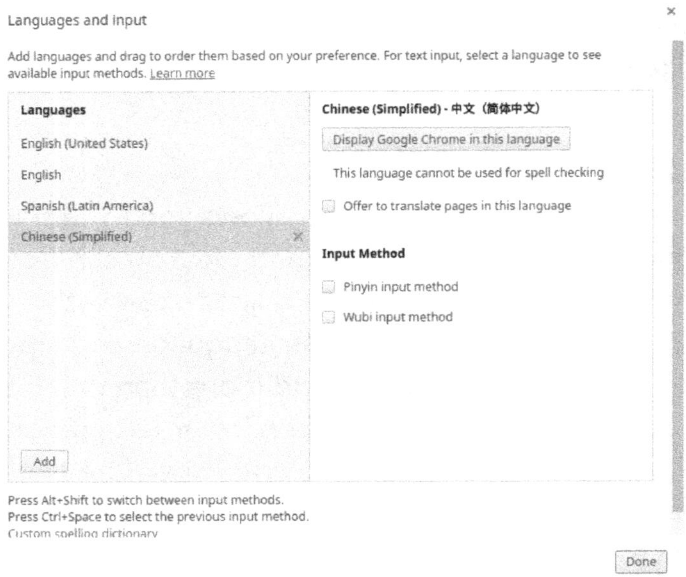


## DOWNLOADS

Here you can change the way your Chromebook handles downloads. Perhaps the most useful feature here is the ability to change the default downloads location to something more accessible than the Downloads folder. Or, if you prefer, you can tell Chrome that you want it to always ask you where you want to save downloads. You can disable Google Drive here as well, though we don't recommend it.

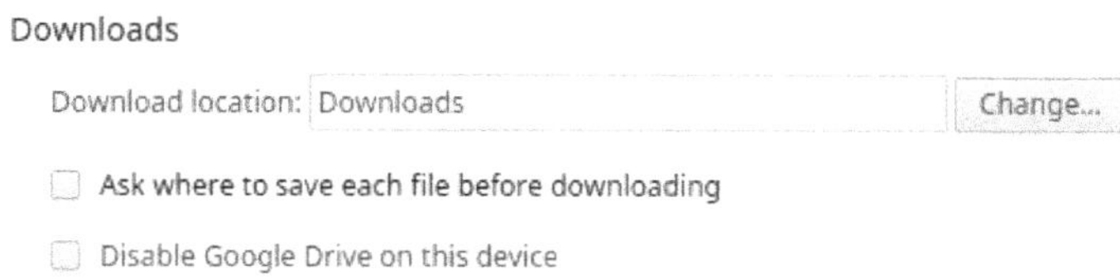


## HTTPS/SSL CERTIFICATES

This area of your settings allows you to view and manage security certificates stored on your computer. The average user won't have too many reasons to make changes here, but it's good to know it's there if you're ever prompted to install or uninstall a certificate.

## GOOGLE CLOUD PRINT

Google Cloud Print is Google's printing service. It allows users to send a print job over the web to their printer, rather than the traditional methods of wired or wireless printer connections. To use it, you'll need to connect your printer to your Google Cloud Print account. You'll find instructions and more information about this by clicking Learn more under the Google Cloud Print heading.

## STARTUP

The On Startup heading tells Chrome what to do the first time you open it. You can start with a new tab page, or open the pages that you had open during your last use (the default option). You can also set a page or group of pages that you'd like to open. This is a great way to open your email, Facebook, the news, and your favorite blog without having to do anything but start Google Chrome.

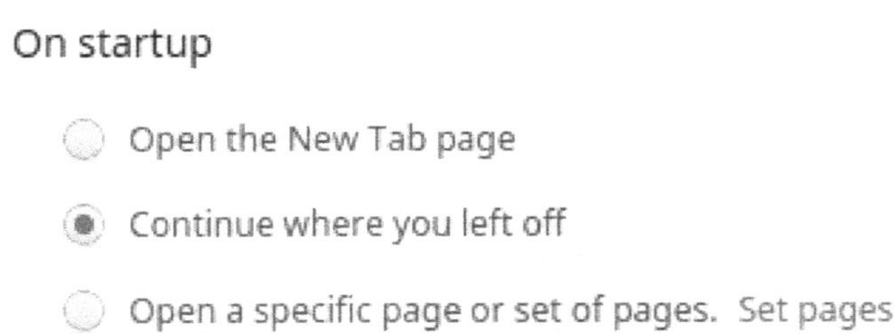


## ACCESSIBILITY

The accessibility heading provides a suite of features designed to make Chromebook more accessible for individuals with impaired vision or certain motor disabilities. Select as many as you like to make your Chromebook experience more comfortable for you.

There is an additional collection of accessibility apps and extensions in the Web Store as well. To view them, click Add additional accessibility features.

## POWERWASH AND RESET

The powerwash and reset options are located at the very bottom of the advanced settings screen. Powerwash is the panic button. This extreme step will completely erase everything on your Chromebook and restore it to factory settings. It can be used as an absolutely last-ditch troubleshooting measure, but just remember that it's permanent—there's no recovering from a Powerwash (though of course you can re-download anything you've purchased through Google, and since almost everything on Chromebook is a web app, you won't lose any of your files stored in Google Drive). Powerwash is also the thing to do if you're selling or giving away your Chromebook.

A less drastic approach is the Reset button. This doesn't wipe your device, but it does restore all system settings to their original defaults. If you've played with your configuration and decided you prefer the original, just hit Reset to get back to square one without losing your apps or data.

## SUPERVISED ACCOUNTS

If you have any children in your house, you may want to set up supervised accounts for them. This will allow them to use your Chromebook, but with a few restrictions designed to keep them safe and you sane. You can restrict web pages and content for supervised users, and you can log in anytime to chrome.com/manage to monitor the account.

To add a supervised user, click Add user on the sign-in screen. A sign-in box will appear. Click Create a supervised user (in blue) on the right side of the box to get started.

Next, you'll name the account and set a password and profile picture. Supervised users aren't Google Accounts users, so there's no need to set up a unique username. You can also set a password that's easy to remember, since it's for a local account instead of an online one.

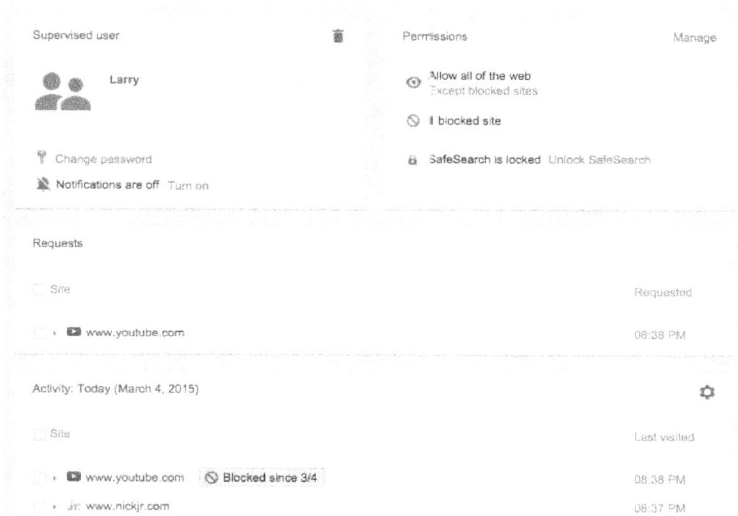


At chrome.com/manage, you can change the supervised user's password, set restricted sites, and deal with requests to unblock sites from the user, as seen above.

## TROUBLESHOOTING AND MAINTAINING YOUR CHROMEBOOK

One of the best things about Chromebook is its simplicity—unlike more complex operating system software like Windows or Mac OSX, there's really very little that can go wrong. However, things can and do happen sometimes, and we'll walk you through some quick and easy troubleshooting methods here.

### Check Your Battery

Also known as the "is it plugged in?" step, this is a frequent culprit in Chromebook problems. Check to be sure that your charger is connected and plugged in before you jump to any conclusions as to why your Chromebook won't wake up.

### Restart

When in doubt, reboot. This often is all it takes to fix frozen systems or other irritating problems. Thanks to most Chrome apps' constant background saving processes, you rarely need to worry about losing work when you do this.

If you're having problems with an app, you can always try closing it and reopening it. If that doesn't work, you may want to try removing it from your device and then re-downloading it from the Web Store.

### Getting Help and Contacting Support

If you're stuck with a Chromebook problem, try the Get Help app. It's a searchable tour of your Chromebook's features and may provide the answer you need. If that doesn't work, you might try the Google user forums at https://support.google.com chromebook-central. Here you'll find frequently asked questions, user forums where you can search for other people with your issue (or post it yourself), and more. You'll find power Google users to be a pretty informed bunch, and the forums are an excellent resource when you run into trouble.

To get official support for your Chromebook, you can either request a call or start a chat session with a Google technician. To do this, visit support.google.com/Chromebook and click Contact Us in the top right corner.

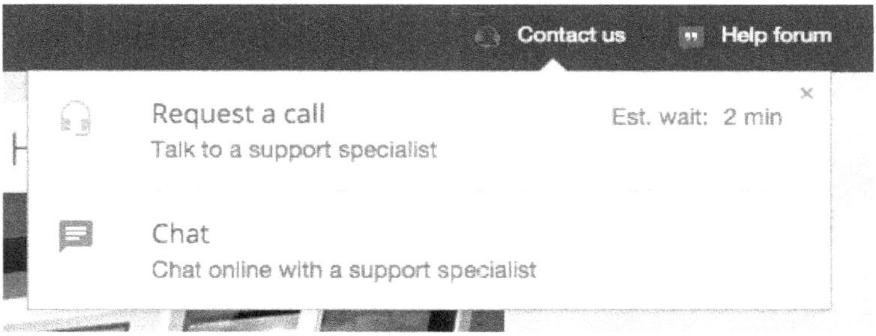


## Updating Your Chromebook

Chromebook keeps itself up-to-date for the most part, so the only thing you need to do is be sure that it's regularly online and in use. Chrome will take care of the rest! If you ever need to see what version of Chrome you're running, you can do so by visiting Chrome Settings. Then click About Chrome OS at the top. This will display your device's update status, as well as its current version.

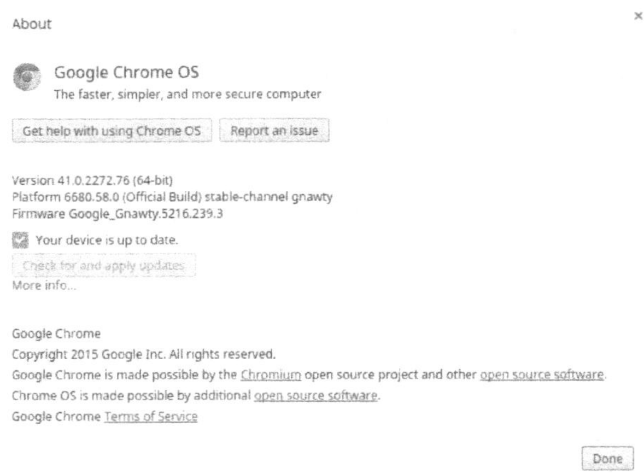


It's a good idea to periodically check that your system is updating itself. You may occasionally need to click Check for and apply updates to manually perform an update check. Sometimes new updates require a system restart, fortunately, most Chromebooks restart within seconds!

# APPENDIX A: SPECS

| Specification | Pixelbook | Surface Laptop | MacBook |
|---|---|---|---|
| **Software** | Chrome OS | Windows 10 S | macOS High Sierra |
| **Display** | 12.3 inches | 13.5 inches | 12 inches |
| **Resolution** | 2400 x 1600 | 2256 x 1504 | 2304 x 1440 |
| **Processor (base)** | Intel Core i5 (seventh-gen) | Intel Core i5 (seventh-gen) | Intel Core m3 (1.2GHz, dual-core, seventh-gen) |

| | | | |
|---|---|---|---|
| **Processor (max)** | Intel Core i7 (seventh-gen) | Intel Core i7 (seventh-gen) | Intel Core i7 (1.4GHz, dual-core, seventh-gen) |
| **RAM (base)** | 8GB | 4GB | 8GB |
| **RAM(max)** | 16GB | 16GB | 16GB |
| **Ports** | USB-C, 3.5mm headphone jack | USB 3.0, 3.5mm headphone jack, Mini DisplayPort | USB-C, 3.5mm headphone jack |
| **Storage** | 128GB, 256GB, 512GB | 128GB, 256GB, 512GB, 1TB | 256GB, 512GB |
| **Weight** | 2.4 pounds | 2.76 pounds | 2.03 pounds |

| **Starting price** | $999 | $999 | $1,299 |
|---|---|---|---|

# APPENDIX B: SHORTCUT KEYS

**Popular shortcuts**

- Open the Google Assistant: Press 
- Search your device, apps, web and more: Press 
- Open the status area (where your account picture appears): Press 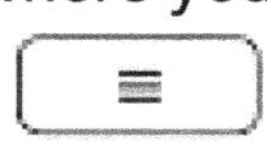
- Take a screenshot: Press Ctrl + 
- Take a partial screenshot: Press Ctrl + Shift + 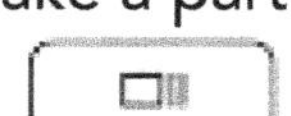, then click and drag

- Turn Caps Lock on or off: Press Alt + Search
- Lock your screen: Press Search + L
- Sign out of your Google Account: Press Ctrl + Shift + q (twice)
- 

## All other shortcuts

Note: If you're using a Windows or Mac keyboard, use the Windows key or Command key in place of the Search key.

**Tabs and windows**

| | |
|---|---|
| Open a new window | Ctrl + n |
| Open a new window in incognito mode | Ctrl + Shift + n |
| Open a new tab | Ctrl + t |

| | |
|---|---|
| Open a file in the browser | Ctrl + o |
| Close the current tab | Ctrl + w |
| Close the current window | Ctrl + Shift + w |
| Reopen the last tab or window you closed | Ctrl + Shift + t |
| Go to tabs 1-8 in the window | Ctrl + 1 through Ctrl + 8 |
| Go to the last tab in the window | Ctrl + 9 |
| Go to the next tab in the window | Ctrl + Tab |

| Go to the previous tab in the window | Ctrl + Shift + Tab |
|---|---|
| Switch quickly between windows | Press & hold Alt, tap Tab until you get to the window you want to open, then release. |
| Open the window you used least recently | Press & hold Alt + Shift, tap Tab until you get to the window you want to open, then release. |
| Go to previous page in your browsing history | Alt + left arrow |
| Go to the next page in your browsing history | Alt + right arrow |
| Open the link in a new tab in the background | Press Ctrl and click a link |

| | |
|---|---|
| Open the link in a new tab and switch to the new tab | Press Ctrl + Shift and click a link |
| Open the link in a new window | Press Shift and click a link |
| Open the link in the tab | Drag the link to the tab's address bar |
| Open the link in a new tab | Drag the link to a blank area on the tab strip |
| Open the webpage in a new tab | Type a web address (URL) in the address bar, then press Alt + Enter |
| Return the tab to its original position | While dragging the tab, press Esc |
| Dock a window on the left | Alt + [ |

| | |
|---|---|
| Dock a window on the right | Alt + ] |

**Page & Web Browser**

| | |
|---|---|
| Page up | Alt or Search and up arrow |
| Page down | Alt or Search and down arrow |
| Scroll down the web page | Space bar |
| Go to top of page | Ctrl + Alt and up arrow |
| Go to bottom of page | Ctrl + Alt and down arrow |
| Print your current page | Ctrl + p |
| Save your current page | Ctrl + s |

| | |
|---|---|
| Reload your current page | Ctrl + r |
| Reload your current page without using cached content | Ctrl + Shift + r |
| Zoom in on the page | Ctrl and + |
| Zoom out on the page | Ctrl and - |
| Reset zoom level | Ctrl + 0 |
| Stop the loading of your current page | Esc |
| Right-click a link | Press Alt and click a link |
| Open the link in a new tab in the background | Press Ctrl and click a link |
| Save the link as a bookmark | Drag link to bookmarks bar |

| Save your current webpage as a bookmark | Ctrl + d |
|---|---|
| Save all open pages in your current window as bookmarks in a new folder | Ctrl + Shift + d |
| Search the current page | Ctrl + f |
| Go to the next match for your search | Ctrl + g or Enter |
| Go to the previous match for your search | Ctrl + Shift + g or Shift + Enter |
| Perform a Google search |  or Ctrl + k or Ctrl + e |
| Add www. and .com to your input in the address bar, then open the page | Ctrl + Enter |

| | |
|---|---|
| View page source | Ctrl + u |
| Show or hide the Developer Tools panel | Ctrl + Shift + i |
| Show or hide the DOM Inspector | Ctrl + Shift + j |
| Show or hide the bookmarks bar | Ctrl + Shift + b |
| Open the History page | Ctrl + h |
| Open the Downloads page | Ctrl + j |

**System & Display Settings**

| | |
|---|---|
| Open the Files app | Alt + Shift + m |
| Preview a file in the Files app | Select the file, then press Space |

| | |
|---|---|
| Display hidden files in the Files app | Ctrl + . |
| Open the status area (where your account picture appears) | 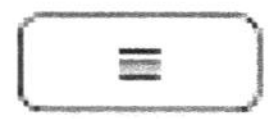 or Shift + Alt + s |
| Click icons 1-8 on your shelf | Alt + 1 through Alt + 8 |
| Click the last icon on your shelf | Alt + 9 |
| Use F keys (F1 to F12) | Search + 1 through Search + = |
| See your notifications | Alt + Shift + n |
| Change screen resolution | Ctrl + Shift and + or - |

| Reset screen resolution to default | Ctrl + Shift + 0 |
|---|---|
| Rotate screen 90 degrees | Ctrl + Shift + 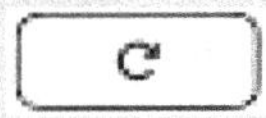 |
| Switch to the next user | Ctrl + Alt + . |
| Switch to the previous user | Ctrl + Alt + , |

**Text Editing**

| Turn Caps Lock on or off | Alt + Search |
|---|---|
| Select everything on the page | Ctrl + a |
| Select the content in the address bar | Ctrl + L or Alt + d |
| Select the next word or letter | Ctrl + Shift and right arrow |

| | |
|---|---|
| Select text to the end of the line | Shift + Search and right arrow |
| Select text to the beginning of the line | Shift + Search and left arrow |
| Select previous word or letter | Ctrl + Shift and left arrow |
| Move to the end of the next word | Ctrl and right arrow |
| Move to the start of the previous word | Ctrl and left arrow |
| Go to end of document | Ctrl + Search and right arrow |
| Go to beginning of document | Ctrl + Search and left arrow |

| | |
|---|---|
| Copy selected content to the clipboard | Ctrl + c |
| Paste content from the clipboard | Ctrl + v |
| Paste content from the clipboard as plain text | Ctrl + Shift + v |
| Cut | Ctrl + x |
| Delete the previous word | Ctrl + Backspace |
| Delete the next letter (forward delete) | Alt + Backspace |
| Undo your last action | Ctrl + z |
| Redo your last action | Ctrl + Shift + z |

| Switch between the keyboard languages you've set. Learn how to choose your keyboard language. | Ctrl + Shift + Space |
|---|---|
| Switch to the previous keyboard language you were using. Learn how to choose your keyboard language. | Ctrl + Space |
| Dim keyboard (for backlit keyboards only) | Alt +  |
| Make keyboard brighter (for backlit keyboards only) | Alt +  |

**Accessibility**

Learn how to make your Pixelbook accessible.

| Turn ChromeVox (spoken feedback) on or off | Ctrl + Alt + z |
|---|---|
| Turn on high contrast mode | Ctrl + Search + h |

| Highlight the launcher button on your shelf | Shift + Alt + L |
|---|---|
| Highlight the next item on your shelf | Shift + Alt + L, then Tab or right arrow |
| Highlight the previous item on your shelf | Shift + Alt + L, then Shift + Tab or left arrow |
| Open the highlighted button on your shelf | Shift + Alt + L, then Space or Enter |
| Remove the highlight from a button on your shelf | Shift + Alt + L, then Esc |
| Switch focus between:<br>• Status area (where your account picture appears)<br>• Launcher | Ctrl + 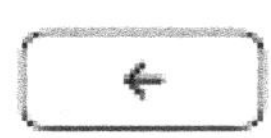 |

<table>
<tr><td>

- Address bar
- Bookmarks bar (if visible)
- The webpage that's open
- Downloads bar (if visible)

</td><td></td></tr>
<tr><td>Highlight the bookmarks bar (if shown)</td><td>Alt + Shift + b</td></tr>
<tr><td>Highlight the row with the address bar</td><td>Shift + Alt + t</td></tr>
<tr><td>Open right-click menu for highlighted item</td><td>Shift + </td></tr>
</table>

# GOOGLE APPS

# INTRODUCTION

Chances are you grew up a Word and Office user. Maybe you were a rebel and committed your herd to OpenOffice, or, dare I say, WordPerfect—but for the majority of people, our lives were loyal to Microsoft.

In 2005, a small little startup named Upstartle developed something unheard of at the time: a web-based word processor called Writely. It pioneered the idea of writing on the "cloud" and changed the way people thought about word processing.

Google noticed the little upstart, and in 2006, they acquired the company. The software was abandoned and turned into what everyone knows today as Google Docs. It disrupted the industry—namely, Microsoft's industry.

Today, Google has a whole suite of productivity apps; from documents to spreadsheets, you can do just about anything from the cloud. Microsoft and Apple have each made big attempts to create cloud-based environments of their own for office productivity, but Google pioneered the idea and its collaborative, online environment make it hard to beat. It's become so feature-rich that many businesses are finding it to be the preferred way to conduct business.

If you are thinking about making the switch to Google, or have already made the switch but want to make sure you are using it correctly, then this guide will walk you through it. It will show you all the basic features to make sure you can get up and running as quick as possible.

Let's get started!

# Google Drive

# [1]

# THE GOOGLE DRIVE CRASH COURSE

This chapter will cover:

- Why is it free?
- Creating files
- Finding files

## Why Is It Free?

You are probably wondering "If it's so great then why is it free?" You don't give away great software for free, right? There has to be a catch! There's always a catch! Are they taking your data and selling it on the black market? First, no!

Second, not everyone is out to get you, so just simmer down!

The Google you know gives all their tools away. How exactly do they make money? Does some rich guy donate a penny every time someone Googles "cute cat photos"? Definitely not—no one is that wealthy! Google makes money by selling ads, cloud services, selling apps, and a number of other things which all adds up to billions of dollars.

So there are ads in Google Docs? Nope! It all goes back to Google's business model. Unlike Microsoft, who is trying to make money off its software, Google is trying to make money off its service. It wants schools and businesses to use its enterprise services.

The Google Docs that we use is free; but for businesses that want to add dozens of workers, or schools who want to add hundreds of students, there is a charge.

If you are a small business, then there's a good chance you could probably make do with the free version. Plus, if Google is managing your company's email account, then you are paying for the service already.

**Google Drive Overview**

Every computer has "local" storage, which is where all the stuff (files, photos, documents), is stored directly on the computer. Windows computers have File/System Explorer, Mac Computers have Finder, and Google has Google Drive—it's the same concept you are accustomed to on your home computer, but it's all online.

Google Drive is basically an online version of a file directory; whatever you create in Google is stored here—think of it like Google's version of DropBox. In fact, you can also store files here—photos, videos, PDFs—whatever you want.

To get started, go to drive.google.com. If you are not signed in to a Google account, then you'll be greeted by a lovely screen that looks a little like the one below:

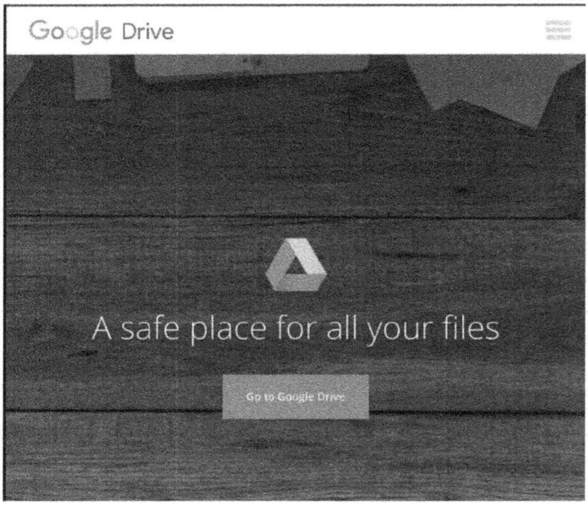


Click that "Go to Google Drive" blue button and you'll see an option that looks like the below:

While Google Docs is free to use, you do need a Google account to use it. So that's the catch, right? Free to use, but you have to pay to get a

Google account? Nope! A Google account is also free. If you use Gmail, then you already have one, and can use that to sign in.

Once you are all signed in you'll see the main interface. The side pane is your main navigation. This is where you will see all of your folders. It's probably empty right now, unless you've started using it.

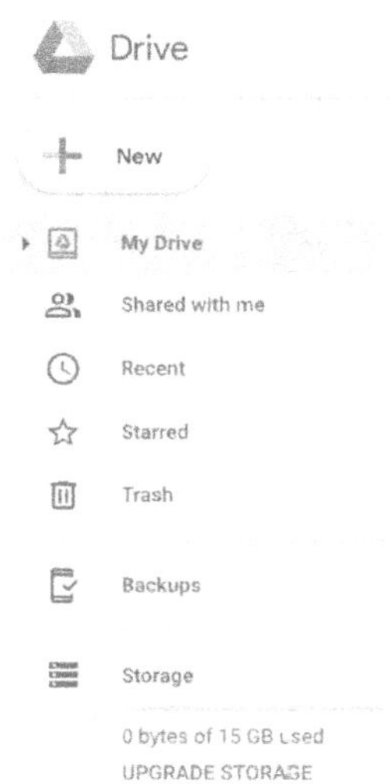


Two things to note here:

1. Shared with me—if people share documents or folders with you, they'll be here unless you move them.

2. Starred—to help you stay organized, you can "star" documents. When you "star" them, they will still be in your main directory, but they'll be here as well.

If you have the basic free plan, you'll have 15 GBs of storage. That's obviously a lot. Considering that a document is very small, you'll probably never want more—unless you are also using Google Drive to store videos and files, or to back up your entire computer.

Why on Earth would you want to pay to back up your computer on the cloud? Because it's surprising cheap! The rates below are what you can expect—they might go up after this book is printed, but not by much since they've been this low for a while.

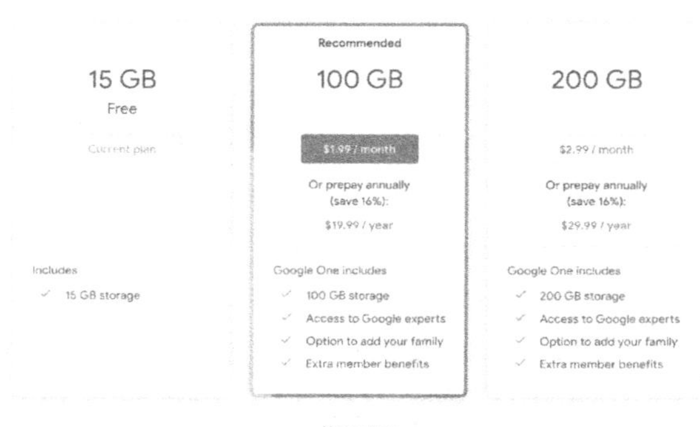

Most people have around 200 GBs of data floating around. That means, for less than a dinner for two at Olive Garden, you can safely know that your data is protected online!

Why back it up online? Two reasons:

1. What if your house floods or burns down and you don't have time to get your computer. Think of all the memories you would lose that are stored on your computer.
2. What if you are away on business or a family trip and you really need a document. It's safely online and you can access it anytime.

If you want to back up your entire computer to Google Drive, you just need to download some software that will sync your computer to the cloud. That means if you save a new file, that file automatically goes to the cloud and you don't have to do a thing. You can also pick and choose what folders are synced to the cloud. To get the software, go to the address below:

https://support.google.com/drive/answer/2424368?co=GENIE.Platform%3DDesktDD&hl=en

## Creating Files and Docs

Once you're ready to create either a document (such as a doc, spreadsheet or presentation), click the new button in the left menu pane:

This will bring up several choices. The main three apps are on the bottom of this menu, but if you click "more" you can see some of the useful, but lesser used, Google Apps (I'm looking at you Google Jamboard!). You can also access this menu by right- clicking inside Google Drive:

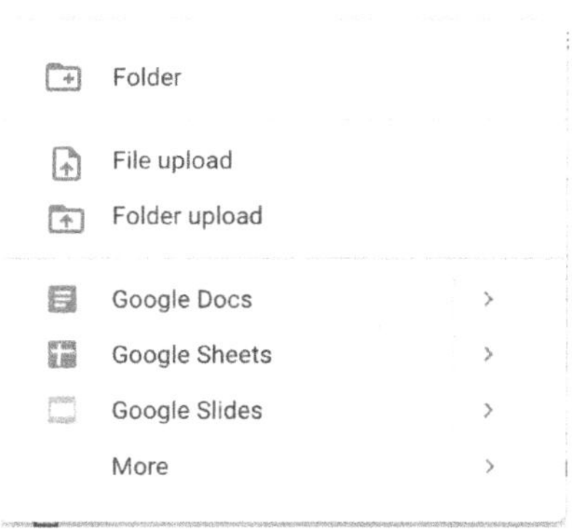

This is also where you'll go to upload files from your computer, or to create a new folder.

Creating folders will help you stay organized. You may, for example, have a recipe folder, or school folder, or a bills folder—you can have as many folders as you want. You can also create folders inside folders (and folders inside the folder you just created inside the folder—go ahead and figure that sentence out…I'll wait!). It's just like file organization on your computer.

If you want to create a folder within a folder, you can either open that folder up and select the new button, or you can right-click inside that open folder and select "Folder."

## Starring and Sharing Files

Once the docs are created, you'll be able to right-click them at any time to bring up a new menu that's just for that specific file. You can add a star to it, rename it, preview it, and, of course, share it.

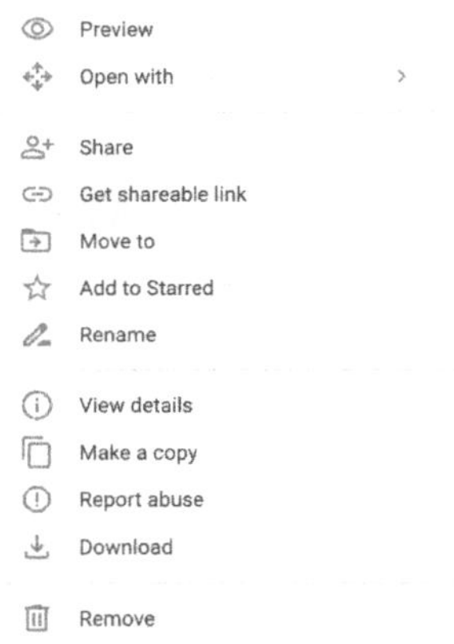


Once you click "Get sharable link" (the option for sharing a file with other people), you'll see something a little like this:

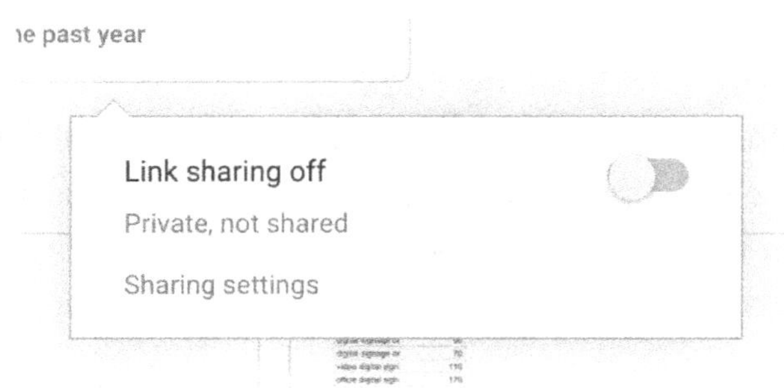


If it's white, like the above, it will note that sharing is off. To turn it on, just click that white box, and it will turn green and note that sharing is turned on. It will also give you a link to the document.

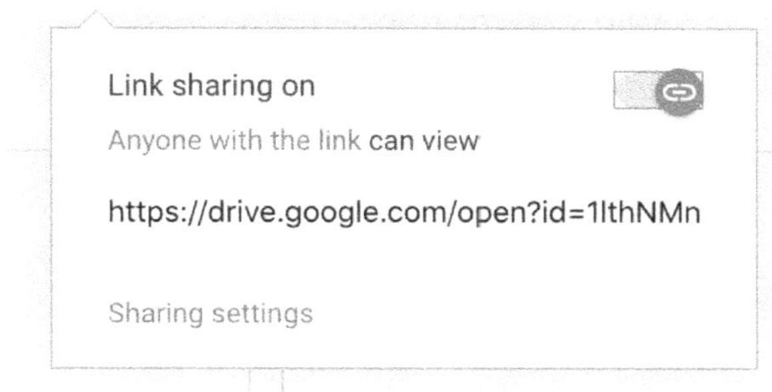


When it's on, by default, it's a non-public link. That means the only way someone is going to find it is if you give them the link.

If you click "Sharing settings" you'll get a few more options. You can email a person the link and also make them an editor, or give them all access.

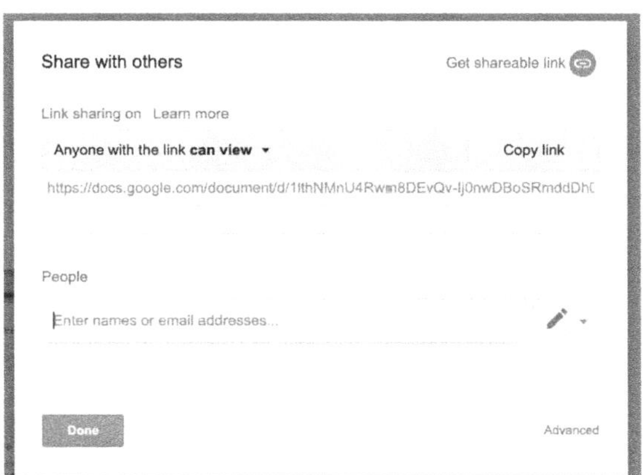

Click the "Anyone with the link can view" drop down and you can manage the access, for example, if you only want certain people that you email to see it—note: if you select this option, they will need to be signed into a Google Account (the one you used in the email name in the box under this), to see the doc.

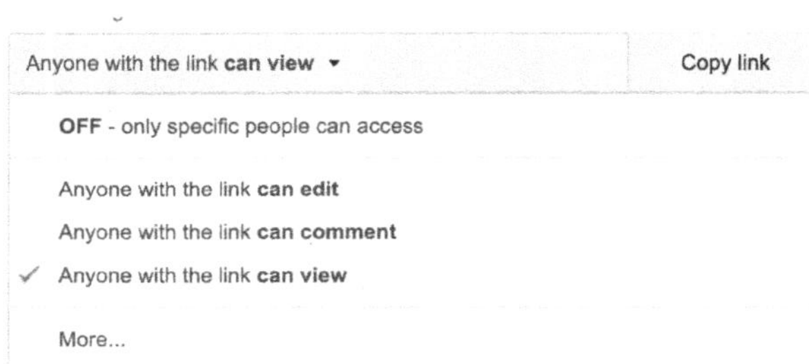


If you select "More" you'll have a few more options. One is to make the file public. This means it's going to be searchable to anyone on Google and people may find it randomly—people you don't know—so it's best if you don't make your Google Sheet with the names and phone numbers of "People with excessive gas" public.

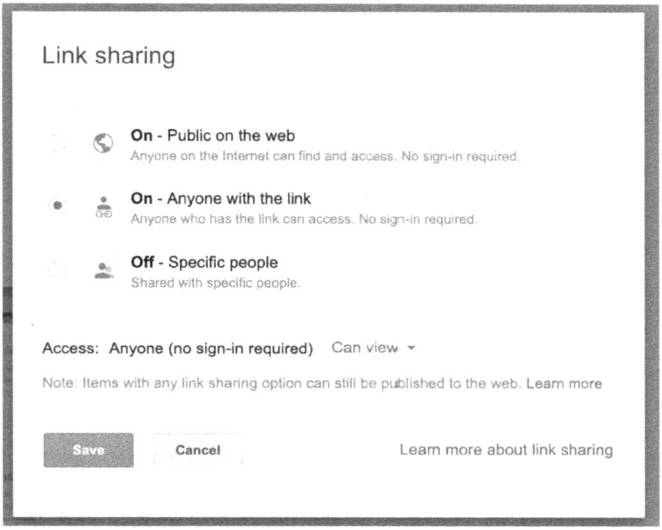


## Find Files

Files are pretty easy to find when you are first getting started. But they add up quickly—especially if you are using them for school or business, or if you are backing up all the files on your computer.

Fortunately, Google has a search bar that works remarkably well—it's right on top of Google Drive. You don't have to know the name of the file—you can search for what's in the document. So if you can't remember what you named your Google Doc, but you know it had the line "And that is why I love competitive dog grooming" (yes, it's a thing!), then just type in that phrase and it will find your doc.

If it's returning too many results—because you have obviously written countless scholarly papers on the subject of competitive dog grooming—then click that little arrow next to the search bar.

That brings up an advanced search. You'll be able to search by owner, by those that are starred, when it was lasted opened, what kind of file it is, and more. Once you've added in all your filters, just hit search, and it will return results in seconds.

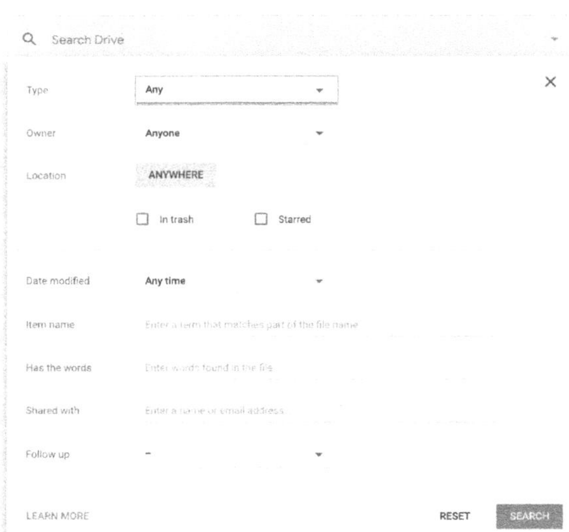

# GOOGLE DOCS

[1]

# Google Docs Crash Course

This chapter will cover:

- Why use Word?
- The Crash Course
- Getting Started

## Should I Throw Away Word and Never Look Back?

Before getting started, let's talk about the elephant in the room: Microsoft Word!

Does Google Docs make Word irrelevant? It really depends on the user. For most people, Google Docs can probably accomplish what you want to do.

Microsoft is paid software, but it's also a lot more powerful. If you are running macros, or doing mail mergers, and need other advanced features, then you'll probably want to stick with Word. There are add-ons for Google Docs, but they just don't beat what you'll find in the full version of Microsoft Word.

If you are just doing basic writing, then Google Docs will be just fine. When it comes to collaboration, it's more than just fine; while Microsoft has made great strides towards making it easier to share and collaborate in Word, Google is the one who mastered the idea. Google also has plug-ins for editing tools such as Grammarly, and is making a big push to be more responsive to catching basic grammatical errors.

Personally, I use Google Docs almost daily, but I still have a copy of Word on my desktop, and that's what I use for my final draft. Once collaboration is finished, I copy and paste it into Word and apply all the final touches.

## The Crash Course

Before we jump into creating our first document, I'll go over the main Google Docs toolbar. If you've ever used Word, then you'll probably know what most of these do already. If you ever get stuck, then hover over the icon and it will give you a description of what it does.

The first two icons are your undo, redo icons. This undoes or redoes whatever you just typed:

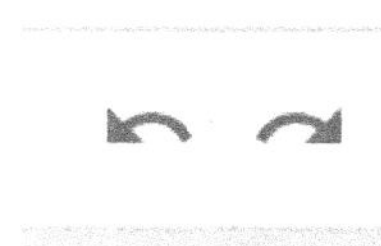

Next is the Print, spellcheck, and formatter. You probably know what the first two are. The last one is a handy little tool; it copies the format of the text. So let's say I have text that is bold, 14- point in size. I can highlight that text, select the paint roller, then click on the text I want to apply the style to. Instantly that text is changed to the same style.

The 100% is the zoom. If you want to zoom out to see more (but smaller) text on the screen, then click on that:

Fonts and style is next to that. This is where you can select the style (if it's a Heading, for example), the font family, the font size, and if you want to bold, italicize, underline, or change the color of the text.

The insert options is the next section. These are all the things you may want to insert into a doc. That includes a link, a comment, and an image:

Justification is next to that. If you want to right align, center align, or change the line spacing, you'll use these options:

If you want to create a numbered or bulleted list, you can use the next two icons; next to those are the indentation:

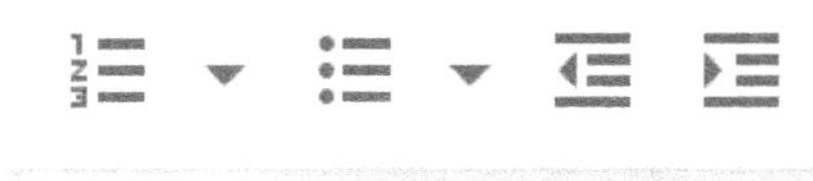

If you have formatting you want to reset, you can use the icon below. This is good if you've copied text from the web and you want to reset it to the default Google Docs text size:

The last two options change how you are viewing a document and to hide the toolbar:

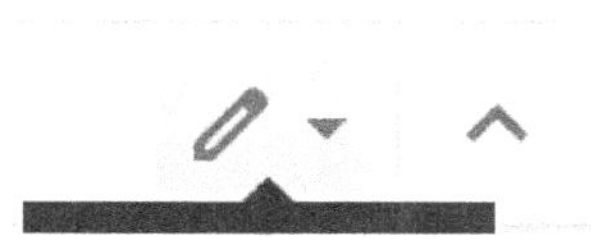

That's a high-level overview. These things will make more sense as we go.

**Getting Started**

Okay, so how exactly do you use Google Docs? There are several ways, but the quickest is to just type in drive.google.com.

Once you have your Google account, then you are all set. Repeat the step above and the browser Window should look more like the below:

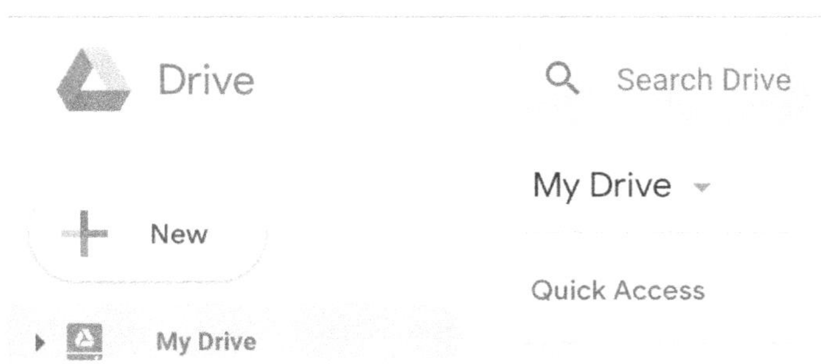


Docs really shines through its connection to Google Drive. Anything you start in Google Docs is automatically saved in your Google Drive account—no need to worry about losing work through power failures, device catastrophes, or really just about any other scenario. Changes are saved as you go, and so are the various versions of your document, so it's easy to revert to an earlier stage of a draft if you need to.

# [3] YOUR FIRST DOCUMENT

This chapter will cover:

- Creating your first document
- Titling your Google Doc
- Opening saved docs

**Creating Your First Doc**

Now that you have your account, let's create a document. Click on the "New" button and then hover over Google Docs; there are two options: Black document and From a template. For now, select "From a template." I'll cover templates a little bit later.

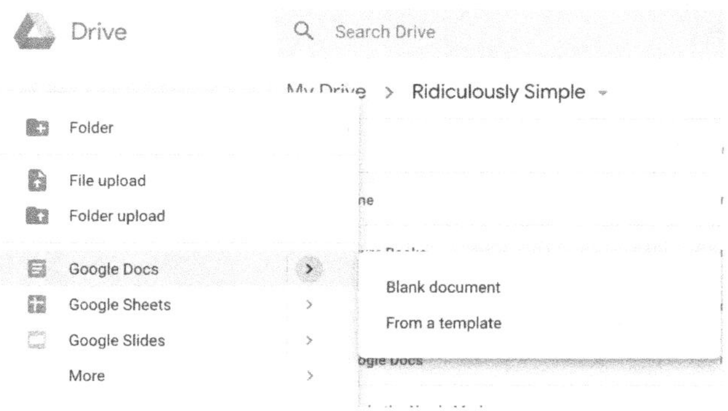


This is going to open up a new tab, and your Google Docs editor will appear.

If you're a Word or Pages user, then you'll be relieved to know everything is designed to work the same way. Many of the buttons look identical.

So, you don't need this book, right?! There's still a difference, and that's what we'll spend the most time with in this book.

Let's have some fun. Pretend the American Revolution is taking place in the year 2019 instead of the year 1776. The British have put fines on our beloved Internet usage, and the people have had enough! Why should you have to pay to see videos of adorable puppies on skateboards?

Michelle Obama is the leader of the American colonies. She's been working on the first draft of a proclamation with her first man, Barack Obama.

The first thing she needs is a title.

**How to title your Google Doc**

Look up in the upper left-hand corner of your Google Docs editor. See the text field that says, "Untitled Document." That's every Google Docs default title. Click on it.

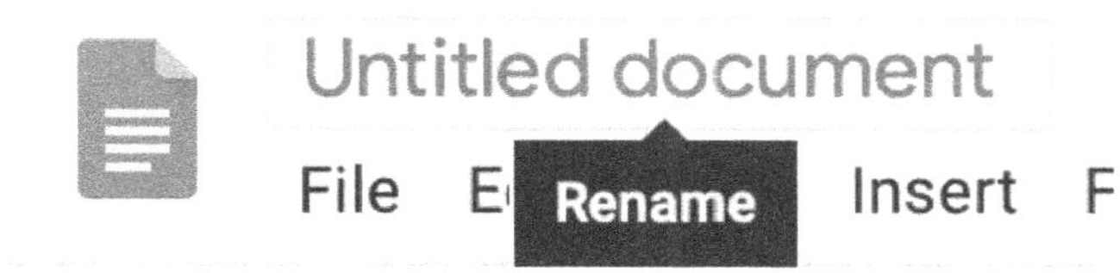


You can now add any title you want by typing. I'll pick something highly original: "The Declaration of Independence," but you can pick anything you want. When you finish, hit the enter key.

In a flash, watch that top bar change with your new title. As long as it shows the new title, then it worked.

Need even more assurance? Look to the right of it: it should say "All changes saved"? Guess what?! It saved!

It may not seem all that revolutionary today, but everything saves automatically. You don't need to hit CTRL S every few seconds. Google saves as you type. If you are the paranoid type, then you still can save manually.

Let's start things off by creating a headline for our doc. Let's go crazy and use Corsiva, 18-point font. You only live once, right?

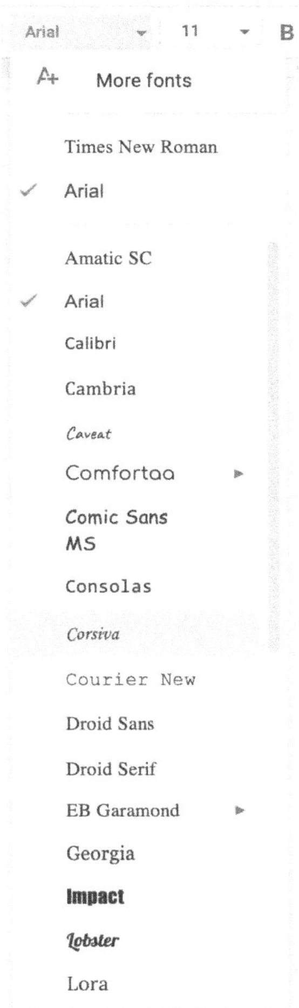


This hopefully feels familiar to you—it's essentially the same way you do it in other document editors. I bet you've used this type of toolbar hundreds of times before. Here's the take away here: icons that look like they do in another app tend to do the exact same thing they did in that other app.

So let's write the title and first paragraph of our declaration, then in a moment we'll send it off for review.

Everything is looking good so far, right? But what happens if there's a power outage? In a blink of a second, it all goes dark. How do we get back to where we left off?

## Opening a saved document

Close your browser. Make sure Google Docs has completely gone away.

Now go right back to drive.google.com.

Unless you are on a public computer (like at a library), Google will show you all the files you have created. Since it was the last thing you worked on, you should see The Declaration of Independence right at the top in the Quick Access list.

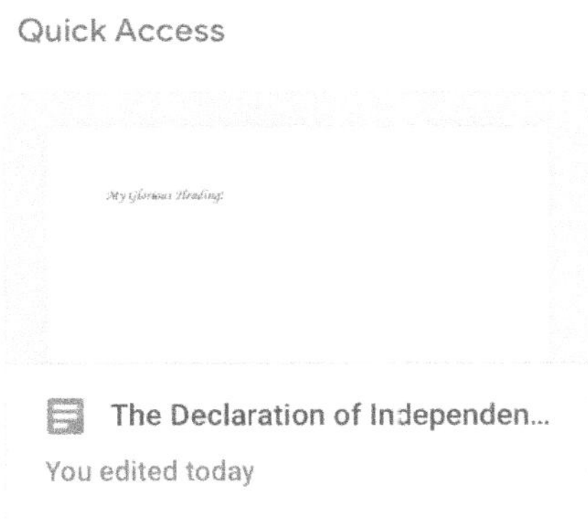


If you are just getting started, it will also be the only doc you see, and you can access it below the quick access; it will look a "little" like this:

I say "little" because you might be in list view or you might be in grid view. What's the difference? List view looks like the above—it gives the name, who the owner is, and the time it was edited. Grid view is more of a thumbnail preview of the doc, like this:

Notice how author and time lasted edited is gone?

What's better? It's a preference, but if you are working with dozens of documents, then Grid view probably will not be ideal unless you need to see previews.

To toggle between the two, click these icons in the upper corner:

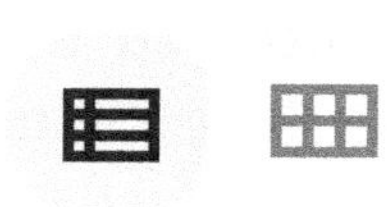

List is the horizontal lines, and grid is the six square boxes.

The top spot goes to documents that have been recently edited.

When you double-click on "The Declaration of Independence," it opens up in a new tab. It's basically the same as opening a document back up in Word—the difference: It's in the cloud.

You can also right-click it to see more options—one of them is "Open with" and you can open it by clicking Google Docs.

This option would be useful if you have a Chromebook that has other editing tools installed and you don't want to use Google Docs to edit it. For it to work, however, you need to have those other apps installed.

You can do that by going to the Chrome extensions store:

https://chrome.google.com/webstore/category/extensions

This is a marketplace for all things Chrome, and most of the extensions (or apps) are free. Just make sure you are using Chrome—hence the name. If you aren't, you can still see the page, but you'll be greeted with this subtle notice:

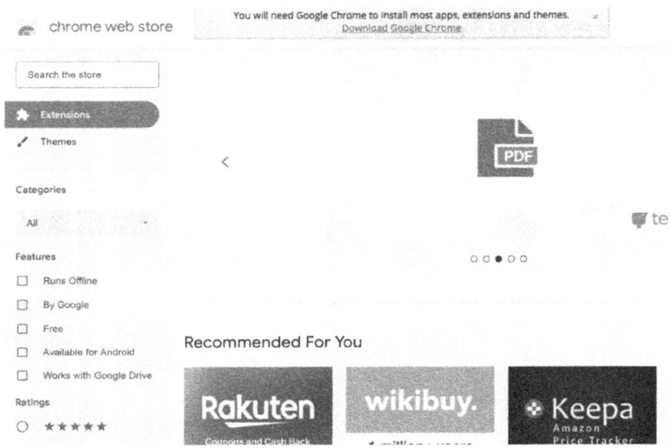


Like most Word Processing editors today, if you open it on a different device (i.e. smartphone or tablet), it's going to look pretty similar. Anything you change on those devices will reflect the document everywhere. It's all in the cloud.

Users of mobile devices (such as iPhones and iPads) can see Google Docs will need a native app to make edits, but what I'm talking about in this book is essentially identical on the apps.

Unfortunately, you'll need a separate app for every app you are using. So you need to get the Google Drive app and the Google Docs app—and if you plan on using Google Slides or Sheets, you'll need to get those apps too. Fortunately, they're free.

Your device has an app store, and that's where you'll download them—just type in the name of the app. The exception here is Fire tablets; these tablets have a not-so-nice relationship with Google that I won't go into here. Google won't put their apps in the app store because of that not-so-nice relationship. You can still install them, but you would need to do something called "side load app." That basically means you are downloading the app onto an SD card, putting the card into the tablet, and installing it manually. I'm not covering how to do that in this book, but if installing it on a Fire device is a must, then there are plenty of tutorials for that. Do so at your own risk, as it's not exactly supported by the device.

# [4]
# SHARING IS CARING

This chapter will cover:

- How to share docs
- Editing and collaborating

## How To Share Your Google Docs

Google Docs is hands-down one of the easiest ways to work on a group document.

When two or more people are editing a document at the same time, you'll be able to see that person's cursor position and watch edits in real time. If you're concerned about losing work, remember that Google Docs saves the version history for you, so it's easy to revert if you need to. Click File > See revision history (or press CTRL+ALT+SHIFT+G). By default, revisions are shown grouped into daily periods, but if you want to see changes made by the minute, click "Show more detailed revisions" at the bottom of the revisions panel. You can see which collaborator made each change in a group document. Of course, the slightly less elegant Undo and Redo functions are always available as well!

Back to your masterpiece in progress: The Declaration of Independence. Michelle is ready for a second opinion of what she's done.

She knows Barack is a master orator, so she knows he's going to have some good input.

Look up in the upper right corner. See the blue button that says Share? Click on that. It's going to open up several different sharing options.

There's a few ways to share it:

1. Type their email address and let Google do the rest.
2. Manually (covered below).

When you email someone, you can also manage exactly what they can do. Click that little pencil icon. By default, it will say they can edit the doc. You can change it so they can only comment on the doc, or they can only view the doc:

You can also hit advance at the bottom of the share menu, and have a few more features—such as disabling print:

But let's say you don't want to email the first man. Let's say you just want to give him a link—that way he doesn't need to use his Google account to open it. To do that, follow the steps above, but in the upper corner of the box, click "Get shareable link."

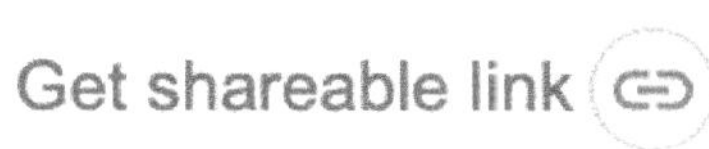


Once you click that, it will give you a sharable link—it even copies the link so if you hit CTRL-V (or right-click paste) you can paste that link anywhere you want.

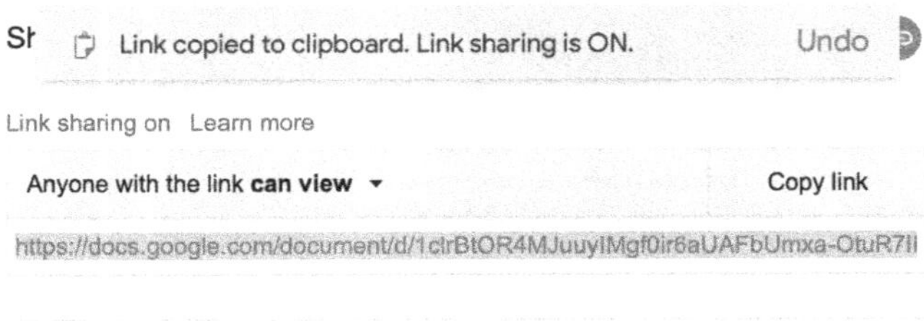


If you click on can view, it will give you a drop-down menu with more features. It looks sort of like the other drop-down menu above, but there's an option that says "more."

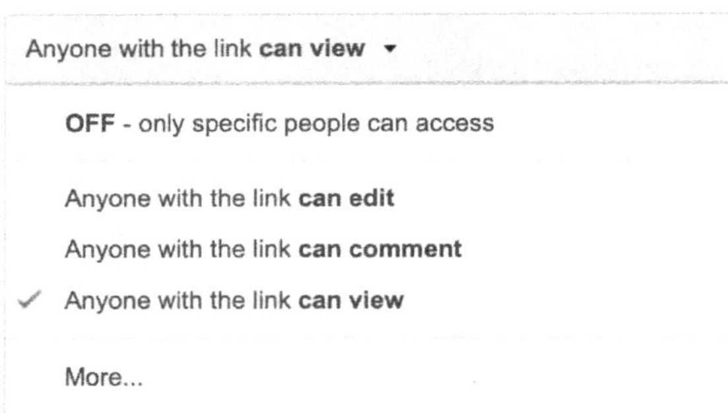


When you click on "More," it gives you a few extra features—such as making the document public in search engines so anyone can find it.

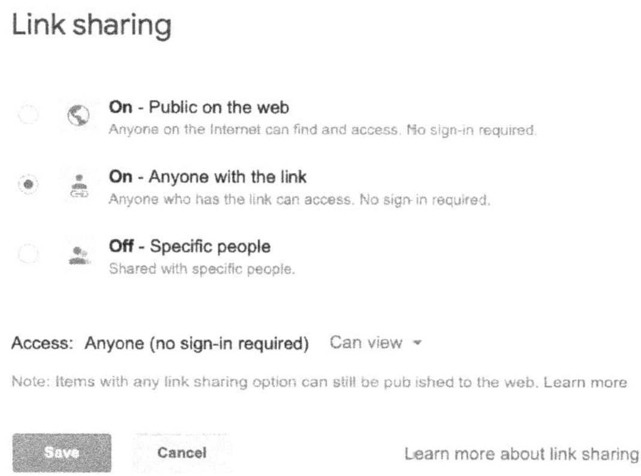


You can turn sharing off at any time, by hitting the "Share" button; once it's turned off, anyone who goes to that link—even if they've been there before—won't be able to see it. If you've emailed a person, they are still a viewer until you remove them.

If you have a person who really hates Google Docs and refuses to view your document in anything but Word, Google Docs allows you to export your work to a Word Document so you don't have to do all of the copying and font processing yourself. Just click on file > download as > Word; there's a whole host of other exports here as well.

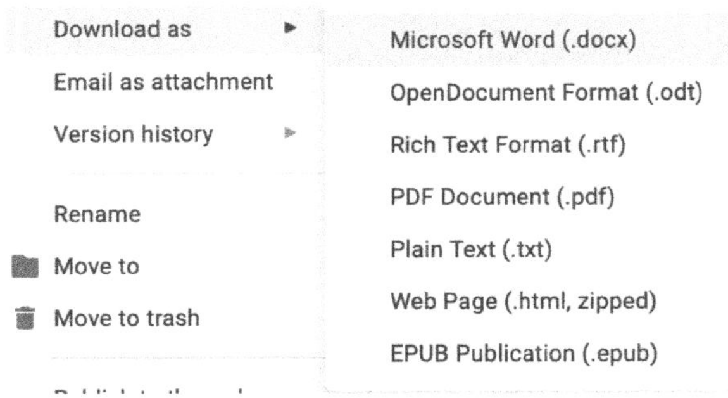


## Editing and Collaborating with Others

Let's pretend for a moment the first man is in the document and he's ready to make some changes and add some notes.

As he goes through the document, he's going to make some notes. There are a few ways to do it; the easiest way is to right-click and select "Comment."

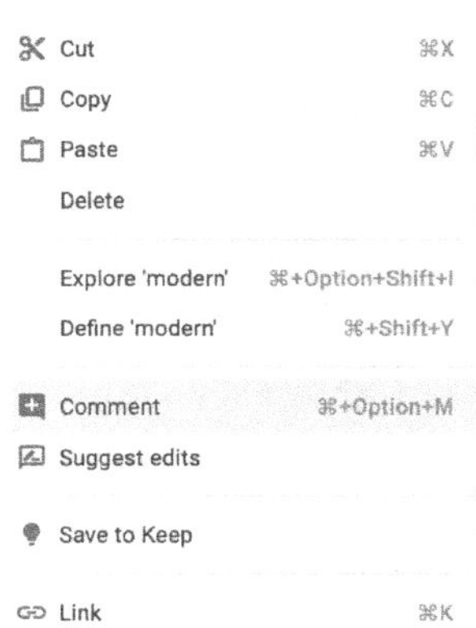

You can also get this, by selecting Insert on the toolbar, and Comment:

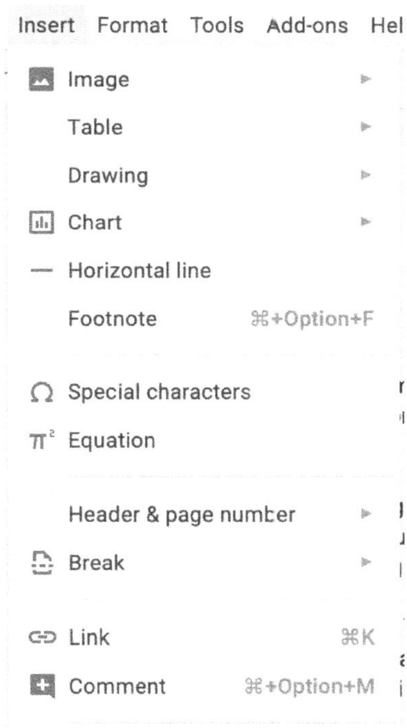


Either of these will bring up the comment box. Add your comment, and select the blue comment box when you are ready to post it. When you add a comment (or make a change), it's in real-time; that means if the person who is collaborating with you has the document open, they can actually watch you make the edits and add the comments.

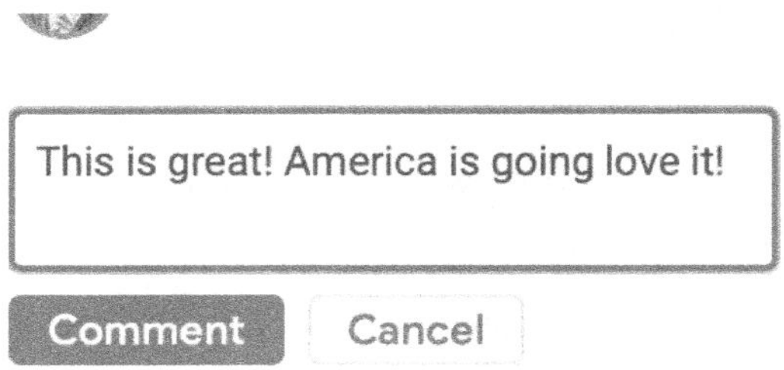


If you have multiple people working on the doc, you can type "@" and see a list of people you can mention; if you mention them, Google will notify them so they can add a reply to your comment.

Once the comment is posted, it will show up on the side of Google Docs.

You can delete or edit the comment by clicking on those three little dots on the side of the box:

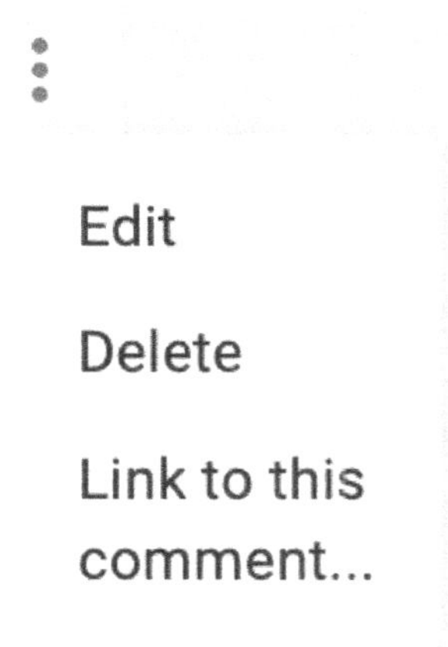


The person on the other end will be able to resolve the comment (that makes it disappear, but they can undo it).

Or they can reply to it.

When others are editing a doc I created, my personal preference is to tell them to edit with suggestions. This lets me see the changes they have made. You can turn it on by clicking on the pencil icon in the menu, and selecting "Suggesting."

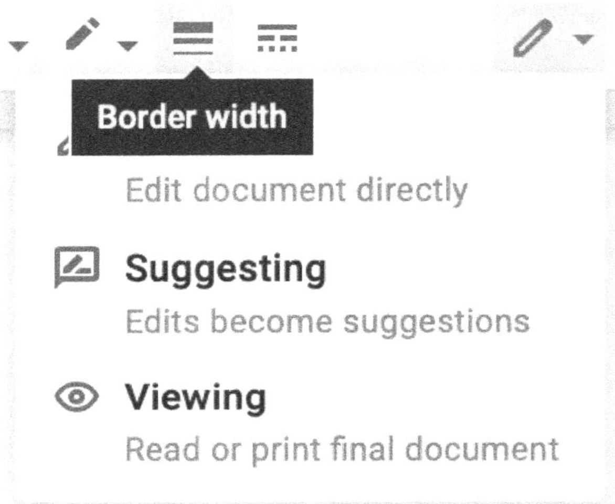


Now when they edit the doc, it will show up as a different color.

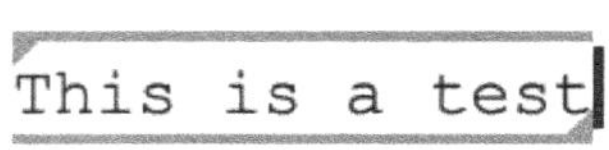


If you click on what they changed, you can accept the change with the check mark, or ignore it with the X. You can also ask questions about it and they can reply.

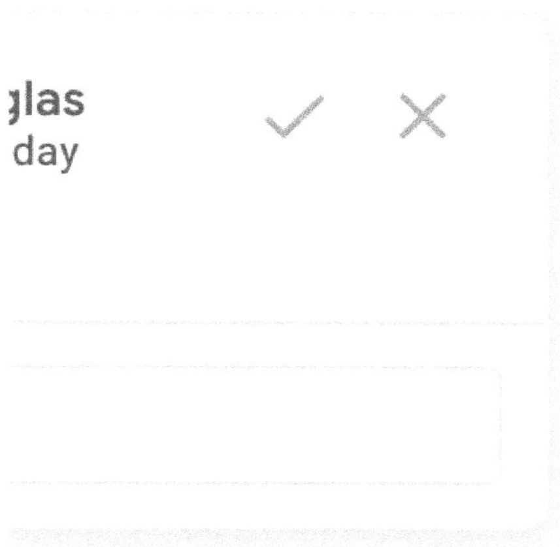


To see all the versions of a document, go to "file" and see versions.

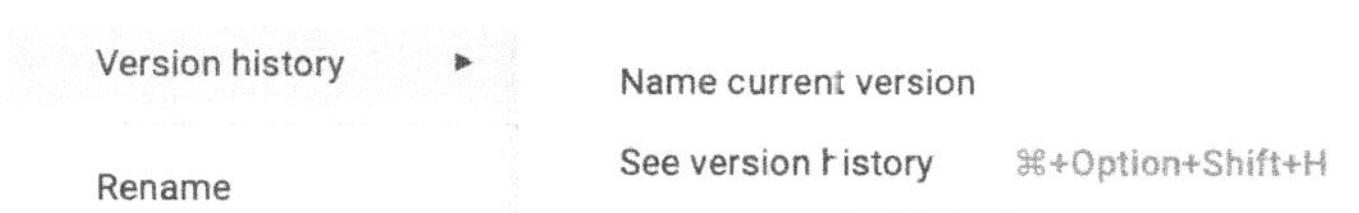


If there is going to be a lot of versions, then one suggestion is to name each one—which you can do here.

When you click "See version history", you'll get a list of all the versions. Clicking on any one of them will bring up that version. You can view it, or even restore it.

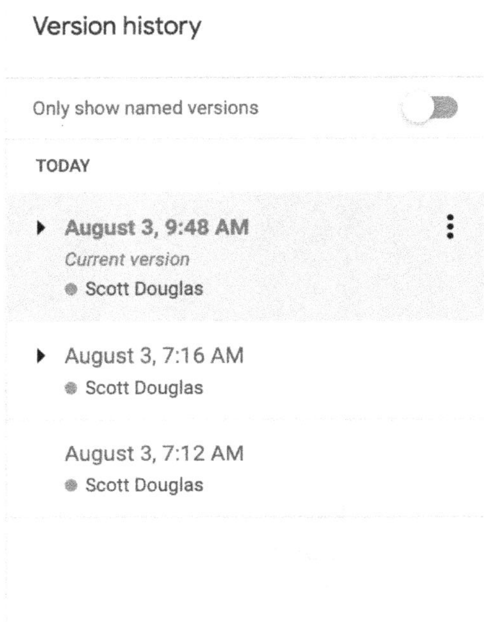


To get back to the document, just hit the back button in the menu (not the browser back button):

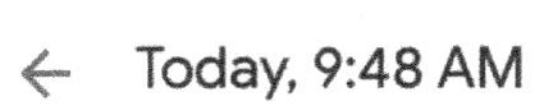


# [5]

# BEYOND THE BASICS

This chapter will cover:

- Printing
- Adding photos
- Adding tables
- Adding spreadsheets
- Adding a table of contents
- Templates

## Printing From the Cloud

Michelle's pretty happy with her declaration, but she's still a little old school—she likes to read through her work the old fashion way with that little thing called paper. So, she obviously needs to print it.

You probably can guess that you do this a way you are familiar with: File > Print.

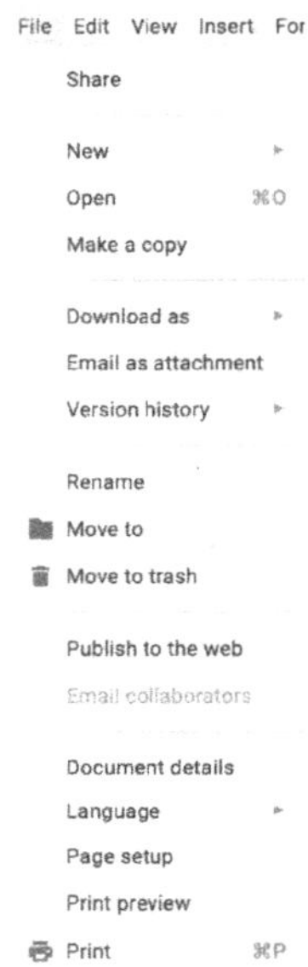


From here, it gets a little…complicated. Printing is not something Google Docs excels at.

You have two main options:

Save it to your computer and then print it from your computer.

Add your computer to Google

If you want to add your computer to Google Cloud print, then click the link.

It will walk you through the steps. The steps change depending on the kind of printer you have. It's not rocket science, but you'll need to pay attention to details.

If you want to skip the fuss there's a longer, but less hassle, way: export as a PDF, open the PDF on your computer, print it from your computer. Because you already have a printer on your computer, it will show up when you do File > Print.

## Adding Photos to Google Docs

Okay, so you've printed it, you've agreed the text is where you want it to be by collaborating with others—now you want to jazz it up.

Google Docs works just like any other word processor. You can add in images wherever you want, either by copying and pasting, or by adding them in from Insert > Image.

Just find a place where you want to add an image. If you have found the image online and copied it, then just do CTRL-V, and it will be added in.

If you have the image stored on your computer, in your Google Drive, or any number of other places, then you can do one of two things. One: click Insert > Image:

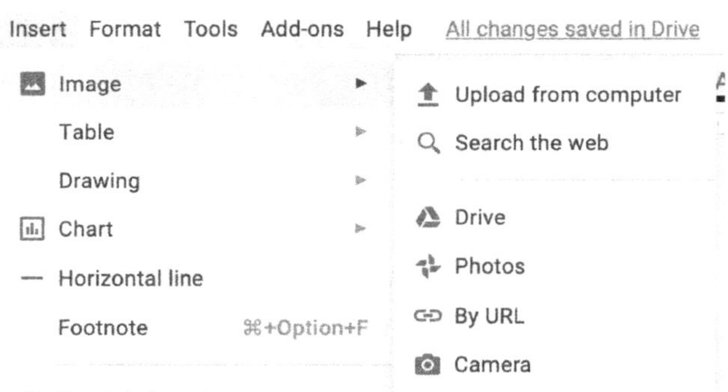


Or, two, click the Picture icon in the toolbar:

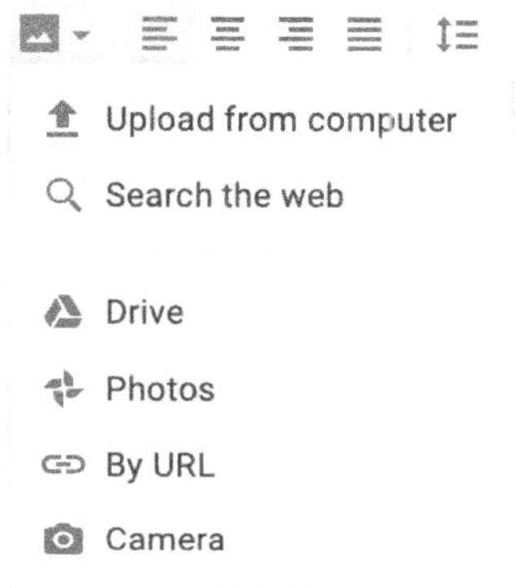


If you simply want to add the image from your computer, then choose "Upload from computer" and find it on your computer. You can also search the web for the file, paste a link to the file, or, if you are using a device that supports it, use the computer's built-in camera to add an image.

Once the image is in your document, click on it. You'll see little blue squares around it—and a small blue dot:

Clicking on these lets you resize the image; clicking on the dot will let you rotate the image. You can also choose how the text communicates with the image. By default, it will be Inline—that means the text will go above and below it. "Wrap text" will mean the text will go on all sides of it. "Break text" lets you put a margin around the text—if you want a little white space, for example.

If you right-click, you'll also see some extra options for the image:

Most options you probably understand. "Alt text" is handy if you'll be publishing this online—it is text that shows if the text can't be seen; you are basically describing the image.

Clicking on "Image options" will bring up even more options:

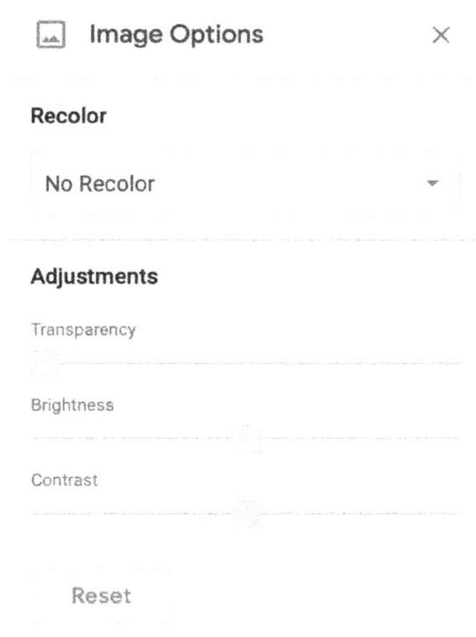


Here you can make it brighter, for example; you can also make it semi-transparent—which is great if you will be using it as a watermark.

If you change your mind about the image, you can delete it or you can just click "Replace image" when you click on it:

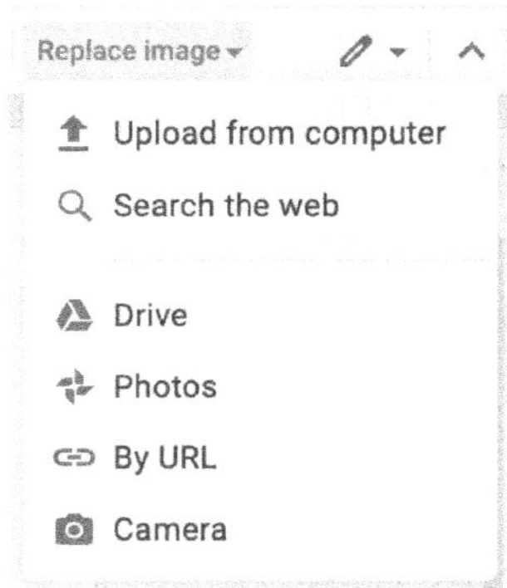


## Getting Really Fancy

We have photos. It's looking snazzy, right?! Now let's dig in deeper.

Next, we are going to learn how to add in tables and spreadsheets. This might not be for everyone, but it's still good to know.

First, let's see how to do this the manual way. This is a good option if you don't have a lot of data you are working with—let's pretend here that you want to show the week's lunch menu.

Go to "Insert" on the toolbar and "Table":

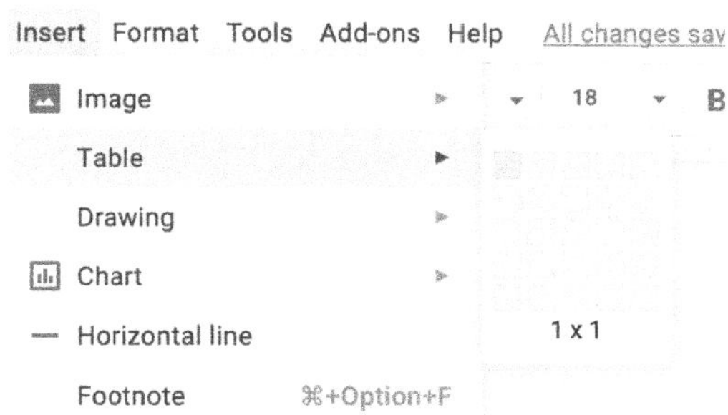


From here, you'll drag the number of boxes based on how big you want your table to be. This is a lunch menu, and I'm going to make it seven days with two rows.

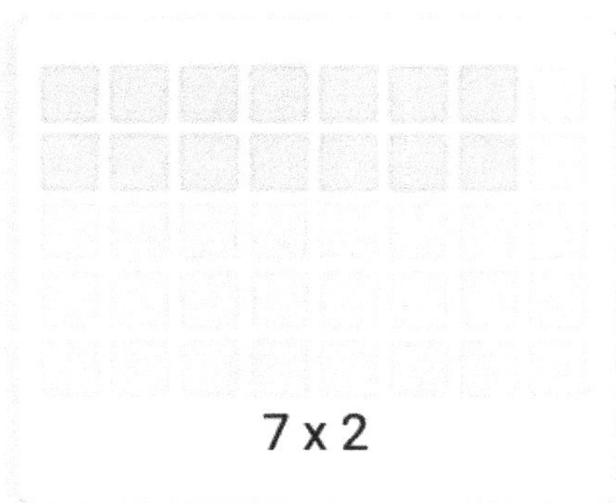


It will show up blank:

| | | | | | | |
|---|---|---|---|---|---|---|
| | | | | | | |

Next, I'll add in my menu. I'm personally excited for Saturday, where lunch will be a bag of Doritos—I really put a lot of effort into that lunch!

| Sunday | Monday | Tuesday | Wednesday | Thursday | Friday | Saturday |
|---|---|---|---|---|---|---|
| Green eggs and ham | Lobster | Hamburger | Lambchops | Fish & Chips | FREE DAY | Bag of doritos |

That table is nice, but it doesn't really visually illustrate anything. Next, I'm going to change the color of the top row so it stands out a bit more. Highlight that entire top row:

| Sunday | Monday | Tuesday | Wednesday | Thursday | Friday | Saturday |
|---|---|---|---|---|---|---|

Next, right-click, which will bring up your "Table" menu. Select "Table properties." This kind of sounds like the properties for the entire table, but because we highlighted and then right-clicked, it will only change the style of the row highlighted (if we had right-clicked without highlighting, it would have changed everything).

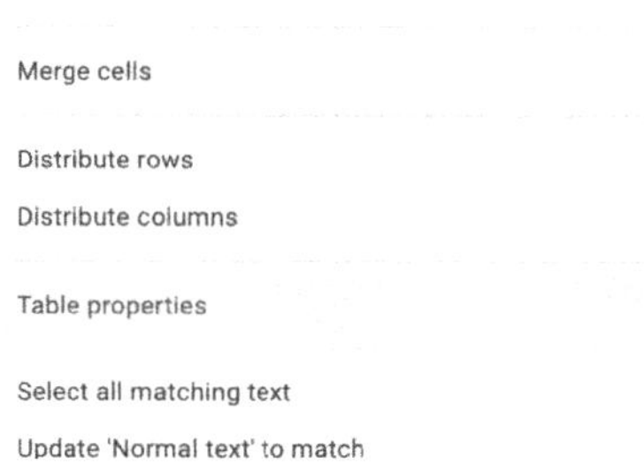


There's a lot of properties here, but the one we want for this row is "Cell background color":

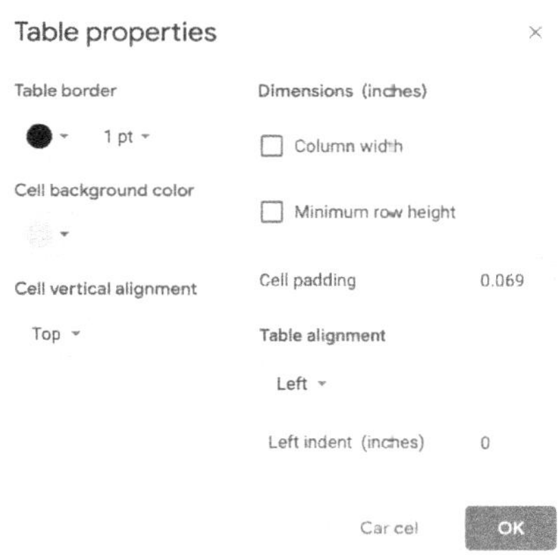


Once you change the background, click "OK" and the table will look similar to the below:

| Sunday | Monday | Tuesday | Wednesday | Thursday | Friday | Saturday |
|---|---|---|---|---|---|---|
| Green eggs and ham | Lobster | Hamburger | Lambchops | Fish & Chips | FREE DAY | Bag of doritos |

You can also highlight one row and change the color. I'll change Friday because it's a free day and I want it to stand out more.

Let's pretend we don't want cow meat this week—we want two days of lobster! Delete "hamburger," highlight both the Monday and Tuesday boxes, right-click, and select "merge cells":

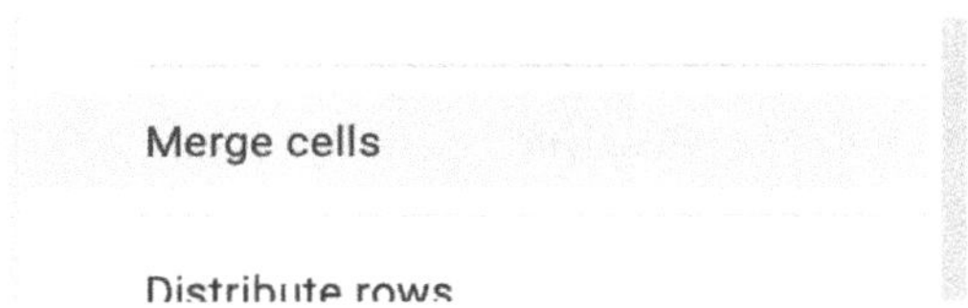


The cell is now one box:

| Sunday | Monday | Tuesday | Wednesday | Thursday | Friday | Saturday |
|---|---|---|---|---|---|---|
| Green eggs and ham | Lobster | | Lambchops | Fish & Chips | FREE DAY | Bag of doritos |

Now, let's make that menu a little taller. Right-click, "select table properties," and check off "Minimum row height." I'll make it one inch. This means if the text is longer, it could be more than 1 inch, but it will be at least one inch:

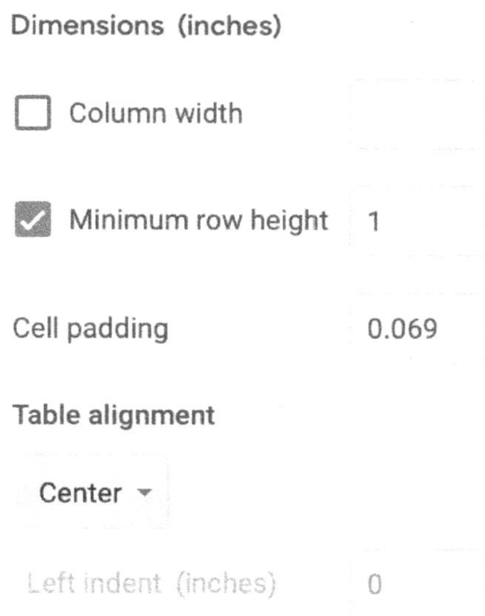


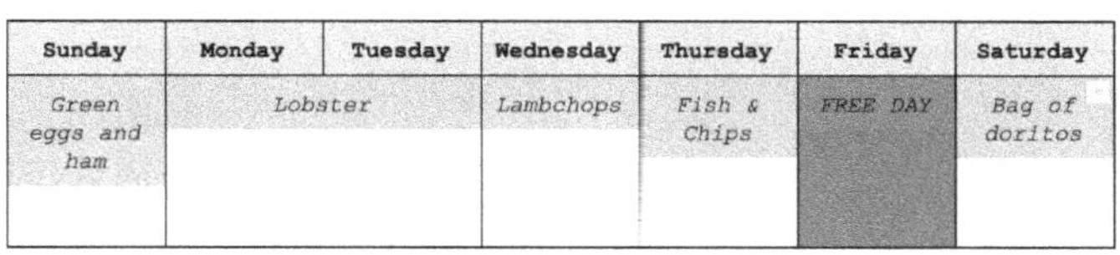


We almost have the menu where we want it, but there's still a little work to be done. Let's make the cells show the text in the middle of the cell. Go to "Table properties" and under "Cell Vertical Alignment," select "middle":

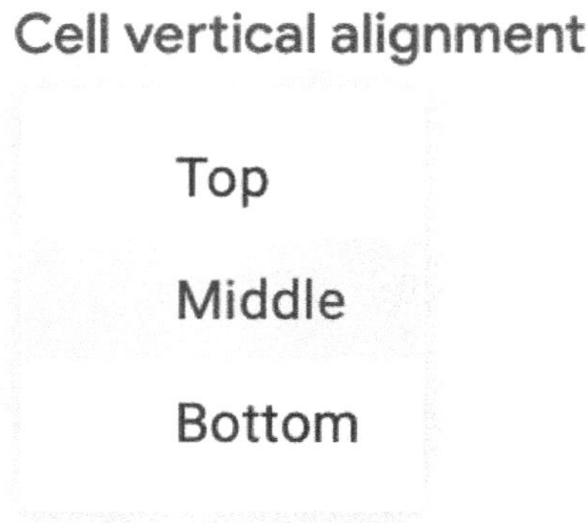


Now everything is evenly aligned in the middle:

| Sunday | Monday | Tuesday | Wednesday | Thursday | Friday | Saturday |
|---|---|---|---|---|---|---|
| *Green eggs and ham* | *Lobster* | | *Lambchops* | *Fish & Chips* | *FREE DAY* | *Bag of doritos* |

Right now, all the columns are the same width. You can make the table larger by dragging either end of the table:

| Sunday | Monday | Tuesday | Wednesday | Thursday | Friday | Saturday |
|---|---|---|---|---|---|---|
| *Green eggs and ham* | *Lobster* | | *Lambchops* | *Fish & Chips* | *FREE DAY* | *Bag of doritos* |

## How to insert spreadsheets from Google Sheet

Google Docs integrates all things Google into it. Let's take that to heart and look at another Google app quickly: Google Sheets.

Go ahead and go back to drive.google.com and create a new document—this time a spreadsheet (hint: click the new button and then select spreadsheet)

In a flash you have a spreadsheet in the cloud. All the menus are pretty similar to Google Docs, and you enter text the same way.

For this example, I'm going to use a library database that's already been created. Let's pretend I want to copy some of it (though I could also do all of it) into my Google Doc. I just need to highlight what I want to copy, then either right-click and choose "copy" or do CTRL-C on the keyboard.

Next, I'll go back into my Google Doc and hit CTRL-V on the keyboard to paste it. It's going to ask us if we want to paste it in Linked or unlinked:

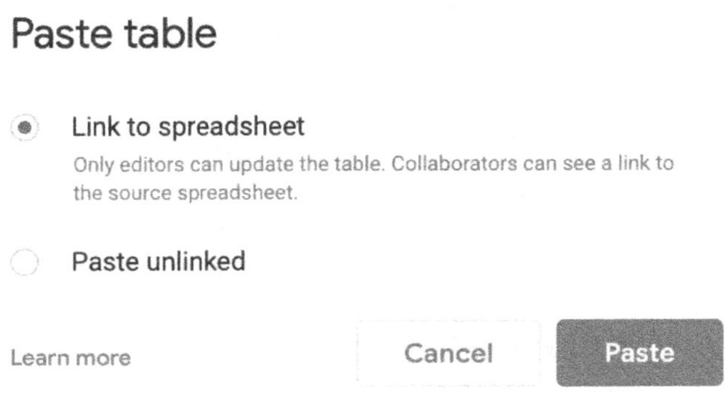


What's the difference? Linked lets a person go to that original spreadsheet—they can view other rows and make changes. Unlinked pastes it in as a new table and if you make changes to the spreadsheet, it won't show up in your Google Doc.

I'm going to pick Linked. It will paste in and look pretty...basic:

| | | | | | | | |
|---|---|---|---|---|---|---|---|
| A brief history of time | Stephen W. Hawking | Hawking, Stephen W. | Bantam Books | | Astronomy | 198 | QB981 .H377 1988 |
| A Career as an Electrician | Daniel E. Harmon | Harmon, Daniel E. | The Rosen Publishing Group, Inc | 2010 | Juvenile Nonfiction | 80 | TK159 .H37 2011 |
| A Child's Garden of Verses | Robert Louis Stevenson | Stevenson, Robert Louis | Chronicle Books | 1989 | Juvenile Nonfiction | 30 | PR5489 .C5 1989 |
| A Concise Guide to Technical Communication | Laura J. Gurak, John M. Lannon | Gurak, Laura J. | Pearson/Longman | 2004 | Technology & Engineering | 17 | T10.5 .G83 2004 |
| A Concise Public Speaking Handbook | Steven A. Beebe, Susan J. Beebe | Beebe, Steven A. | Allyn & Bacon | | Performing Arts | 292 | PN4129.15 .B42 2012 |
| | | | | | Techno | | TK786 |

Just like the table we created earlier, however, you can go in and create all sorts of styles for it. For example, I chose "table property" and changed the background color for the first two rows:

| | | | | | | | |
|---|---|---|---|---|---|---|---|
| A brief history of time | Stephen W. Hawking | Hawking, Stephen W. | Bantam Books | | Astronomy | 198 | QB981 .H377 1988 |
| A Career as an Electrician | Daniel E. Harmon | Harmon, Daniel E. | The Rosen Publishing Group, Inc | 2010 | Juvenile Nonfiction | 80 | TK159 .H37 2011 |
| A Child's Garden of Verses | Robert Louis Stevenson | Stevenson, Robert Louis | Chronicle Books | 1989 | Juvenile Nonfiction | 30 | PR5489 .C5 1989 |
| | | Gurak, | Pearso | | Techno logy & | | T10.5 |

These changes don't show up in the original spreadsheet.

So let's pretend that you also linked your sheet into Google Docs. If you click on the link button in the upper corner, then you'll get new options:

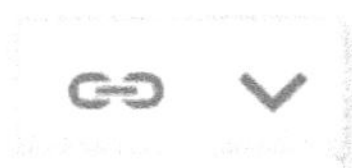

You can unlink the document, for example, or open it. If sharing is not turned on, the other person won't be able to access it.

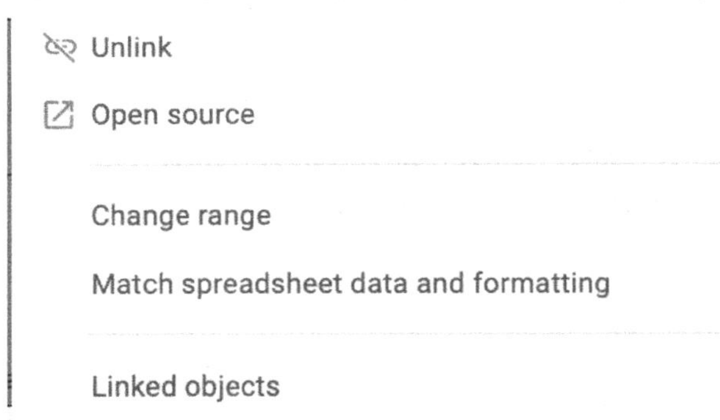


## There's a Template for that

Once you know your way around Google Docs, you can save time by using one of the pre-created Google Templates for Docs. To use one, go to drive.google.com and create a Google Doc—but instead of blank, select from template.

A new window is going to open with all of your options. Unlike Word and Pages, Google isn't huge on templates, but they do allow others to add templates, and you can find plenty of others by doing a quick Google search for Google Docs templates.

## Table of Contents

One useful feature is the table of contents. This would more commonly be used in a book or long-form document. You hopefully won't use it to share a love letter with your wife, but you might want to use it if you are using Google Docs for a dissertation.

You can see/add the table of contents by going to Insert > Table of contents. You can do it either with or without the page numbers:

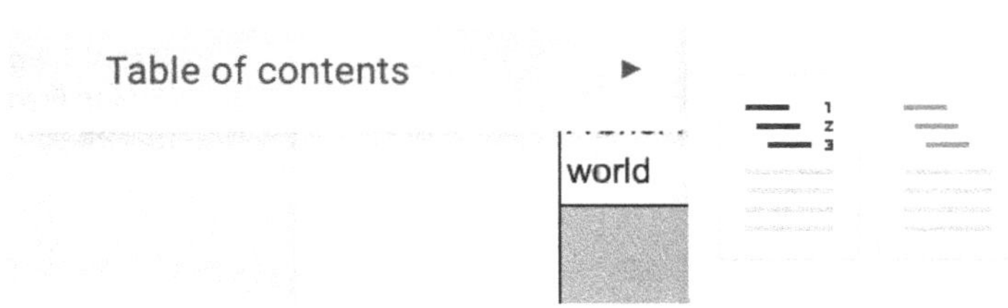

If you don't see your table of contents after adding it, there's likely a good reason: you haven't added any headings to the Doc.

Click on Normal text from your drop down. See all the different options?

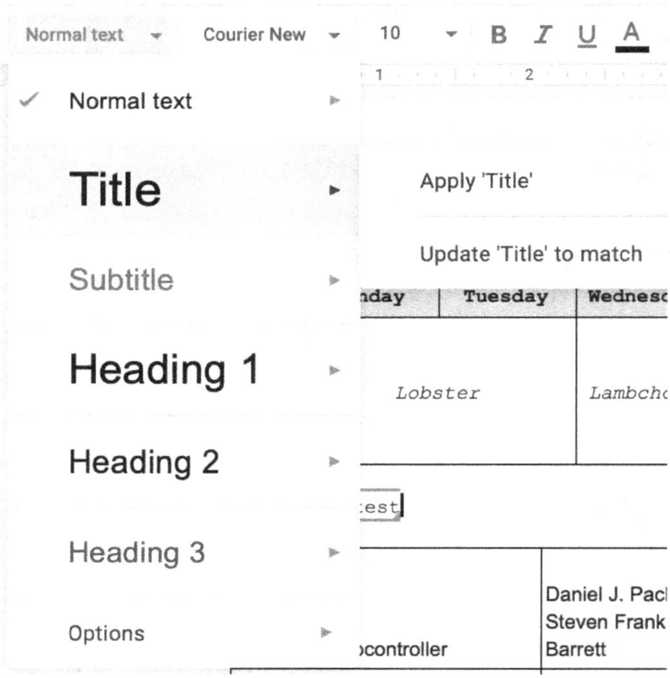


If this were a book, then "Title" would be the title on the first page. "Heading 1" would be the chapter title, "Heading 2" and "Heading 3" would be sections within that chapter.

For each one you can select "Update 'Title' to match." Let's say "Title" changes the text to size 24 but you want it to be size 36. If you change your text to size 36, then highlight it and select "Title" and update it. Then, every time you add a new Title in the doc (not other docs) it will update it to that style.

If you want it to apply to every doc going forward, then go to "Options" in that same section and select "Save as my default styles":

[5]

# THIS AND THAT

This chapter will cover:

- Google Docs menus

In this section, I'll cover some final things you need to know about Google Docs. This isn't comprehensive—I'm not going to cover Script Editor, for example, because the point is to keep things simple and show you the features you'll most likely be using.

### File menu

We've covered all the important things in the file menu, but there's one thing of note: File > Language:

By default, it will be in English; that means if you start typing a document in Spanish, then you'll see all kinds of grammatical errors. Changing the language adds in a new dictionary so it doesn't think you are just typing gibberish.

### View Menu

There are two things I'll point out under the View menu. First, Print layout. By default, it's checked off. Clicking it will show the document in a long scroll view—so no page breaks:

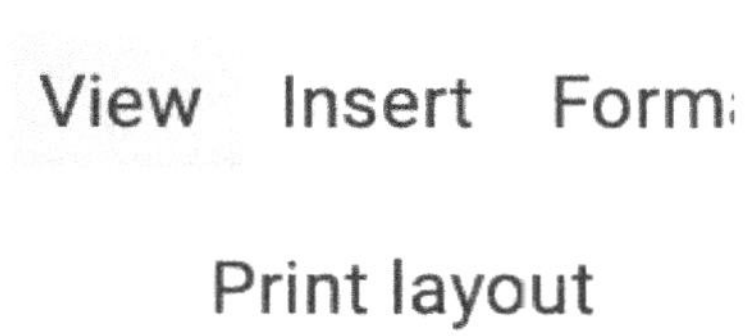

"Show document online" will bring up a side panel to show all the headers in your document:

**Insert Menu**

If you want to add a header (such as every page has your last name on top), or add in page number, then head to "Insert" and "Header & page number."

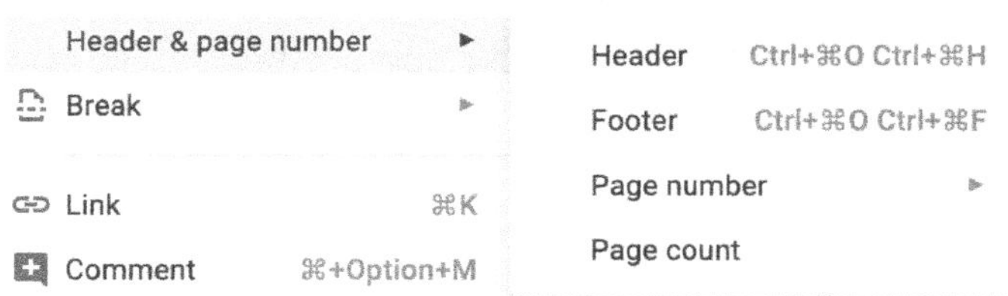


Insert > Break will add in a page break. By default, Google does this automatically, but if you are doing a new section that you want on a new page, then you can do it manually here:

Insert > Special characters is where you can grab symbols like the © sign:

Insert > Bookmark is helpful in longer documents. You can create bookmark links, so whenever you are referencing something, you can send them right to that section so they don't have to scroll to find it:

**Tools Menu**

The tools menu is where you'll find Spell checker and word count.

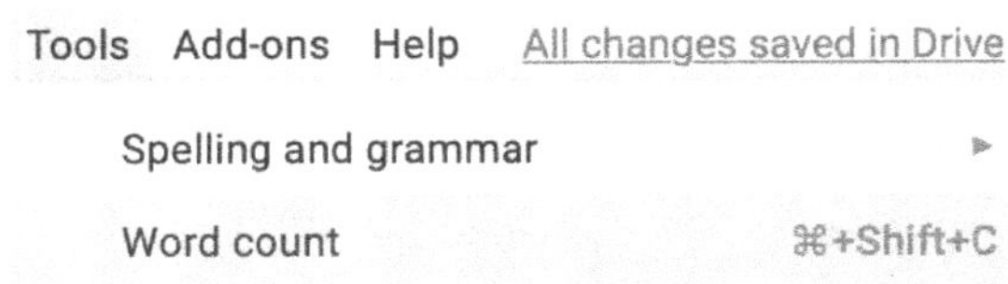


You can also see the built in dictionary and where you can translate the document into another language. I should note here that this is obviously a computer translation, so don't expect perfection.

"Explore" is helpful in research papers. It keeps you in the doc so you don't have to go to a tab to look something up:

In the below example, I typed in "Stephen Colbert" and it gave me basic information about him in a side menu:

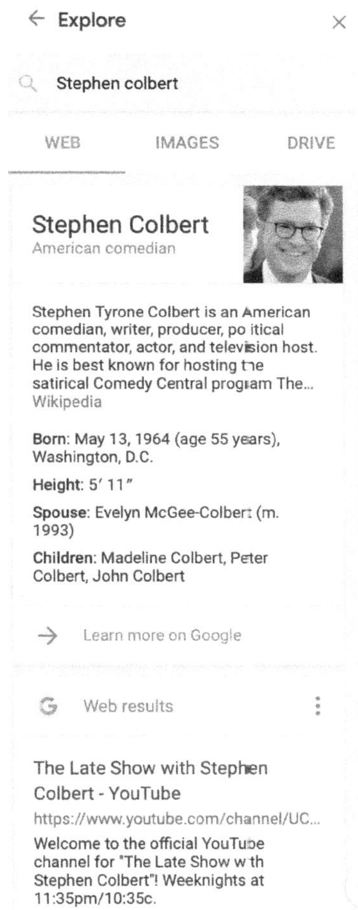


### Add-ons Menu

This is where you can add on extensions if you don't go to the Google store:

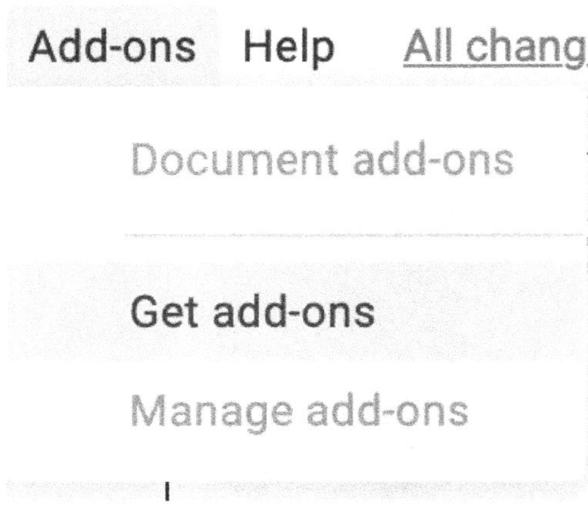


**Help Menu**

And finally, the help menu will let you search for common tasks, see updates to Google Docs, and even get training:

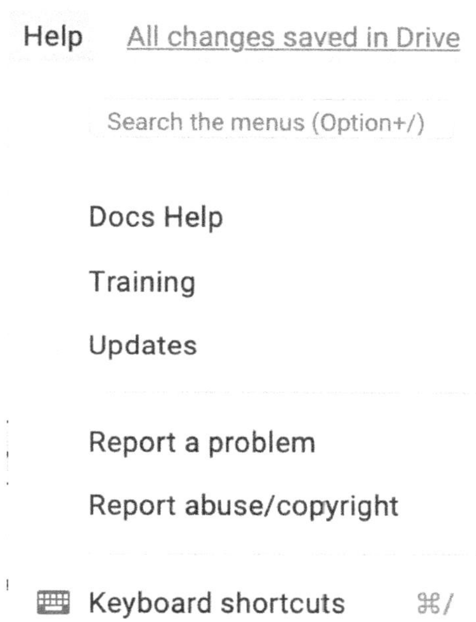
Help
All changes saved in Drive
Search the menus (Option+/)
Docs Help
Training
Updates
Report a problem
Report abuse/copyright
Keyboard shortcuts
⌘/

# [6] Google Docs Keyboard Shortcuts

You can see all the keyboard shortcuts in Google Docs by selecting Help > Keyboard shortcuts.

For your reference, below are some of the most common ones you'll use.

| **Common actions** | |
|---|---|
| Copy | Ctrl + c |
| Cut | Ctrl + x |
| Paste | Ctrl + v |
| Paste without formatting | Ctrl + Shift + v |
| Undo | Ctrl + z |
| Redo | Ctrl + Shift + z |
| Insert or edit link | Ctrl + k |
| Print | Ctrl + p |
| Open | Ctrl + o |

| | |
|---|---|
| Find | Ctrl + f |
| Find and replace | Ctrl + h |
| **Text formatting** | |
| Bold | Ctrl + b |
| Italicize | Ctrl + i |
| Underline | Ctrl + u |
| Strikethrough | Alt + Shift + 5 |
| Superscript | Ctrl + . |
| Subscript | Ctrl + , |
| Copy text formatting | Ctrl + Alt + c |
| Paste text formatting | Ctrl + Alt + v |
| Clear text formatting | Ctrl + \ |
| Increase font size | Ctrl + Shift + > |
| Decrease font size | Ctrl + Shift + < |
| **Paragraph formatting** | |
| Increase paragraph indentation | Ctrl + ] |
| Decrease paragraph indentation | Ctrl + [ |
| Apply normal text style | Ctrl + Alt + 0 |
| Apply heading style [1-6] | Ctrl + Alt + [1-6] |
| Left align | Ctrl + Shift + l |
| Center align | Ctrl + Shift + e |
| Right align | Ctrl + Shift + r |
| Justify | Ctrl + Shift + j |
| Numbered list | Ctrl + Shift + 7 |
| Bulleted list | Ctrl + Shift + 8 |
| **Comments** | |
| Insert comment | Ctrl + Alt + m |
| Open discussion thread | Ctrl + Alt + Shift + a |
| **Menus** | |
| File menu | Alt + f |
| Edit menu | Alt + e |
| View menu | Alt + v |

| | |
|---|---|
| Insert menu | Alt + i |
| Format menu | Alt + o |
| Tools menu | Alt + t |
| Help menu | Alt + h |

# GOOGLE SHEETS

# [1]

# Google Sheets Crash Course

This chapter will cover:

- What is Sheets?
- Should you still use Excel?
- The Google Sheets crash course

## What is Google Sheets, Anyway?

For 30-some-odd years, the world of spreadsheets has been ruled by one king: Microsoft Excel. Sure, there were far away challengers that tried to overtake the beast—I'm looking at you, Lotus 1-2-

3—but none have come close to dethroning the powerful tool...until Google Sheets.

So what is Google Sheets? It's a cloud-based spreadsheet. Think Excel, but online. "But Excel is online," you say. Yes! But Google was there first, and really has the advantage over Excel in this arena. It's quicker and easier to use for collaboration.

Google Sheets is also free; Excel has monthly/yearly subscriptions.

**Excel vs. Google Sheets: What's Right For Me?**

If you are judging Google Sheets by mere looks, you might think it was a clone. It has tabs, it has cells, and, heck, even the formulas are largely the same!

So what is the difference?!

Let's go with the obvious one. As of this writing, you can add 5,000,000 cells to Google Sheets; Microsoft Excel? 17,179,869,184 cells.

How embarrassing, right? How on Earth can you get anything done with only 5,000,000 cells!

Kidding aside, that number does tell you one thing: Excel is the best software for large corporations managing budgets spanning dozens of years. But for the rest of us, that number really doesn't matter. A spreadsheet with 5,000,000 cells is plenty. The moment you get to cell 5,000,001 you have hopefully made it in the world and have sold your business. You now live on a private island where you ride llamas bareback on the beach. Why llamas? Because you are ridiculously wealthy and horses just seem too middleclass.

There is one other thing that's telling about that number, however. It's speed.

What do I mean by that? The reason Google limits cells is because in a cloud-based environment, the more cells you add, the slower it gets. Excel can afford crazy amounts of cells because it's locally installed. As long as you have a good computer with plenty of memory, you can have a nearly endless number of cells and not have to worry about things slowing down.

Again, most of us probably don't care about speed. We're working with smaller spreadsheets and never notice lags. But, and it's a big but, things do slow down when you start working with thousands of cells in Google, and that can be problematic for productivity.

The biggest reason people are switching to Google Sheets, however, is collaboration. Google is king when it comes to collaboration. If you are working on a budget with a group of people, then Google is hands down the way to go.

## The Google Sheets Crash Course

The first three buttons are pretty straightforward: undo, redo what you have typed and print. The last one is the format painter; this lets you copy the style of one cell into another cell. To use it, click the cell you want to copy, select the format painter, and then click the cell you want to put the style in.

By default, a spreadsheet is viewed at 100%; if you are working with a larger sheet and want to see more cells on your screen, you can use this to zoom out—or also to zoom in and see less cells on your screen.

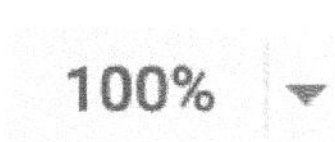


The next five options tell the cell what the content is. $ turns it into currency; % turns it into a percentage; the next two move the decimals forward and backward; and finally, the 123 gives you additional options to telling the cell what it is—plain text, a scientific formula, a date, etc. This is also useful if you have a number, but you want Google to treat it like plain text.

If you have used any kind of productivity software, then you should know the next two options; if you've been under a rock: this is the font and font size.

Next to the font is the font formatter; here you can bold, italicize, strikethrough (i.e. put a line through the middle of the text), or change the number.

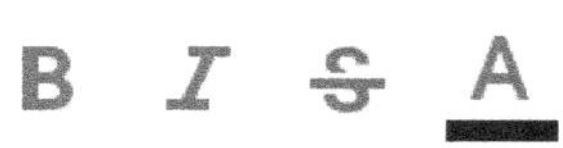

The next set of options is for the cell style; you can change the fill color, the cell border, and merge cells. To merge cells, highlight the cells you want to merge and then click this option.

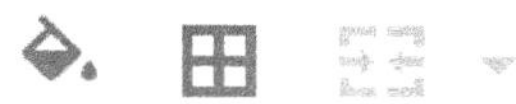

Justification and placement are managed in the next four options. Here you can center/right/left align, move the content to the bottom/middle/top of the cell, wrap the text (by default text will just spill over into the next cell unless you resize the cell; this option tells it to make the text go to the next line, sort of like hitting the enter key, since the enter/return key doesn't work in Sheets); and finally rotate text, which also lets you change the direction of the text.

The last set of options is to insert things into a cell. You can insert a link, comment, chart, filter, or function.

On the far side, is an up arrow. This just hides or unhides the toolbar.

# [2]

# GETTING STARTED WITH GOOGLE SHEETS

This chapter will cover:

- Your first Sheet
- Opening saved documents
- The basics

Okay, so how exactly do you use Google Sheets? Like everything else in the Google Suite family! The beauty of Google is once you learn one, learning others is pretty easy.

Here's a refresher: type in drive.google.com.

Once you have your Google account (hopefully you do by now), then you are all set. Repeat the step above and the browser Window should look more like the below.

**Creating Your First Sheet**

Now that you have your account, let's create a document. Click on the "New" button and then hover over Google Sheets; there are two options: "Blank document" and "From a template." For now, select "From a template." I'll cover templates a little bit later.

At this point, you'll be taken to Google's Sheets editor. This is where you do the actual work. Everything is designed to function just like Excel or Numbers.

Have a look in the upper left-hand corner of your Google Sheets. You'll see a text field that says "Untitled Document." Click on that.

You will now be prompted with a box asking you to rename the document. I chose "My Glorious Google Sheet!," but you can type anything you want. When you finish, hit the enter key.

Once you do that, the top bar will change, reflecting the new name you've chosen:

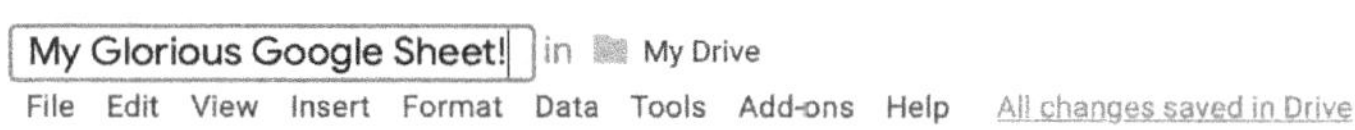


Do you see the text on the right where it says, "All changes saved"? That's another awesome thing about Google Sheets:

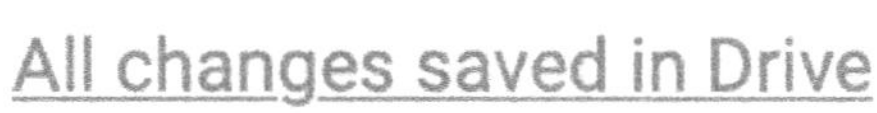


In a stroke of pure brilliance, the folks at Google have decided to completely automate document saves. As you write, Google saves your project and tells you when it last did this. If you want, you can go ahead and save, but it's practically unnecessary. Google Sheets saves after you enter every new word.

## Opening A Saved Document

Don't worry about accidently closing your tab. When you open it back up, Google will take you right back to your list of documents. You should see your document at the top of that list in "Quick Access."

If you are just getting started, it will also be the only sheet you see, and you can access it below the quick access

List view looks like the above—it gives the name, who the owner is, and the time it was edited. Grid view is more of a thumbnail preview of the Sheet.

Notice how "author" and "time lasted edited" is gone?

What's better? It's a preference, but if you are working with dozens of files, then Grid view probably will not be ideal unless you need to see previews.

To toggle between the two, click these icons in the upper corner:

List is the horizontal lines, and grid is the six square boxes.

The most recently viewed and edited files gets the top spot.

When you double-click on the Sheet or document you want, it'll open right up in the browser, and we can get back to writing. It's just like opening up an Excel or Numbers document on your home computer.

## The Basics

Now that we've gotten our quick crash course, let's add some numbers and see how this thing works.

I'll start by adding some years; like any good spreadsheet software, Google is pretty good at guessing. If there's a pattern, then you can autofill the cells. In the example below, I've added two years: 1900 and 1901. When I highlight those two cells, there's a tiny blue box:

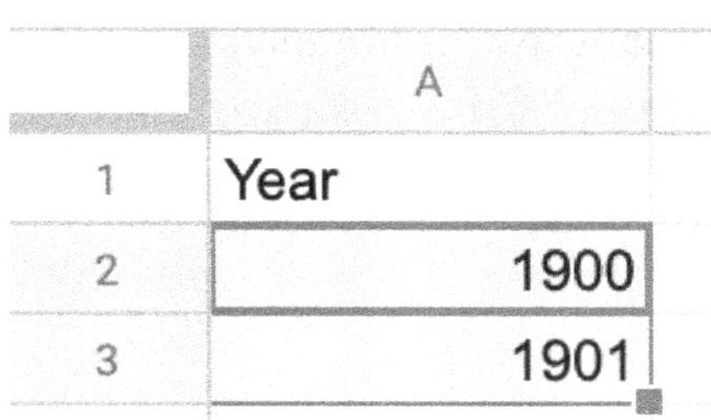

If I drag that blue box down, Google will correctly predict that I am putting years in and add one year per cell for as long as I drag:

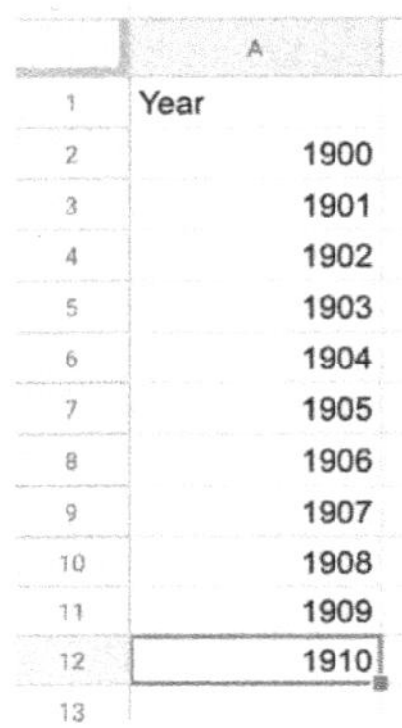


For this example, I'm going to create another column that shows how many babies were born, then two fields to show the total babies and average babies born.

To get the total number, go to the cell and type "=sum(". Google will probably highlight what it thinks you want automatically, but if it doesn't, then just highlight the cells you want to add up and then hit Enter/Return:

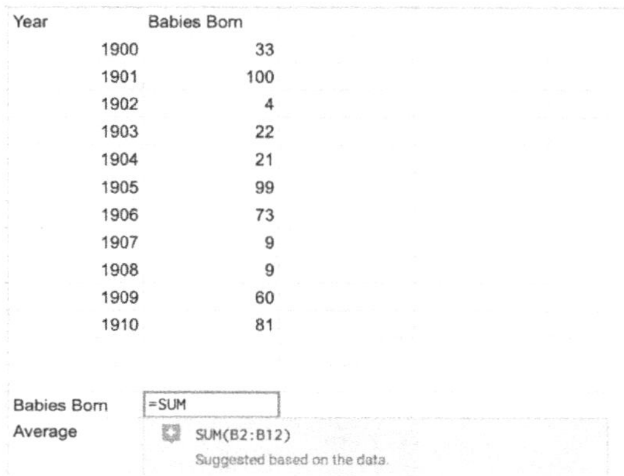

| Year | Babies Born |
| --- | --- |
| 1900 | 33 |
| 1901 | 100 |
| 1902 | 4 |
| 1903 | 22 |
| 1904 | 21 |
| 1905 | 99 |
| 1906 | 73 |
| 1907 | 9 |
| 1908 | 9 |
| 1909 | 60 |
| 1910 | 81 |
| | |
| Babies Born | =SUM |
| Average | SUM(B2:B12) Suggested based on the data. |

The same method is used for averages, but you type =average( instead of sum:

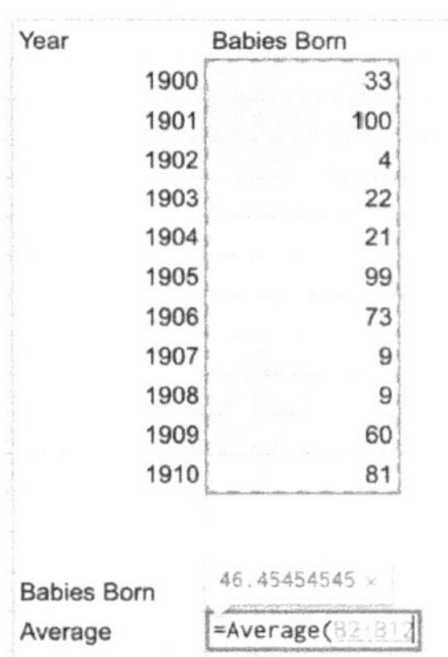

| Year | Babies Born |
| --- | --- |
| 1900 | 33 |
| 1901 | 100 |
| 1902 | 4 |
| 1903 | 22 |
| 1904 | 21 |
| 1905 | 99 |
| 1906 | 73 |
| 1907 | 9 |
| 1908 | 9 |
| 1909 | 60 |
| 1910 | 81 |
| | |
| Babies Born | 46.45454545 |
| Average | =Average(B2:B12 |

In seconds, we now know the number of babies born as well as the average for all years:

| Year | Babies Born |
|---|---|
| 1900 | 33 |
| 1901 | 100 |
| 1902 | 4 |
| 1903 | 22 |
| 1904 | 21 |
| 1905 | 99 |
| 1906 | 73 |
| 1907 | 9 |
| 1908 | 9 |
| 1909 | 60 |
| 1910 | 81 |
| | |
| Babies Born | 511 |
| Average | 46.45454545 |

Not happy with how it looks? You can apply basic formatting the same way you would in a Google Doc or Word Doc:

| **Year** | **Babies Born** |
|---|---|
| 1900 | 33 |
| 1901 | 100 |
| 1902 | 4 |
| 1903 | 22 |
| 1904 | 21 |
| 1905 | |
| 1906 | 73 |
| 1907 | 9 |
| 1908 | 9 |
| 1909 | 60 |
| 1910 | 81 |
| | |
| Babies Born | 412 |
| Average | 41.2 |

# [3] Beyond the Basics

This chapter will cover:

- Creating charts
- Functions
- Scripts

## Creating a Chart

People are visual. Numbers aren't very sexy. You need visuals to make them pop.

Before we go deeper into the fun world of functions, let's take the fun out of functions and do something fun: a chart.

I'll take the example above and create a chart that shows the babies born per year a little more visually.

To get started, I'll highlight what I want to show; in my example, only the top portion—the chart doesn't need to show the totals or averages:

| | A | B |
|---|---|---|
| 1 | Year | Babies Born |
| 2 | 1900 | 33 |
| 3 | 1901 | 100 |
| 4 | 1902 | 4 |
| 5 | 1903 | 22 |
| 6 | 1904 | 21 |
| 7 | 1905 | 99 |
| 8 | 1906 | 73 |
| 9 | 1907 | 9 |
| 10 | 1908 | 9 |
| 11 | 1909 | 60 |
| 12 | 1910 | 81 |
| 13 | | |
| 14 | | |
| 15 | Babies Born | 511 |
| 16 | Average | 46.45454545 |

Next, go to the toolbar and click the chart icon:

And just like that, we have a pretty line graph that represents our data:

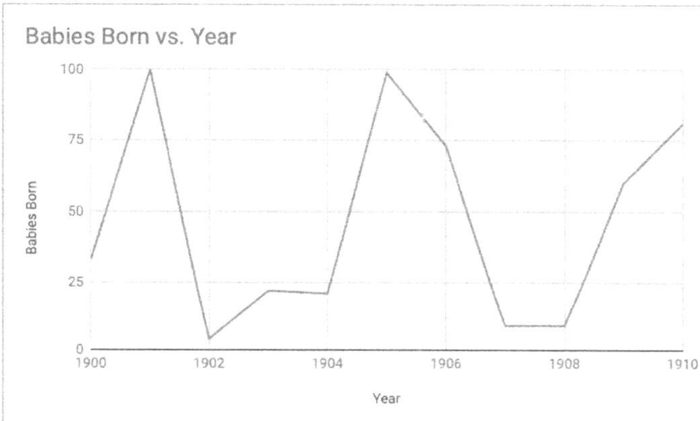


I know, I know...you're sitting there thinking: Lines! I hate lines!

Don't fret! You use the chart editor that opens a chart library to create dozens of other charts:

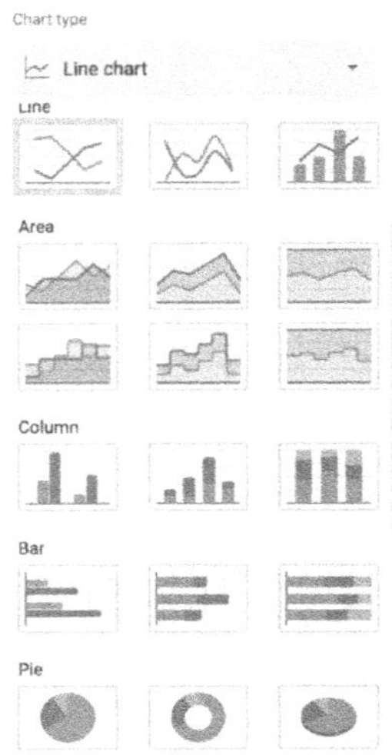


If you got so excited when the chart came up on your screen that you accidentally closed the chart editor, then just double click the chart and it will open back up:

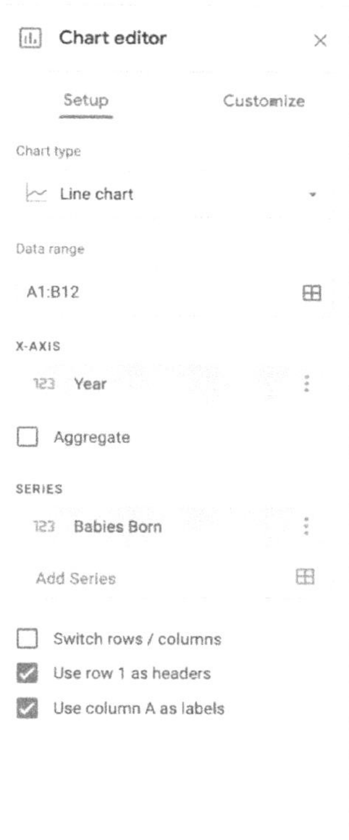


You can use this editor to change the range (you add some more rows, for example, and want them represented) or reverse the data shown—you want to show the years on the lines, not the number of babies born.

Google has its own idea of what is pretty. It's probably different from yours. You don't want a blue line! You want a red line! You hate the black text! You want green! If there's one thing

Spreadsheet people are known for, it's their incredible talent for making numbers look sexy. Don't worry! You can customize almost everything here.

If you need to bring sexy back to your chart, then just go into your editor and select "Customize" right next to "Setup."

From here you can go section-to-section and change colors, fonts, and more:

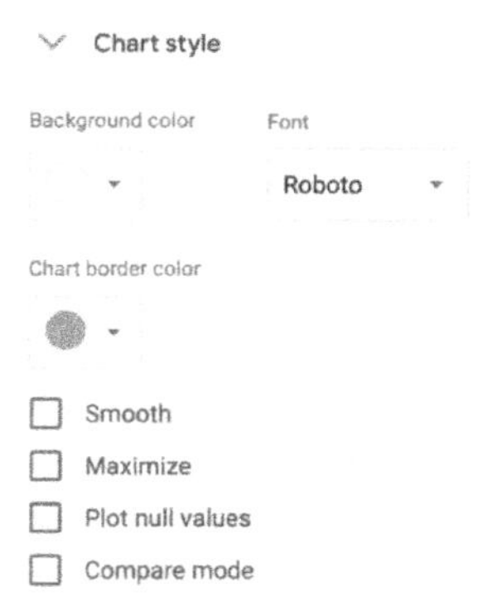


You can also change gridlines around on the bottom:

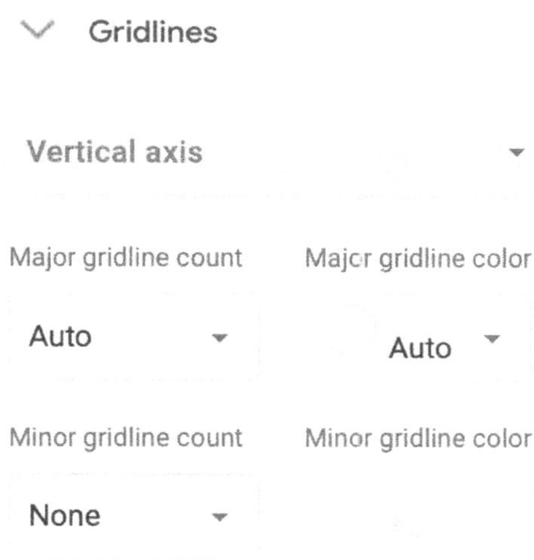


By default, Google will just stick the chart inconveniently over your data. If you click on it, you'll see a bunch of little blue boxes. That means you can either resize it (click on one and drag in/out to make it larger/smaller) or move it:

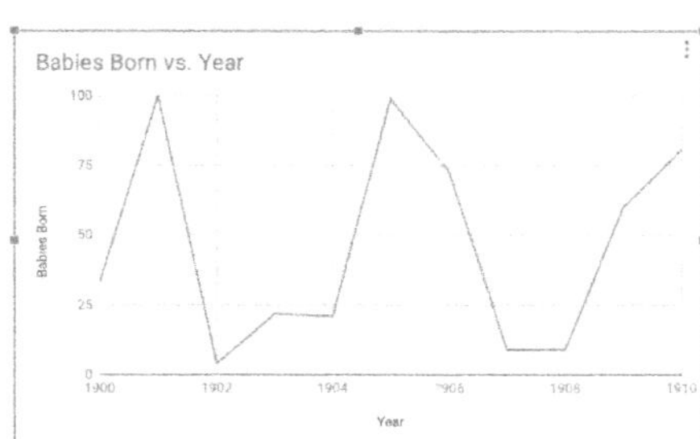

You'll also notice three little boxes in the upper right corner of the chart. That's your chart menu. Click that and you'll see several options:

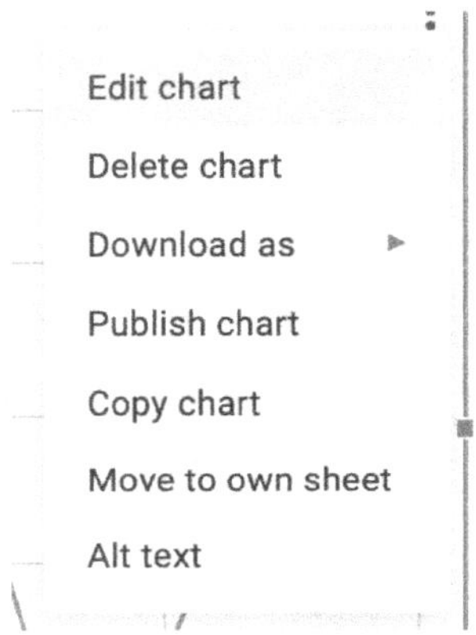


Download as is helpful if you want to insert it into emails as attachments or presentations. You can download it as an image or PDF.

You can also copy and paste the chart into other Google app—like Google Slides or Google Docs. Just click it and do CTRL+C on your keyboard to copy it, and CTRL+V to paste it.

## Functionally Yours

Now that we had some fun, let's get serious and learn about functions.

What is a function exactly? Well, we already learned about two: Sum and Average. Functions are the formulas you put into cells to tell Google to calculate an equation.

There are a lot of functions. Go to your toolbar and click the function key, and you can see what I mean!

The main ones you use will be right at the top, which is helpful; below that, Google has categorized additional ones.

Because this book is meant to get you started quickly and not teach you all the features that you will never use, I won't cover every single function here. The goal is to show you how they work, so if there's one not covered here that you want to use, you'll know how.

I recommend you spend a few minutes looking at the list above and see if there's something that would be useful to what you are doing. There are hundreds of functions.

To use any of the functions in this list, go to the cell you want to show the equation in, and then click the function option and select the one you want to do; from here, select your data range. Once it's selected, hit return/enter.

If you decide later that you need to edit the function, go to the upper left corner—just under the tool bar. See the fx? When you select a cell with a function, it will show up here. Click in there, and then update the range that you want.

That's also the same place you go to edit anything in a cell—function or no function.

## So Many Functions...That I Don't Want

Google Sheets has a lot of functions. It's overwhelming, but it doesn't have everything. If you become a power spreadsheets user, you might find it would be helpful to do something that there is no function for.

That doesn't mean you can't do it. It's just a little more involved. There are many more things you can do by creating a script. Scripts let you basically program your own function.

Scripts can be found by going to Tools > Scripts Editor.

This is going to launch a separate Google app for creating a script:

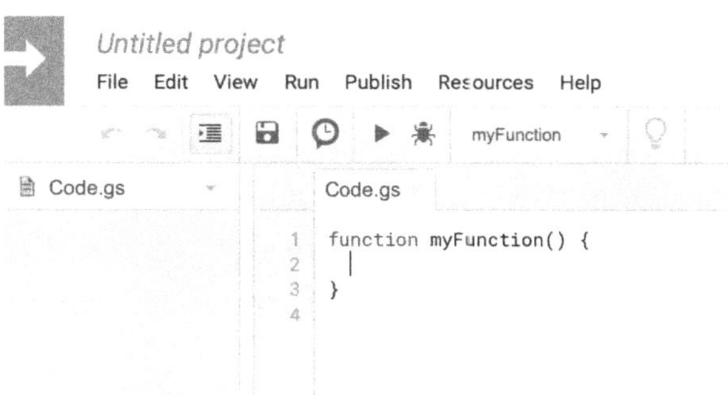


Below is an example of what a script might look like:

```
var ss = SpreadsheetApp.getActiveSpreadsheet();
 var sheet = ss.getSheets()[0];

 // The size of the two-dimensional array must match the size of
 var values = [
   [ "2.000", "1,000,000", "$2.99" ]
 ];

 var range = sheet.getRange("B2:D2");
 range.setValues(values);
```

Once you have your script written, go to Publish > Deploy as Sheets add-on:

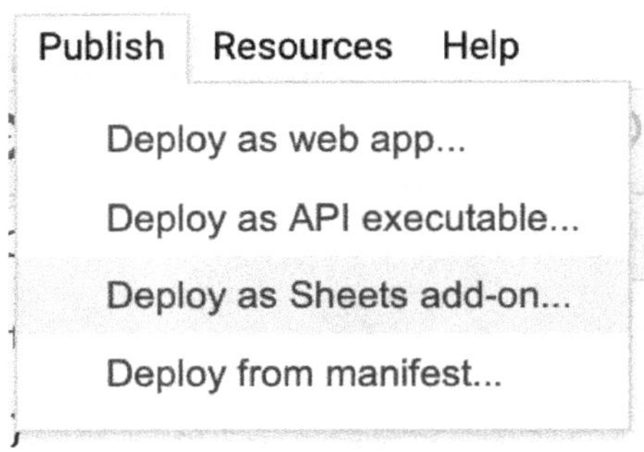


The topic of scripts is much too complicated for this book, but there are plenty of resources both in the Scripts app and online if this is an arena you'd like to dig deeper into later.

# [4]

# SHARING IS CARING

This chapter will cover:

- Sharing your sheet
- Editing and collaborating sheets
- Protecting sheets
- Data validation

## Sharing Your Sheet

Now that you know your way around, you're ready for feedback from others.

If you know how to share a Google Doc, then you are in luck! Sharing Sheets is the same. Need a refresher?

Look up in the upper right corner. See the blue button that says Share? Click on that. It's going to open up several different sharing options.

When you click on that, a share box opens up, and you get a bunch of different options.

There's a few ways to share it:

1. Type their email address and let Google do the rest.
2. Manually (covered below).

When you email someone, you can also manage exactly what they can do. Click that little pencil icon. By default, it will say they can edit the doc. You can change it so they can only comment on the doc, or they can only view the doc:

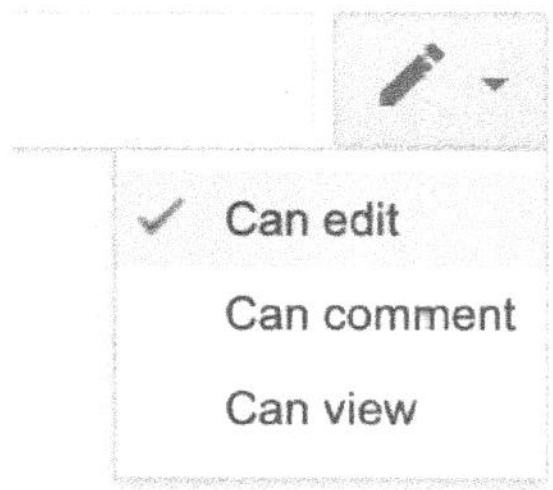


You can also hit advance at the bottom of the share menu, and have a few more features—such as disabling print:

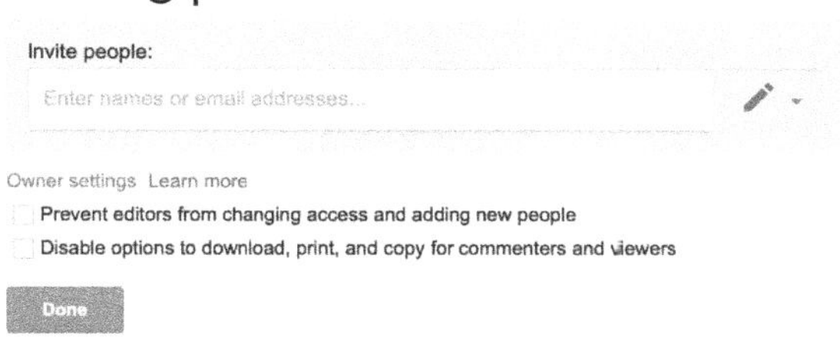


But let's say you don't want to email the first man. Let's say you just want to give him a link—that way he doesn't need to use his Google account to open it. To do that, follow the steps above, but in the upper corner of the box, click "Get shareable link."

Once you click that, it will give you a sharable link—it even copies the link so if you hit CTRL-V (or right-click paste) you can paste that link anywhere you want.

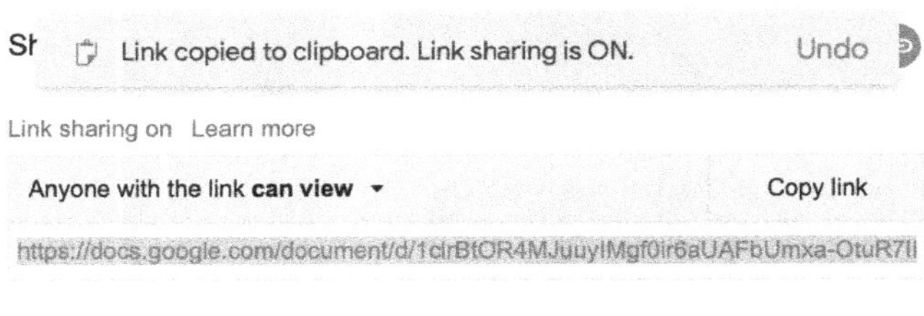


If you click on can view, it will give you a drop-down menu with more features. It looks sort of like the other drop-down menu above, but there's an option that says "more."

When you click on "More," it gives you a few extra features—such as making the document public in search engines so anyone can find it.

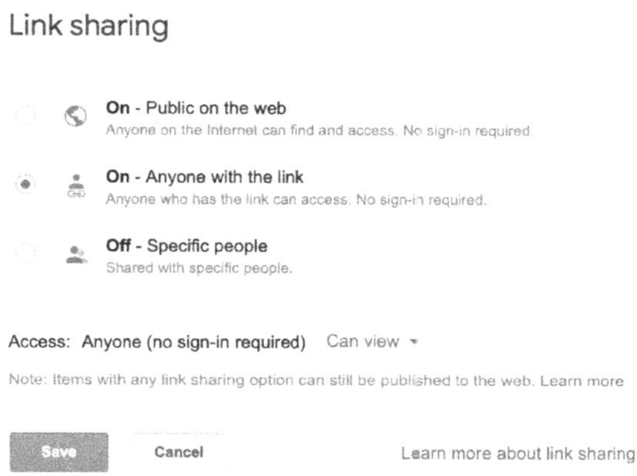


You can turn sharing off at any time, by hitting the "Share" button; once it's turned off, anyone who goes to that link—even if they've been there before—won't be able to see it. If you've emailed a person, they are still a viewer until you remove them.

If you have a person who really hates Google Sheets and refuses to view your document in anything but Word, Google Docs allows you to export your work to a Excel Document so you don't have to do all of the copying and font processing yourself. Just click on file --> download as --> Excel; there's a whole host of other exports here as well.

## Editing and Collaborating With Others

The easiest way to make comments in a spreadsheet is to right-click and select Comment.

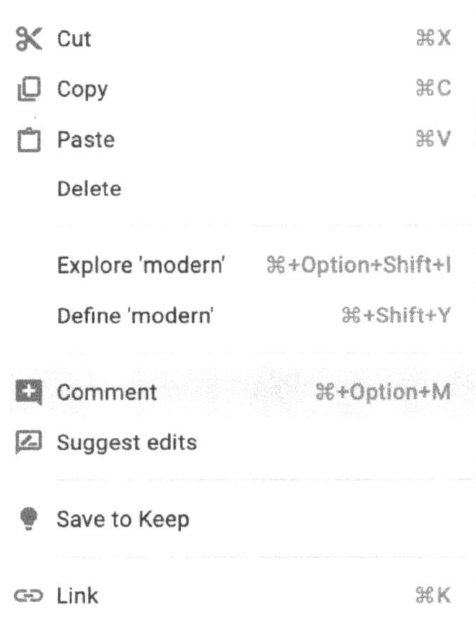


You can also get this, by selecting Insert on the toolbar, and Comment.

Either of these will bring up the comment box. Add your comment, and select the blue comment box when you are ready to post it. When you add a comment (or make a change), it's in real-time; that means if the person who is collaborating with you has the document open, they can actually watch you make the edits and add the comments.

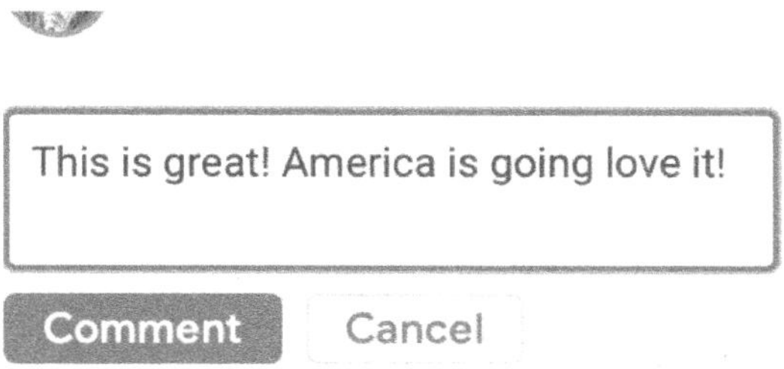


If you have multiple people working on the doc, you can type "@" and see a list of people you can mention; if you mention them, Google will notify them so they can add a reply to your comment.

Once the comments in, it will show up on the side of Google Sheets.

You can delete or edit the comment, by click on those three little dots on the side of the box.

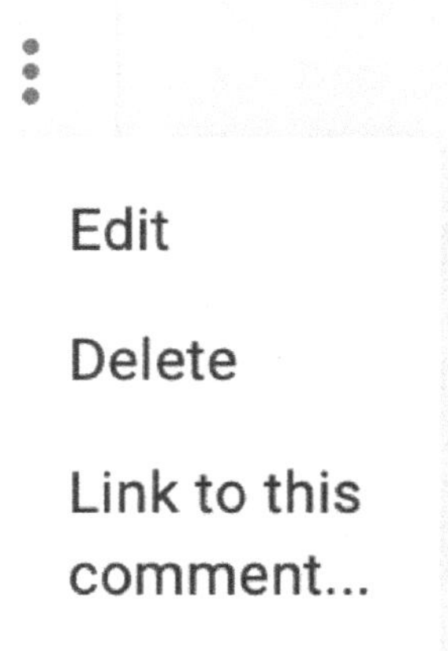


The person on the other end will be able to resolve the comment (that makes it disappear, but they can undo it)

Or they can reply to it.

To see all the versions of a cocument, go to file and see versions.

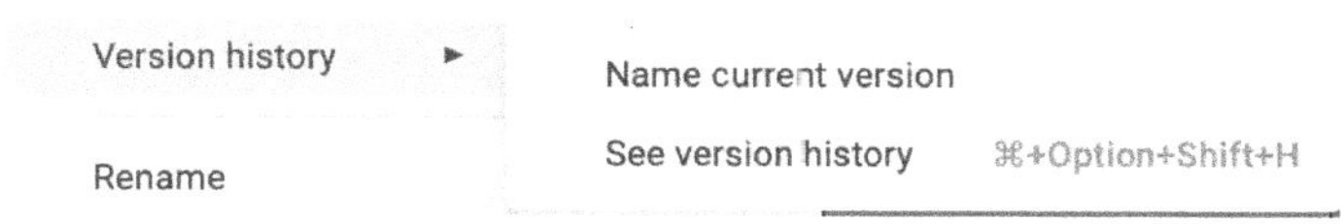


If there's going to be a lot of versions, then one suggestion is to name each one—which you can do here.

When you click See version history, you'll get a list of all the versions. Clicking on anyone will bring up that version. You can view it, or even restore it.

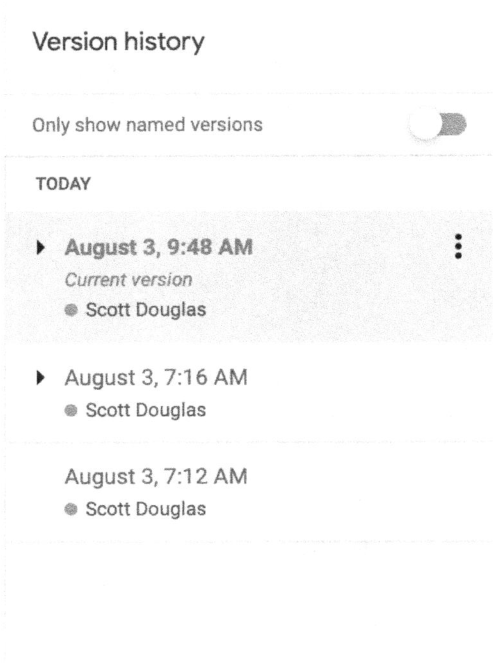


To get back to the document, just hit the back button in the menu (not the browser back button).

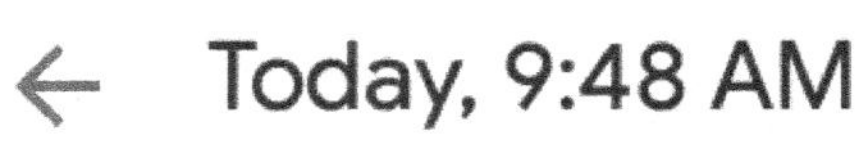

## Protect a Spreadsheet

Google Sheets has an extra layer of protection not seen in Google Docs. To apply it, go to Tools > Protect Sheet.

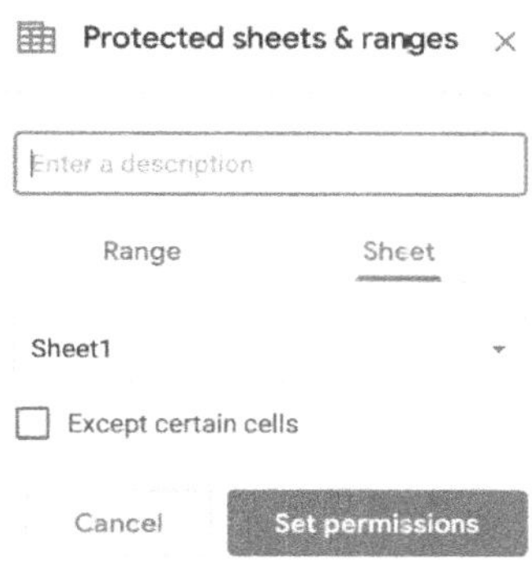


From here you can do several things:

Give it a description – Why does it need a description? Because you can create several difference protections.

Select the range.

Set permissions – you can, for example, give one person the ability to make changes and another the ability only to see it.

## Data Validation

Let's say you give someone permission to edit the sheet and they add in something wrong; that error messes up the entire spreadsheet! Now what? Spent hours trying to figure out the mess they made, right?

Sure, why not! But why don't we make sure they don't make that mess to begin with!

Data validation let's you add in rules so people can't add in things incorrectly. For example, let's say someone doesn't know the answer so they just put in "?" or "N/A." You can set up a rule that forces them only to use a number.

To add one in, highlight the cells you want to apply it to and then go to Data > Data validation. This brings up the option box.

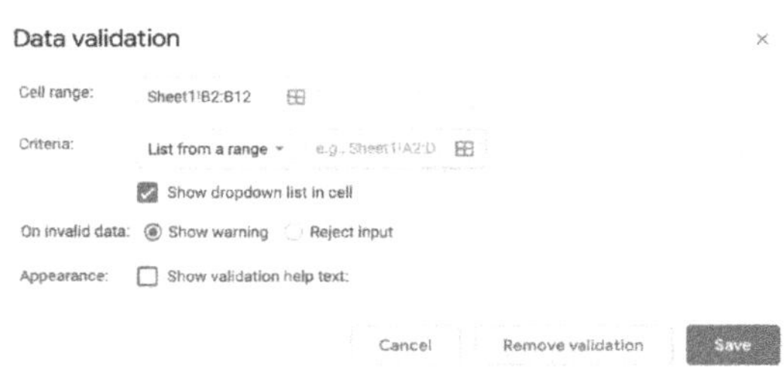


From here you need to set your rule (or criteria).

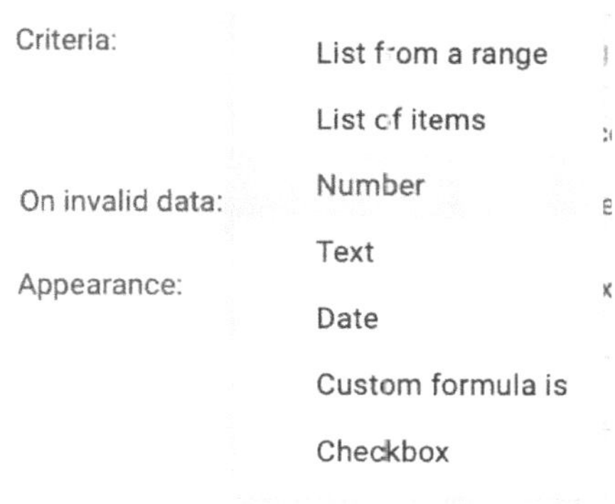


My rule is the data here needs to be a number between 0 and 101. If you want to get really fancy, you can add in a custom formula.

Next, you need to say what happens if they break the rule. Do you want to outright reject it or just give them a warning. In my case, I'm all about rejection. But I'm a nice guy too, so I'm going to tell them why I'm rejecting them.

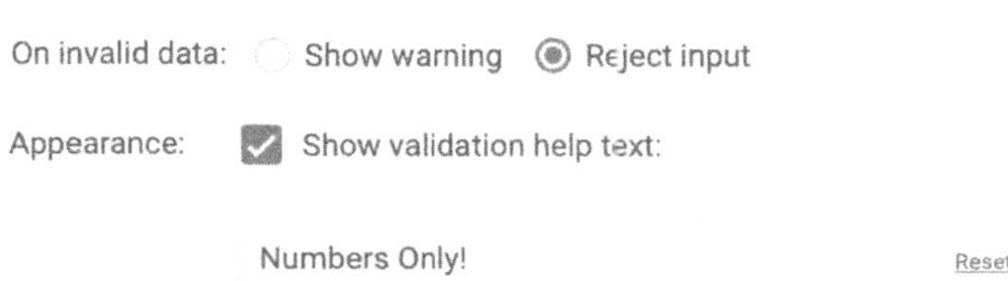

Now if someone tries to add anything but a number, then tell get this message.

# [5] THIS AND THAT

This chapter will cover:

- Surveys
- Google Sheets menus

## Survey's Into Data

One area Google Sheets has Excel and other programs beat is it's survey integration.

Using Google Forms to create a survey, you can have all the answers go right into a Google Sheet so you can collate your results.

To get started go to Insert > Forms.

This is going to launch a separate tab with the Google Forms application.

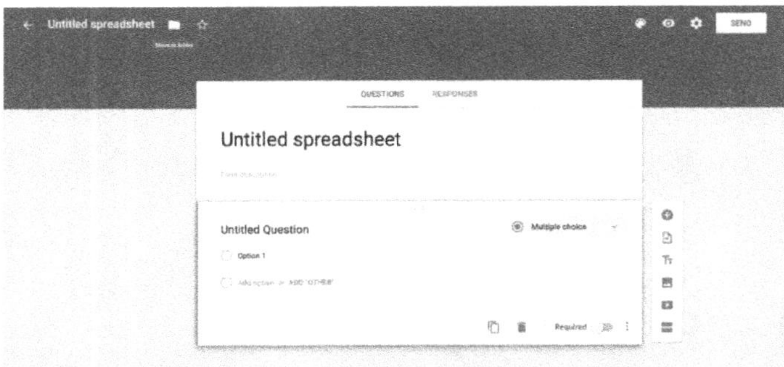


I'm going to make this survey simple, but if you want to jazz it up, there's all kinds of options for adding photos and changing styles around. Use the menu on the right side for those options.

For my survey, I'm going to make it a drop-down survey. You can change the question type by selecting the drop down to the right side of the question name; you can have as many types as you want in the survey—for example, question one could be multiple choice and question two could be a drop down.

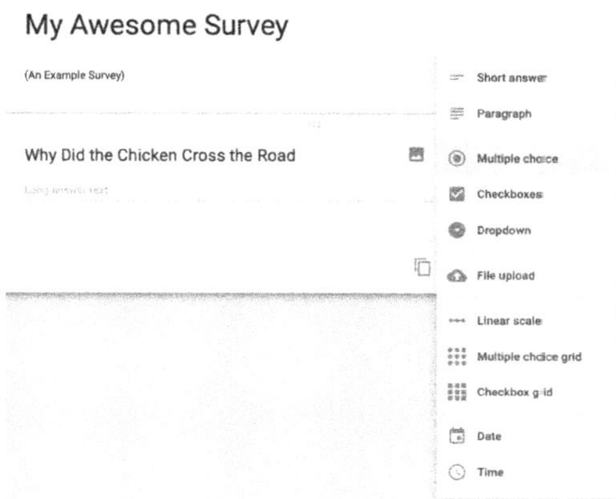


This changes our answers to editable fields. Right now, it has room for two questions. As soon as I stop typing in the second answer, a slot will be added for a third question.

More answer slots are added with each question.

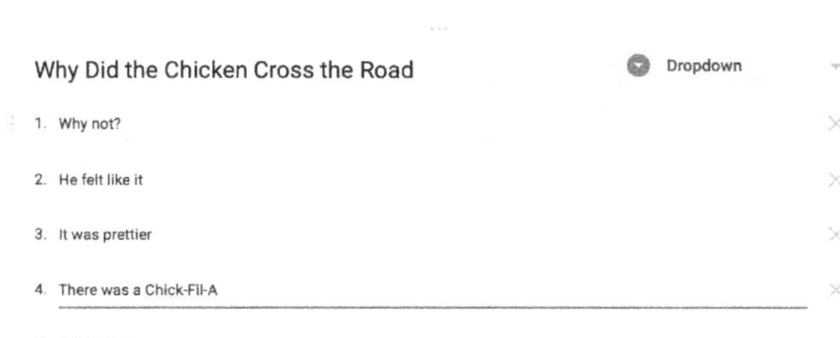

When you are done, click the "Send Form" button in the upper right corner:

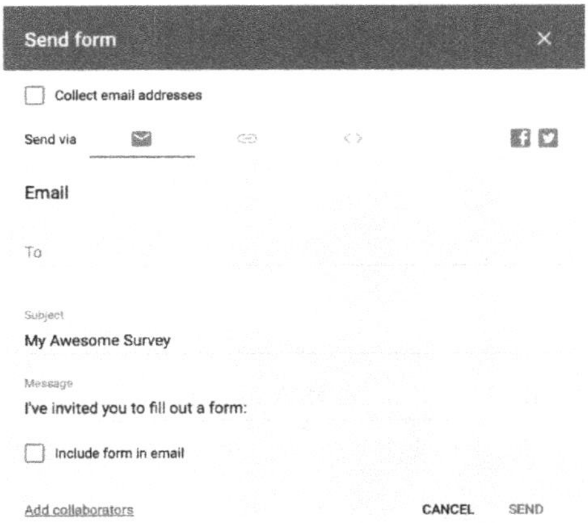


I don't want to send the form to anyone—I want it to be a link. So, I'm going to click the link icon next to the email one (it's the middle one).

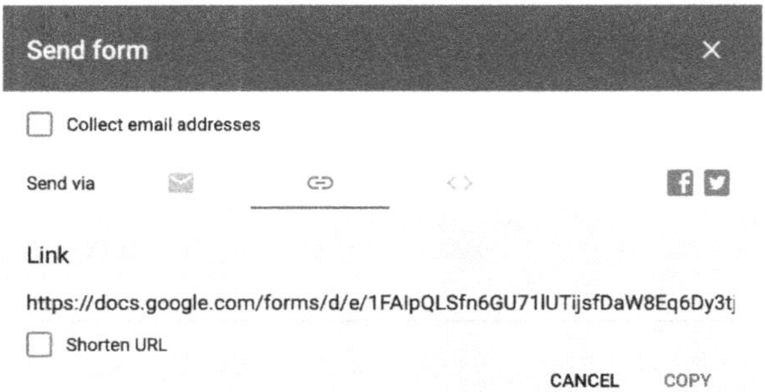

When someone goes to my survey, it will look a little bit different from the one that was in the editor because all the menu fields are gone.

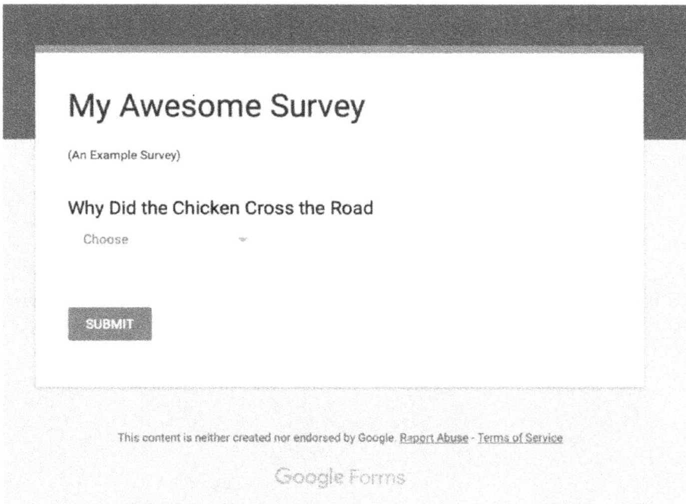


Once they click submit, they'll see a confirmation. You can make this a custom confirmation or use the default Google one.

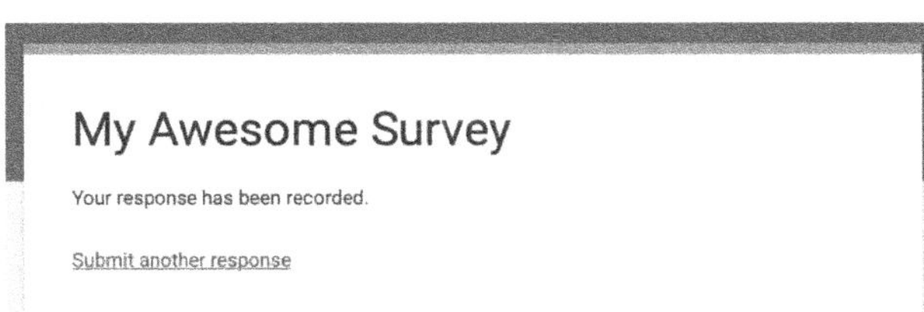

Now that you have a response, go back to your Sheet and you'll see a new tab has been added on the bottom of the sheet for form responses.

Click that and you can see what the person answered.

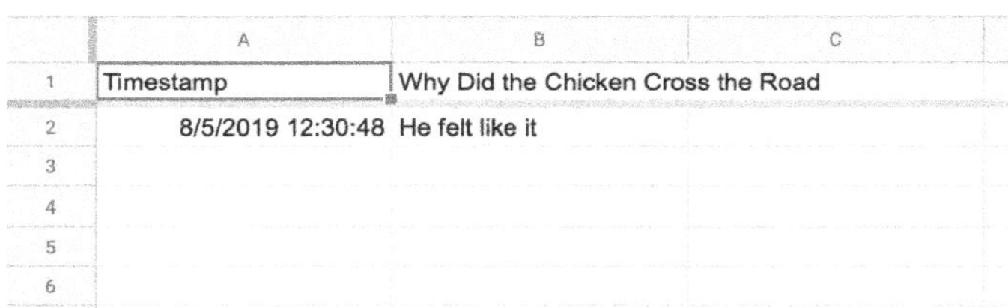

| | A | B | C |
|---|---|---|---|
| 1 | Timestamp | Why Did the Chicken Cross the Road | |
| 2 | 8/5/2019 12:30:48 | He felt like it | |
| 3 | | | |
| 4 | | | |
| 5 | | | |
| 6 | | | |

If you need to make changes to it, just go to Form from your menu bar.

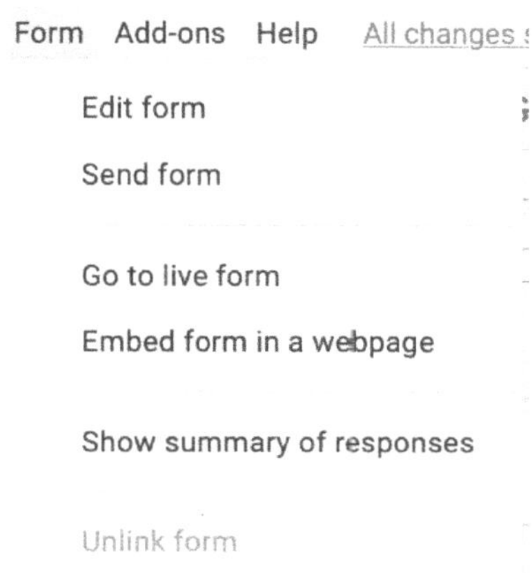


If you have multiple forms, then this option will not show on your menu bar unless you are inside that form tab. So if you don't see the option, then click the tab for the Form responses and then it will appear in the menu.

If you decide to delete the form, it's a little different from a normal tab. A normal tab, you right-click on the tab and hit delete, it will tell you that you can't. You have to unlink it first. How? Easy!

Right-click on the form tab you want to unlink and select Unlink form.

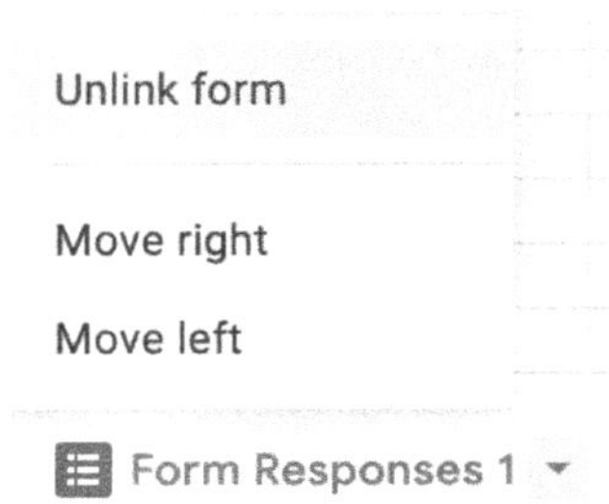


Once it's unlinked, you'll be able to delete it, by right-clicking and selecting delete.

## This and That

By now, you should be have a really good idea how Google Sheets work. Before leaving you, I'll cover a few more features that you should know about.

By default, Google will base the Sheet on your Google Account; if your Google Account thinks you live in Spain, then that's how the Sheet is set up.

You can change this by going to File > Spreadsheet settings.

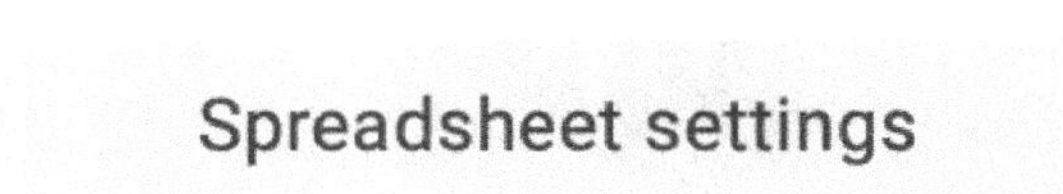


This is helpful if you, for example, live in the United States, but happen to be working on a

Sheet for someone who lives in the UK. You can change the settings, so it shows as pounds instead of dollars.

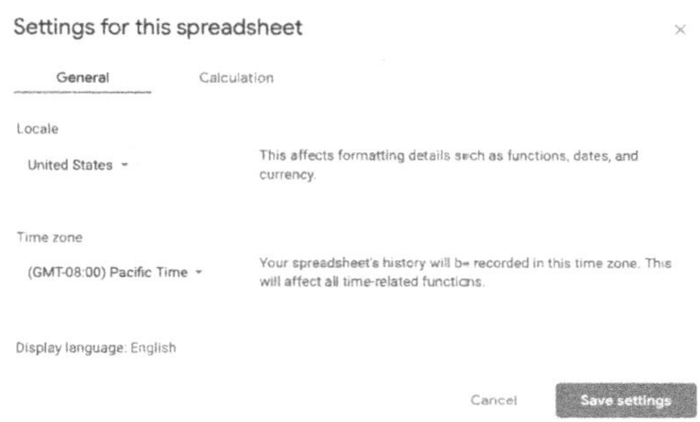


When you start working on large documents, it gets difficult to find things. Imagine you have 100,000 cells and you have to find the one with the number "12a?b44." Good luck with that! Fortunately for you, there's something called "Find and Replace" under the Edit menu.

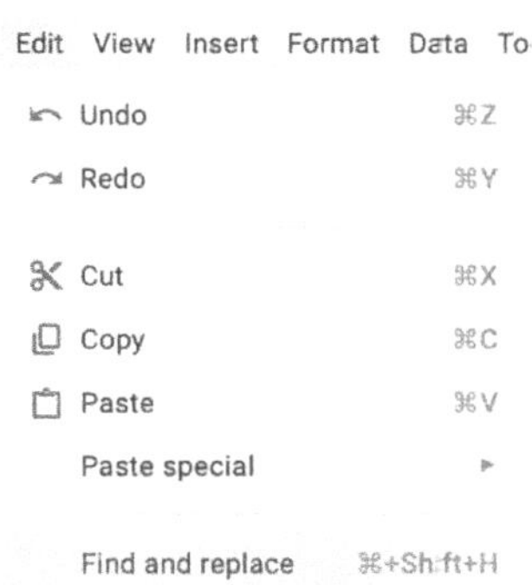

Not only does it find the cell you are looking for, but it let's you replace it with something else. For example, I can tell it to find every example of "California" and replace it with "CA."

Another handy feature if you have lots of rows is the freeze option. That's under View > Freeze.

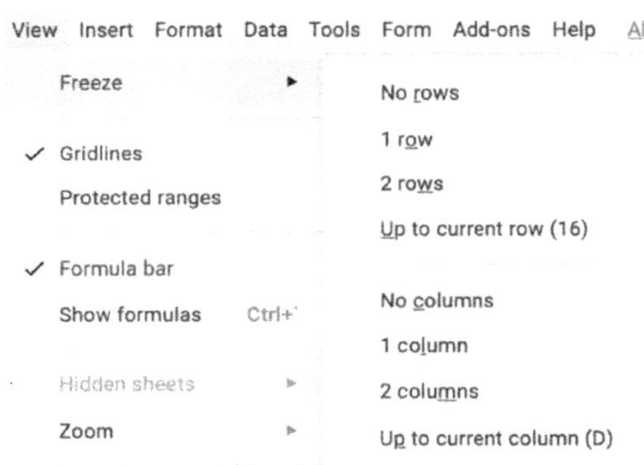


What exactly is freeze? Typically, you have a top row that is sort of like a menu. It tells the view what is in each column. And then you have the first column that has something else descriptive—such as dates. Now imagine you have 10,000 rows. You're on row 2079, column AA. You can't remember what that row stands for. If you had freeze row enabled, then that top menu (or side column) would be frozen, so no matter where you are, you always see it.

If you are editing a lot of formulas, go to View and check off "Show formulas." This will show you the formula instead of the answer. It's helpful for editing formulas.

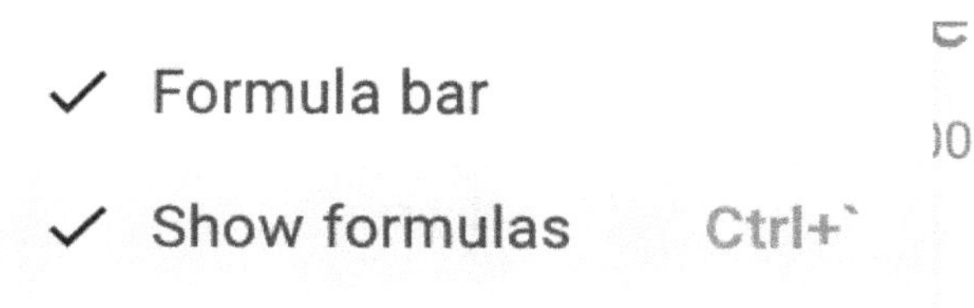


If you are in the middle of a large sheet and need to add in a row in the middle, then select the row you want to add it to, then go to Insert > and select Row above, Row below, or anywhere else you want it.

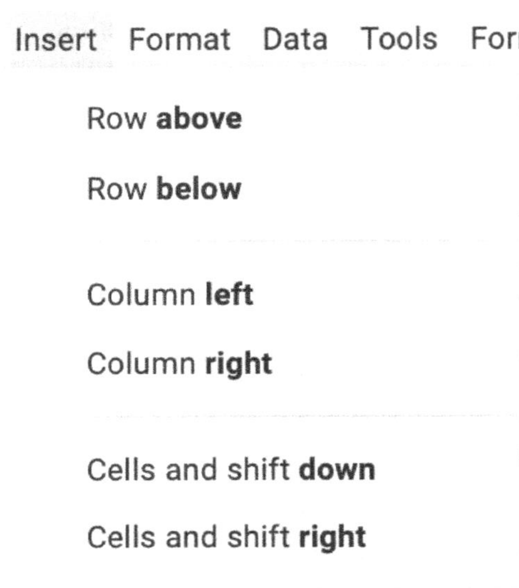


Insert > Checkbox is useful if you have people viewing it and you want them to confirm that they see something.

If you want to add a new tab to the bottom of your sheet, you can either click the + in the lower left corner of the sheet, or go to Insert > New sheet. To delete the sheet, right-click the tab and select delete.

You learned earlier about setting rules to a Sheet with data validation. You can do something similar with format. This is found in Format > Conditional formatting.

With conditional formatting, you can, for example, tell the sheet if the cell is empty, it's green, but if it has content, then it's blue. You can do it for run cell, or highlight multiple cells to do it for several.

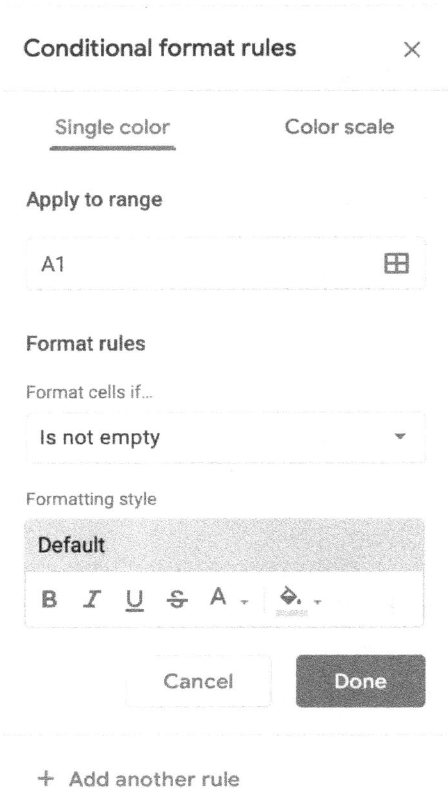


If you are working with a large sheet, and want to make sure there's no duplicate content, then highlight the range, then select Data > Remove duplicates. This will go through the range and remove anything that's the same.

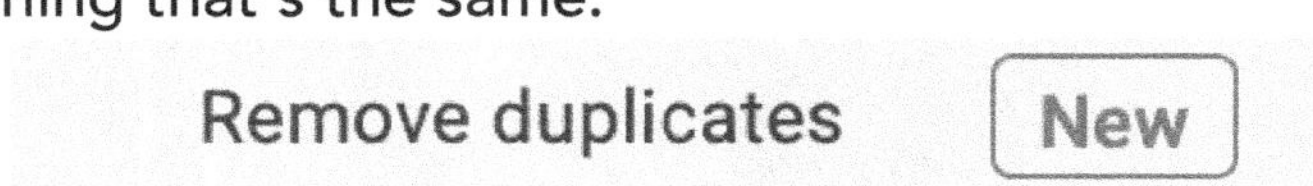

Macros are a bit complex, they help you create sequences to automate certain tasks. I won't cover them here, but if you want to use them, it's under Tools > Macro.

Also under tools is Notification rules.

This is what you will use if you want to be notification when someone edits your document, or adds something to your survey. You can either be emailed immediately or once a day.

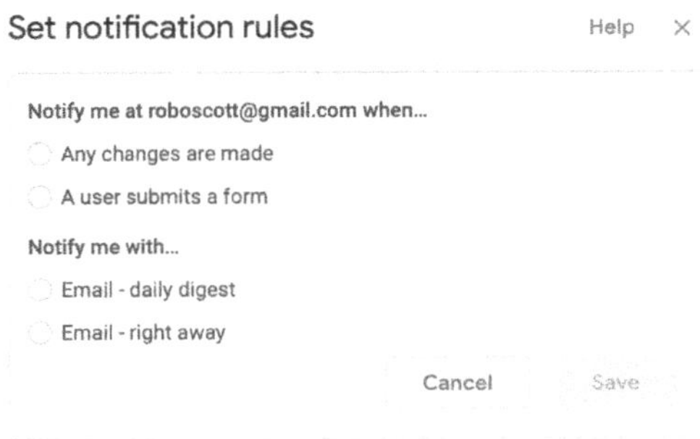


There's still a lot to learn, but I hope you now have the understanding and using Sheets comfortably.

If you find yourself copying a lot of formulas and getting errors, try pasting only the values. That means it will only copy the number and not the actual formula. You can do this by pressing CTRL+Shift+V, or by going to Edit > Paste special.

# [6]

# GOOGLE SHEETS KEYBOARD SHORTCUTS

You can see all the keyboard shortcuts in Google Sheets by selecting Help > Keyboard shortcuts.

For your reference, below are some of the most common ones you'll use.

| **Common actions** | |
|---|---|
| Select column | Ctrl + Space |
| Select row | Shift + Space |
| Select all | Ctrl + a |
| Undo | Ctrl + z |
| Redo | Ctrl + y |
| Find | Ctrl + f |
| Find and replace | Ctrl + h |

| | |
|---|---|
| Fill range | Ctrl + Enter |
| Fill down | Ctrl + d |
| Fill right | Ctrl + r |
| Copy | Ctrl + c |
| Cut | Ctrl + x |
| Paste | Ctrl + v |
| Paste values only | Ctrl + Shift + v |
| **Format cells** | |
| Bold | Ctrl + b |
| Underline | Ctrl + u |
| Italic | Ctrl + i |
| Strikethrough | Alt + Shift + 5 |
| Center align | Ctrl + Shift + e |
| Left align | Ctrl + Shift + l |
| Right align | Ctrl + Shift + r |
| Apply top border | Alt + Shift + 1 |
| Apply right border | Alt + Shift + 2 |
| Apply bottom border | Alt + Shift + 3 |
| Apply left border | Alt + Shift + 4 |
| Remove borders | Alt + Shift + 6 |
| Apply outer border | Alt + Shift + 7 |
| Insert link | Ctrl + k |
| Insert time | Ctrl + Shift + ; |
| Insert date | Ctrl + ; |
| Insert date and time | Ctrl + Alt + Shift + ; |
| Format as decimal | Ctrl + Shift + 1 |
| Format as time | Ctrl + Shift + 2 |
| Format as date | Ctrl + Shift + 3 |
| Format as currency | Ctrl + Shift + 4 |
| Format as percentage | Ctrl + Shift + 5 |
| Format as exponent | Ctrl + Shift + 6 |
| Clear formatting | Ctrl + \ |

| Use formulas | |
|---|---|
| Show all formulas | Ctrl + ~ |
| Insert array formula | Ctrl + Shift + Enter |
| Collapse an expanded array formula | Ctrl + e |
| Show/hide formula help *(when entering a formula)* | Shift + F1 |
| Full/compact formula help *(when entering a formula)* | F1 |
| Absolute/relative references *(when entering a formula)* | F4 |
| Toggle formula result previews *(when entering a formula)* | F9 |
| Resize formula bar *(move up or down)* | Ctrl + Up / Ctrl + Down |

# Google Slides

# [1] Google Slides Crash Course

This chapter will cover:

- What is Slides?
- Slides crash course

How many times do you work on a presentation that you will get absolutely no feedback on and want no help?

Maybe you're the type that likes to whip something up and have no practice or feedback at all? Most of us are the former. Before we stand in front of a group of people, we want to make sure we're as polished as possible.

The problem is PowerPoint wasn't built like that. It was built as a desktop program that one person would use at a time.

Google realized the problem and seized the opportunity when they launched Google Slides over ten years ago.

Google Slides is a cloud-based presentation editor that can replace PowerPoint or Keynote.

If you'd like to get the most out of the software, then let's get started!

## Slides Crash Course

There's a lot to cover. In the next section, we'll start from scratch with a blank presentation, but before we get there, I'm going to quickly go over the main tool bars.

This is going to be a quick overview, so if there's something you don't understand, that's okay—I'll cover it in more detail later in the book.

The first button is one you'll probably use a lot. That's how you add a new Slide. When you click the drop down, you can see all the predefined layouts. Click it and the layout will be added (hint: you'll be able to change it later).

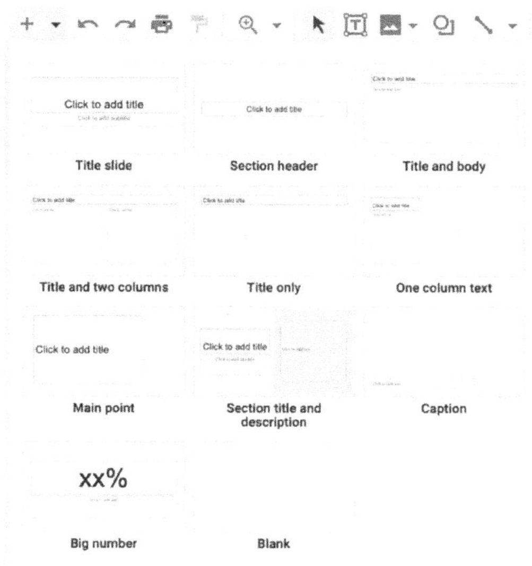


Next to that is the undo, redo, and print icon. The last option is the format painter. This copies one style to another—for example, you want to copy the font color and size of one text, to another text. To use it, just highlight the style you want to copy, select the icon, then click the text you want to copy it to.

Next is the zoom icon. This lets you zoom in or out, so you can see more or less of your slide.

The insert options are next. The first icon (the cursor) lets you select an object, the next lets you add a text box, next to that is the insert image option, and finally, the last, insert a shape.

There's one final insert option: line. There are a couple different lines you can when you select the drop down. The scribble line is if you want to draw the line freehand.

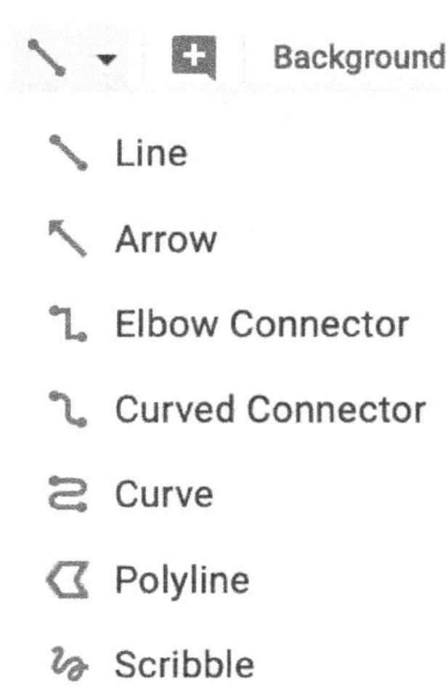

Because Google Slides is so collaborative, you'll probably use the next button a lot: the comment option. This lets you add comments to any slide or text.

The background button let's you add an image or color to your slide background.

The layout option looks similar to the Add Slide button. This lets you change the layout of the selected slide.

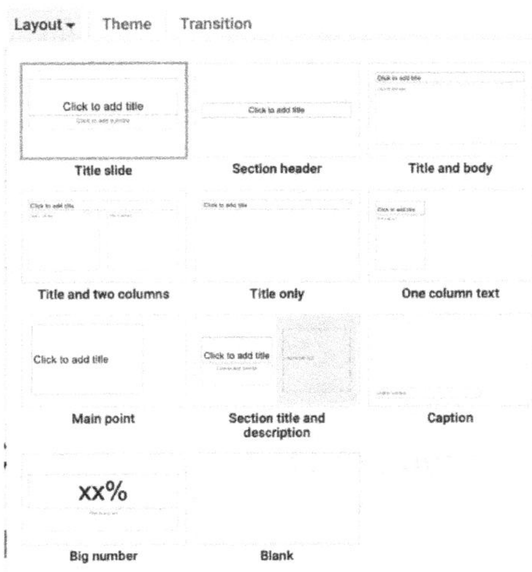


The theme button is similar to layout, but instead of text, it's changing the style of the slide—adding a background image, for example.

Finally, the Transition button is where you tell Google Slides what to do whenever you go to the next slide.

Hanging out at the far right side is the menu hide button. Use this to toggle between hide and unhide.

Over on the far left side, the side menu has three options: calendar, Google keep, and tasks. These are sort of mini apps. They don't change your slide—they just help you keep notes and pull up dates.

[2]

# Getting Started With Google Slides

This chapter will cover:

- Creating your first slide
- The basics

Now that we know the basics, let's dig in and see how to use the features in practice. To get started, head to drive.google.com (create an account if you haven't already) and click the create new button, then Google Slides, and blank presentation.

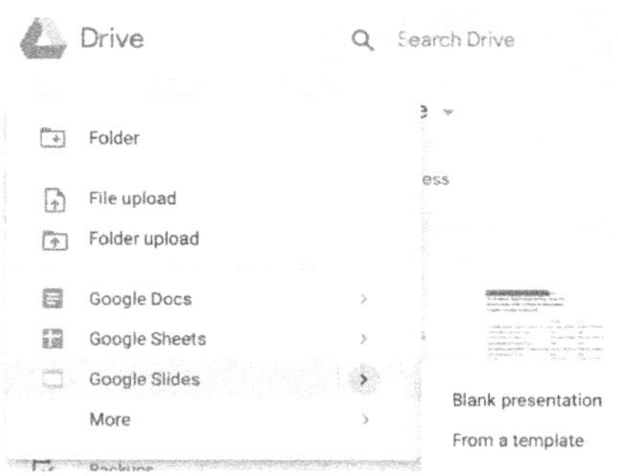


Right off the bat, it probably looks a little familiar to you if you've used PowerPoint or Keynote.

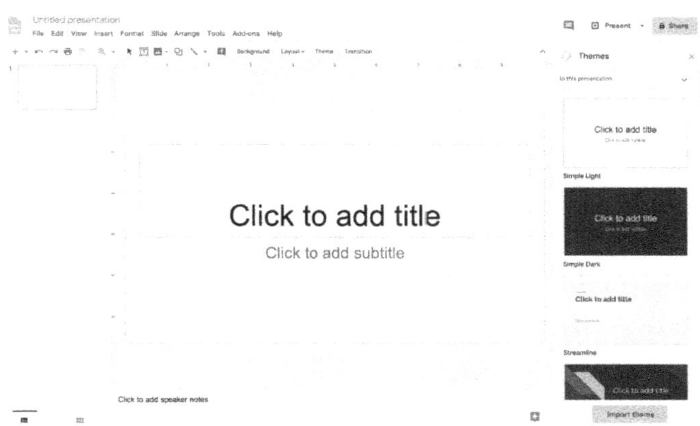


For this book, we're going to create a presentation on how to know if your friend is a monster. How many books on Google Slides, also give you valuable information on friendship?! Your welcome!

I find the best kind of learning is through actually doing something, so fill free to work on a similar presentation as you go.

First, things first: let's rename our document. Technically, this isn't required. You could give it no name and it's still going to be saving in the background. Naming it will just help you find it later.

To name it, just click once on that name area in the upper left corner and start typing. Hit enter when you are done.

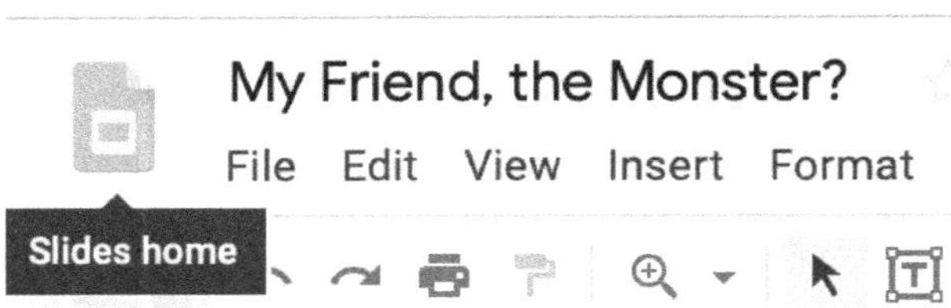


Want to rename it? Simple. Just click in that area again. Gone are the days of File > Save As.

Now let's move to our first slide—the title slide—and give the presentation a name.

That's pretty straightforward, but it's also a little...boring. Let's add a fun background to it.

For this book, I went to google.com/images. That's a nice resource for pictures, but you have to keep in mind that many are copyrighted, so be mindful of what you are using—especially if the presentation is for non-instructional commercial use.

Once you have your image, you can either save it, or just copy and paste it right into your slide.

To add it, there's two methods. I prefer the second, because there's more customation to it, but I'll show you both approaches here.

For the first approach, go to your toolbar and click the Background button. From here you can either give it a solid background color, or make an image a background.

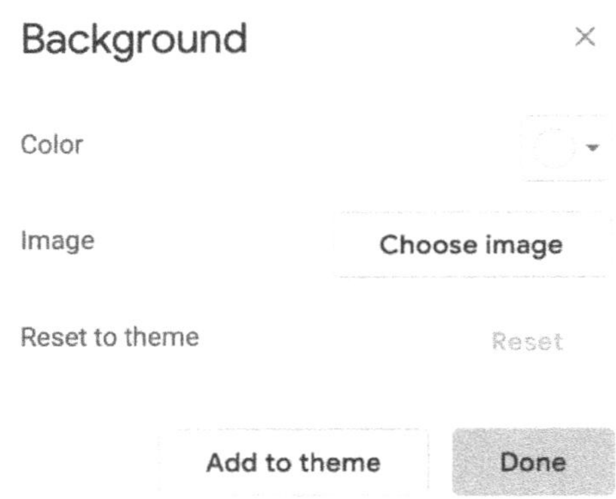


If you are just using a color, then it can work. If you are using an image, then personally I find it problematic because there's not a lot of adjustments that can be made to the image at this level. Take a look at the background below.

Not incredibly easy to see the text, right? How do we fix that? We use the second option. Either copy and paste the image onto the slide or go to Insert > Slide. This will put the image on top of the text. Not much better right? You can fix that by right-clicking the image and selecting "Send to back."

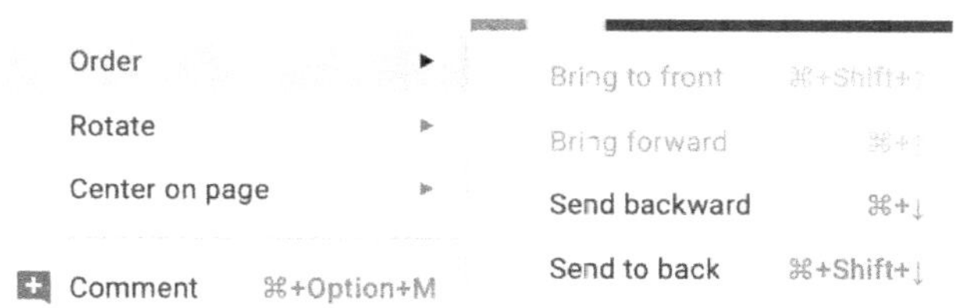


That basically makes it the same as having it as a background image, so it's still not where it needs to be. But now when you click on the image, it brings up a format menu. One option is transparency. Transparency makes the image more see through—like a watermark.

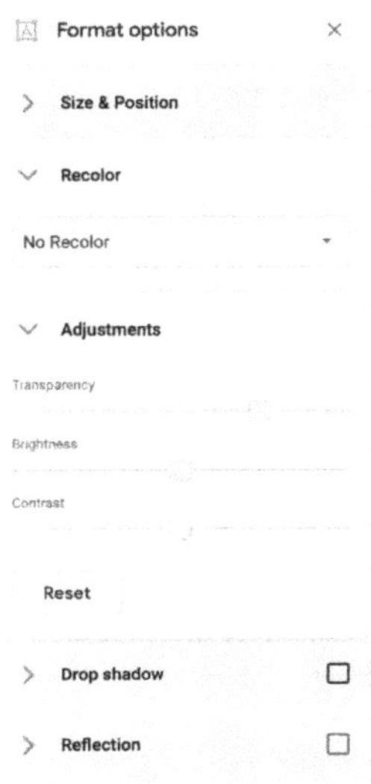


After making it a little transparent, it looks like the below image.

Better, right? But it is bigger than the slide. If you are presenting the slide, it will only show what's in the slide box, but it's much easier to work on a presentation in editor mode when it matches what the presentation will look like, so let's crop it. Right-click on the image, then select "Crop image."

This brings up small blue boxes. Just drag those in so it fits in the slide.

Now we are ready for our next slide. There are two methods to do this. Click the + sign in the menu toolbar.

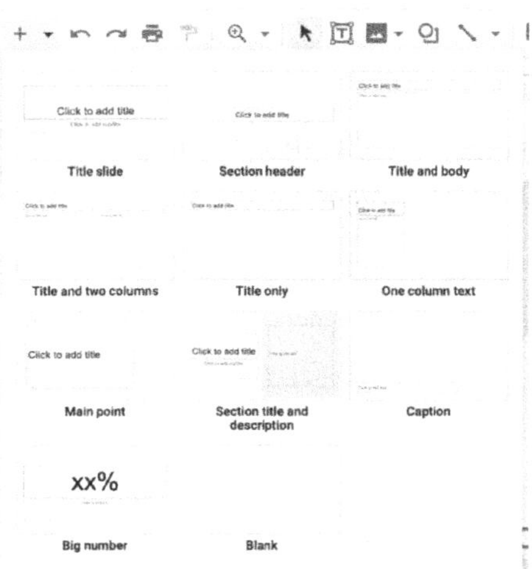

The second method is to click under the first slide and hit the enter / return button on your keyboard.

The default slide will look like the below.

You can change the layout by either right-clicking on the slide thumbnail on the left side. Or going to the menu and clicking on layout.

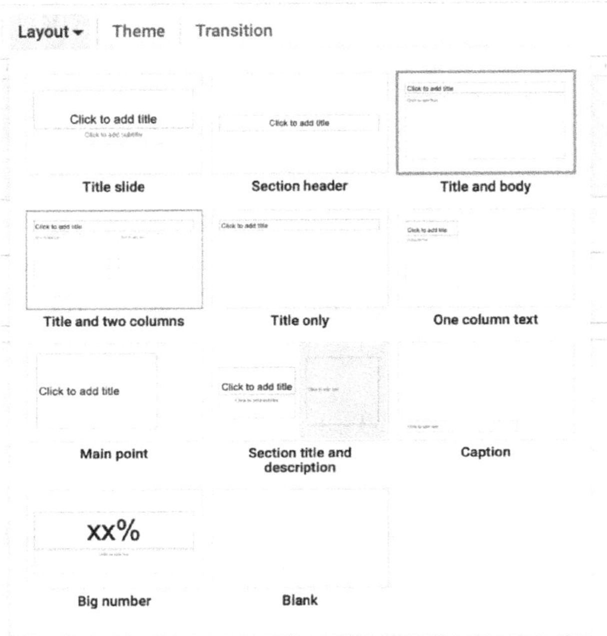


I'll change my layout to two columns.

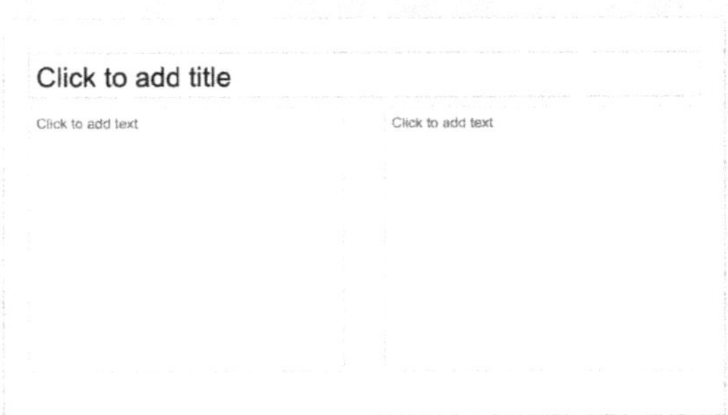


Next, I'll add in some content.

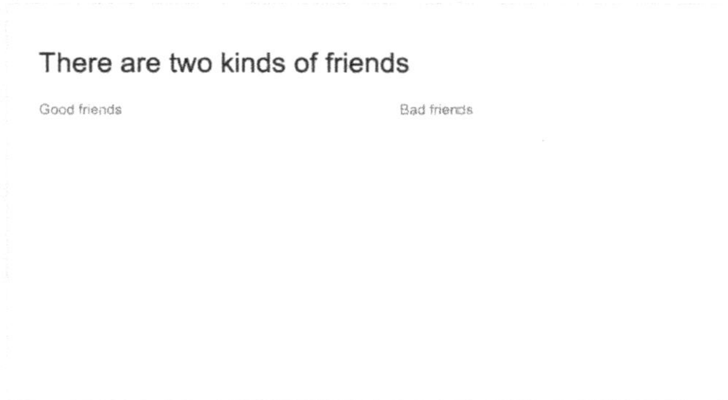


Awesome! Visually stunning! Let's call it a day! Don't get ahead of yourself, cowboy...there's still some work to be done here. Let's throw in some images. Again, you can either do Insert > Picture or just copy and paste it in.

Those pictures are a little...black and white—both literally and figuratively. Right-click on the image, then go format options. For this image, I'm going to check off "Reflection" to make it pop a little. This puts a shadow effect on the image.

The pictures are fine. Now let's work on the text. The header needs to be all caps. We can either type it again with all caps on, or we highlight the text, and then go to Format > Text > Capitalization > UPPERCASE.

Do the same to the text under that, but for that make it Title Case. Next we want to center align it. You may not see this option if you have the format menu open, but it's still there. To the far right of the toolbar, you'll see three dots. Click that, and it will bring up the hidden menu. From here you can center align it.

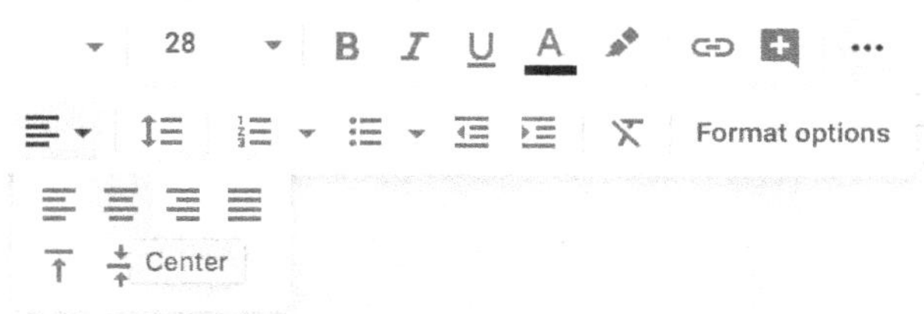


We are also going to change the text color using the button with the A and black line under it.

Now everything will be centered, and a different color.

That's still not very colorful. We could add an image to the background like the first slide, but images as backgrounds can make things look too busy. So let's do a solid color. Click Background from the toolbar and then change it to the one you want.

That's better. But I want the slide header to pop out more. I'm going to put a separate background behind it. Go to the Shapes button on the menu bar and select the rectangle.

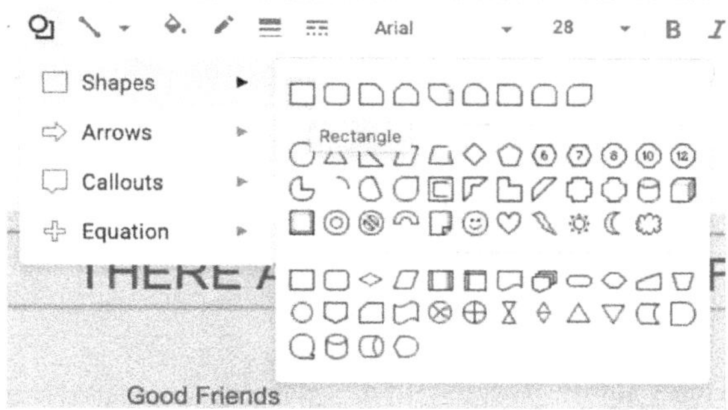


Now drag a rectangle on the upper portion of that slide. I want the box itself to pop more, so I'm also going to right-click, select Format options, and check off "Drop shadow." This gives the box a more 3D effect by putting a subtle shadow behind it.

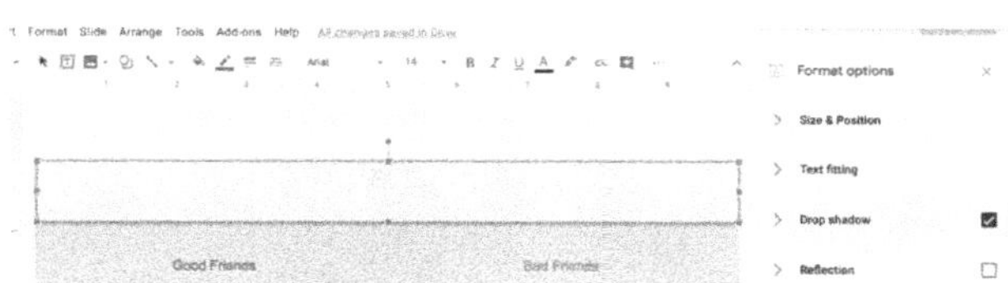


Now we just need to send the box to the back so the text is in front of it. To do that, right-click on the box and under Order select send to back. I also click the text and moved it a little higher up, so it was in the middle of the box.

Now the slide is taking shape, but let's do a few more things. Next, let's make the subtitle text come out more. Click the top box you just created and copy and paste it (CTRL+C and CTRL+V). Then move that box under the top one, right-click it, and do format options; change the color of the box so it's not the same as the other box.

After you change the color, right-click and select Order and send to the back. The text is kind of small, so let's make it bigger and then adjust it so it's more in the middle of the box. Change the font size in the menu bar; by default it's 14.

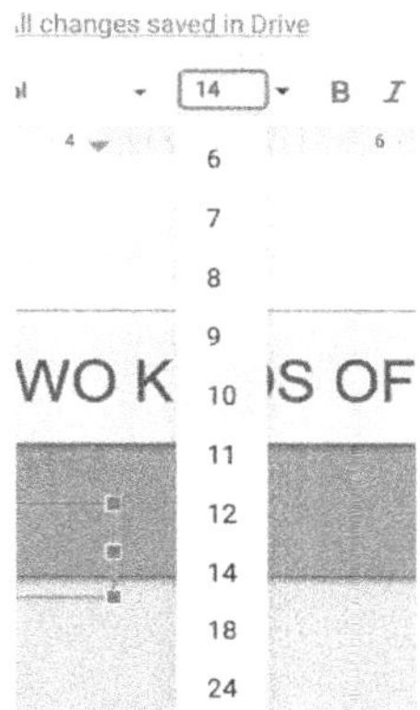


Finally, that dark grey I used doesn't really work. I'm going to make the box white. Right-click, select format options, and then change the color to white.

I want to put a line between friendship to separate the good friends from the bad. Go to the menu bar, click the line option, and select the first line. As you draw the line, hold the shift on the keyboard—that's going to make it a straight line—so it doesn't go diagonal at all.

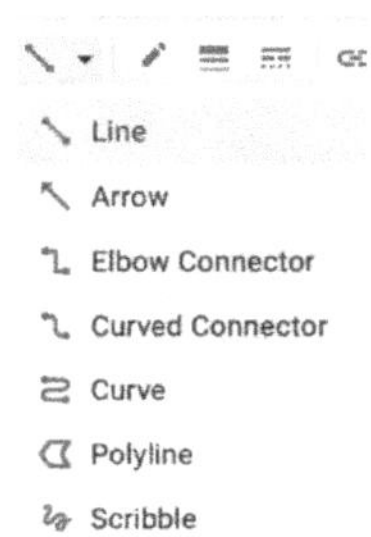


The line is going to be pretty thin; that works for some things, but here we want to beef it up. Click the line, then go to the menu bar. See the box with the lines of different weights? That's what you want. It's like a font size, but for a shape. If you don't see it, then you haven't selected the line. Click it one time.

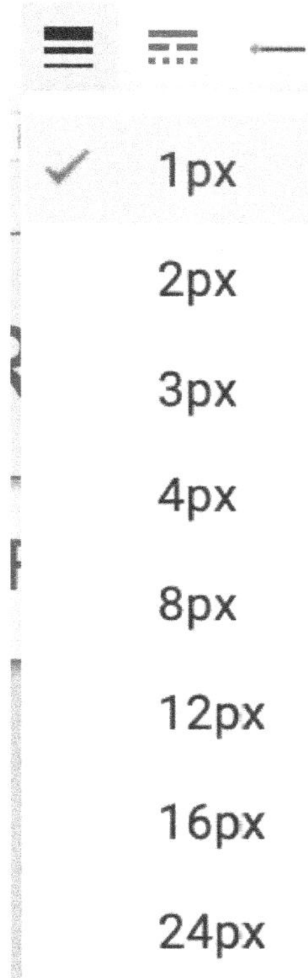


Now that the line is wider, we have everything where we want it to be.

You can create a different look for every slide, but to save yourself a lot of time, copying the slide is a lot faster. Go to the left pane where the slide thumbnails are. Right-click, and select, duplicate slides.

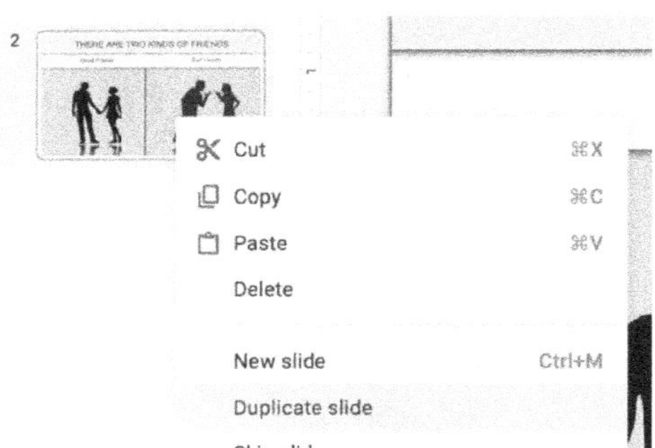


From here, all we have to do is take out the text we don't want and change the images.

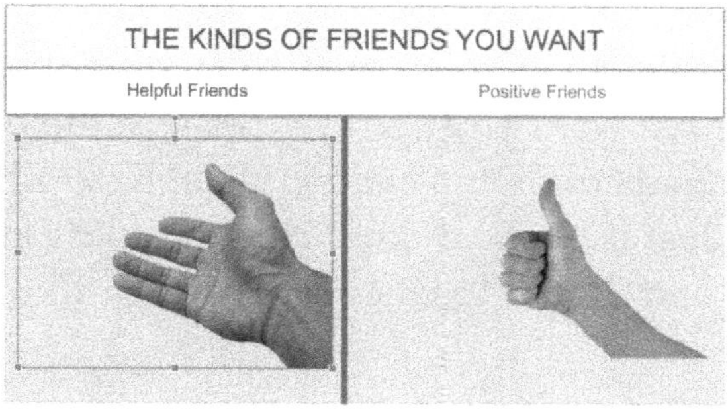


The image above feels a little off. I don't want both hands going the same direction. That's an easy fix. Select one of the images, select format options, and then under rotate, select Flip.

That's going to horizontally flip the image you've selected.

So things are going great! You have three slides! But wait! You just realized that the third slide needs to be the second slide! Now what! Easy! Just click the thumbnail of the slide in the left pane, and drag it to where you want it to go.

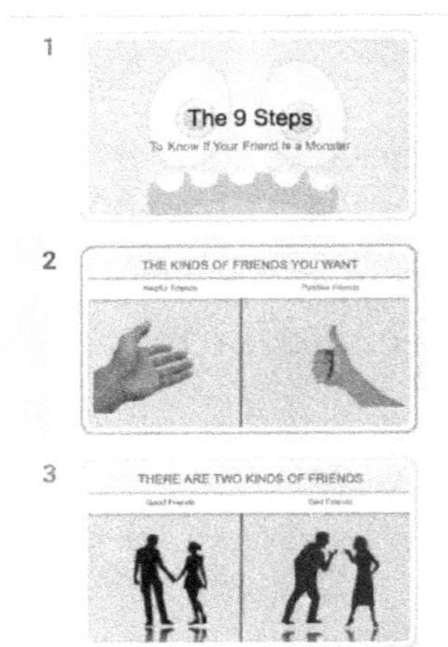


Now that you have the Slides, you need transitions between them. You won't see this in editor mode, but transitions is what happens when you are presenting a presentation between each slide—does it show a dissolve, for example.

To add in a transition, right-click on the thumbnail you want, and then select change transition.

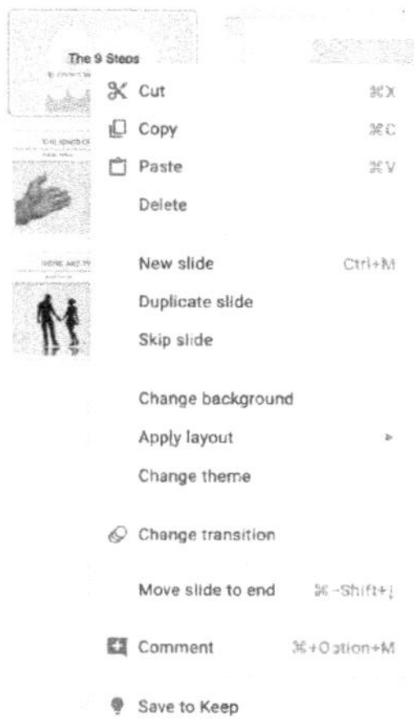


This brings up the Transition menu; you can change one transition or apply the transition to all of the slides.

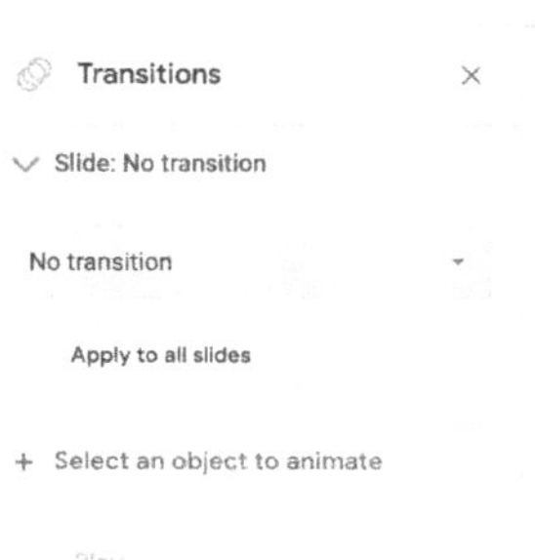

# [3]

# SHARING IS CARING

This chapter will cover:

- How to share
- Sharing settings
- Naming versions

Are you ready to share your slides about friends with your friends? Google Slides is a collaborative platform, so sharing is where things really come together. With sharing you can get feedback and also have others edit your slides (or you can disable editing and only get feedback)

To share, click the Share button in the upper right corner.

If you've used any other Google apps software, then you'll probably know what to do next—they all work exactly the same. You'll have a box to either share the Slide with specific people via email, or you can send them a link to it.

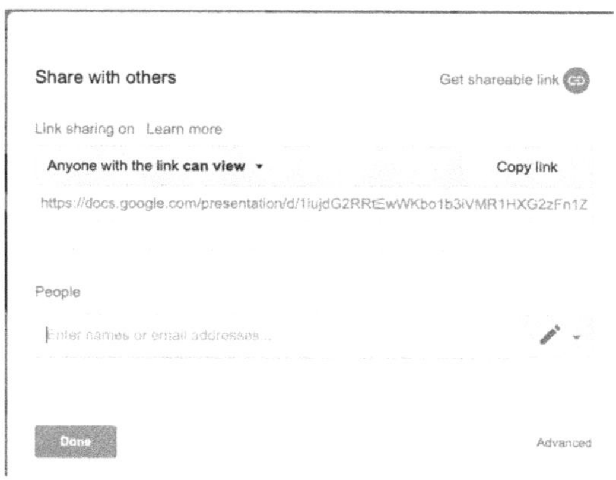


If you click on can view you'll get a drop down with varies options. If you only want people to see it, but not do anything else, for example.

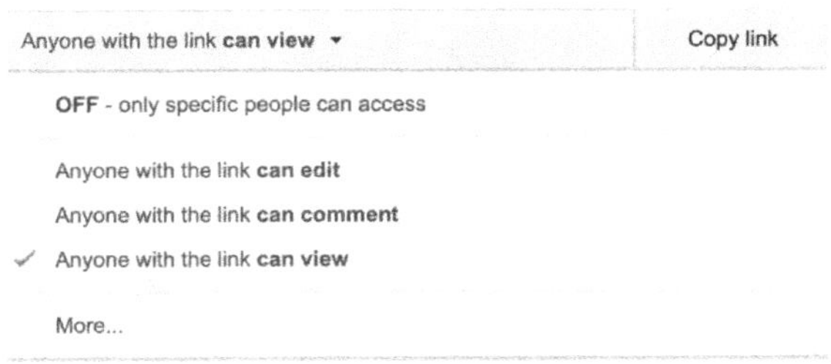


If you click on Advanced, you'll have even more options—such as preventing editors from adding people or disabling copying anything in the doc.

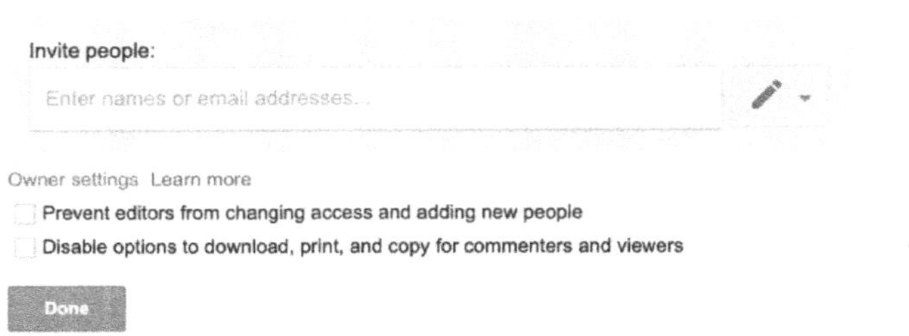


Once people are in your document, and ready to make changes, things get a little—difficult. Unlike Google Docs where you can track changes, Google Slides doesn't have that option. If someone makes a change, there's no good visible way to see it.

You can ask them to comment instead. To do that, have them right-click and select comment. Or go to Insert > Comment:

There's one final way to keep track of changes—albeit, not the ideal one. That way is to view the history. You can see the history by going to File > Version history > See version history.

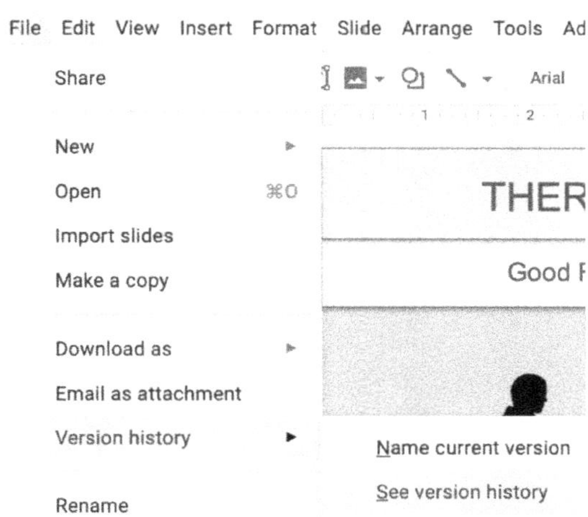

This will show you a list of changes and timestamp when they were made.

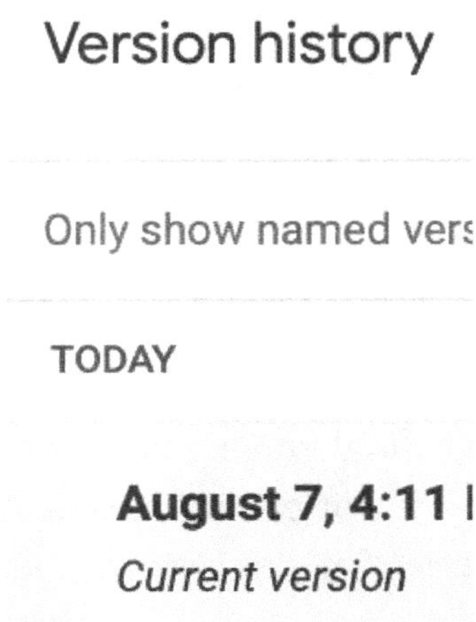


If you are using this method, then my advice is to have people go in after a change and name the version: File > Version history > Name current version.

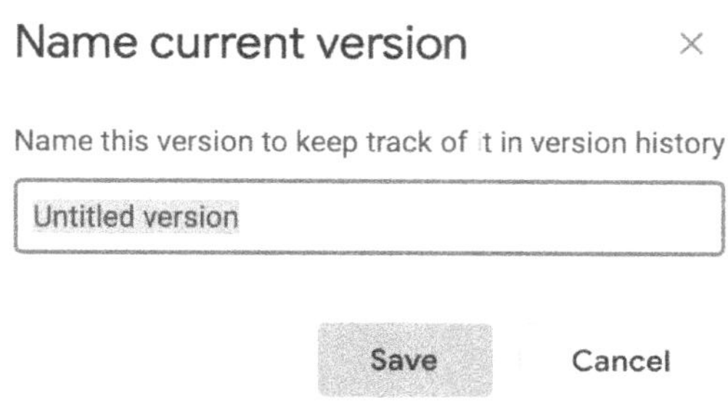


If you have someone whose old fashion—like PowerPoint, old fashion—you can also export it and email it to them. This is under File > Download as. There's all kinds of options.

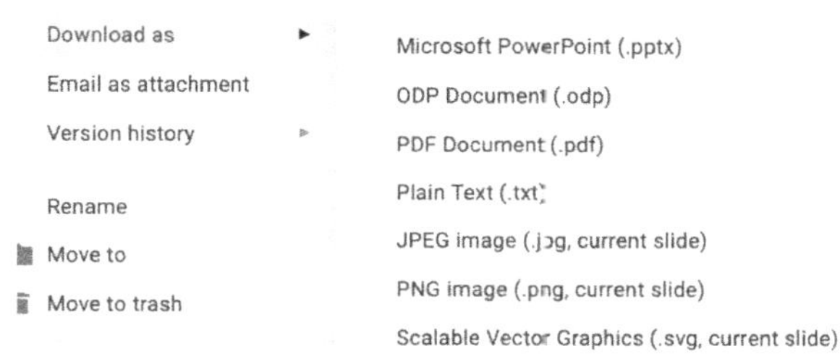


If you are giving a presentation, my advice is to export it as a PowerPoint and PDF. This way if you are ever presenting somewhere and you show up and they say, "Oh, we don't have Internet in this room—and you'll be using a computer without PowerPoint" You'll have something to display.

# [4]

# PRESENTING YOUR BIG IDEA!

This chapter will cover:

- Presenting to others
- Speaker notes
- Audience questions

So speaking of that big presentation, now what?! That's the easy part. See that big Present button in the right corner? Guess what that does?!

But there's more to presenting then, presenting! Click that arrow next to Present, and you'll see a few more options.

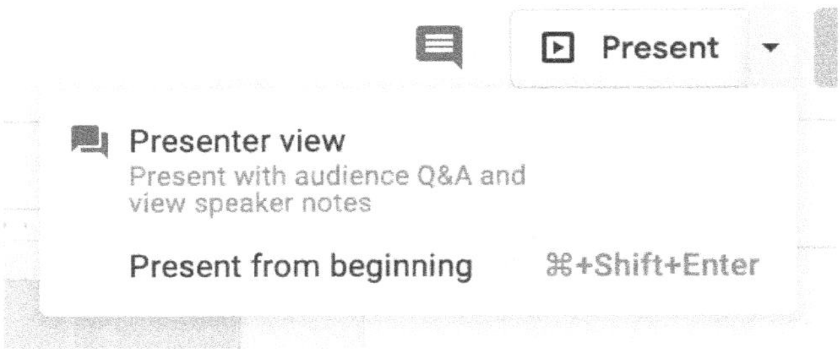


One is Presenter view, which I'll cover in just a few minutes. When your presentation is open, there's a new menu. In this menu you'll be able to turn on Q & A and notes, which will be covered below, and use the pointer. Pointer is kind of like a laser pointer; if you are doing mouse movements, then this will make it easier for viewers to watch themovements.

## Using Presenter mode

By now, you've probably noticed there's a little box on the bottom that says "Click to add speaker notes." Want to take a wild guess and say what that is for? If you guessed, "Speaker notes" then congratulations, you can read!

You can actually make that area bigger or non-existent by clicking on those three dots in the middle and making it go up or down. For the sake of this book, we'll keep them right where they are.

Okay, so what are speaker notes? This is what appears on your screen when you are presenting a presentation. What do I mean by "your screen"? When you give a presentation, you usually will have your laptop connected to either a projector or TV, right? So your screen would be the laptop, and the other screen would be what it's connected to.

Speaker notes is kind of like having paper notes in front of you. It can be whatever you want. Since the audience doesn't see them, it doesn't matter—whatever is helpful when you are giving the presentation.

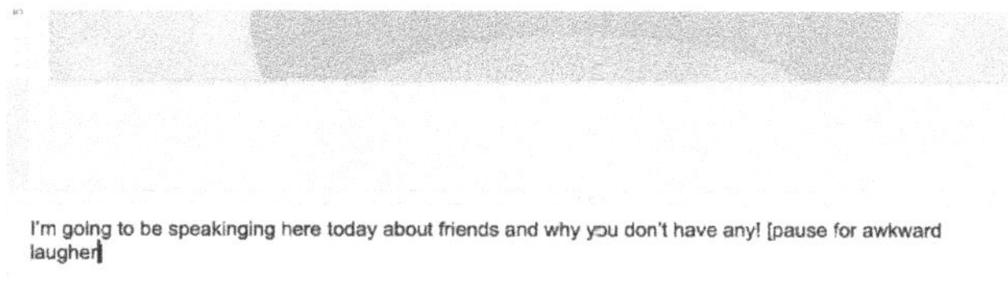

You could technically set it up to mirror your screen, but having a presenter screen is very useful. In speaker mode, you'll see the notes, the amount of time that has passed, and thumbnail of the slide coming up next, and the ability to get audience questions.

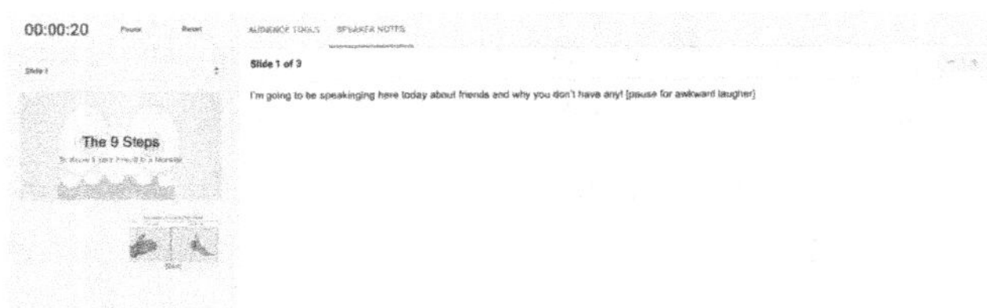


If the notes are too small for you, then you can use the "- | +" buttons to make them bigger.

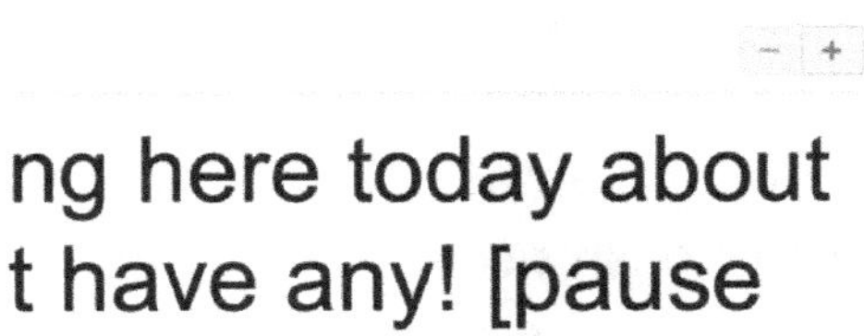


What's really cool about presenting in Google Slides is the audience can ask questions. To accept questions while you present, you just have to turn it on. Next to speaker notes, click Audience Tools, then click the Start Now button.

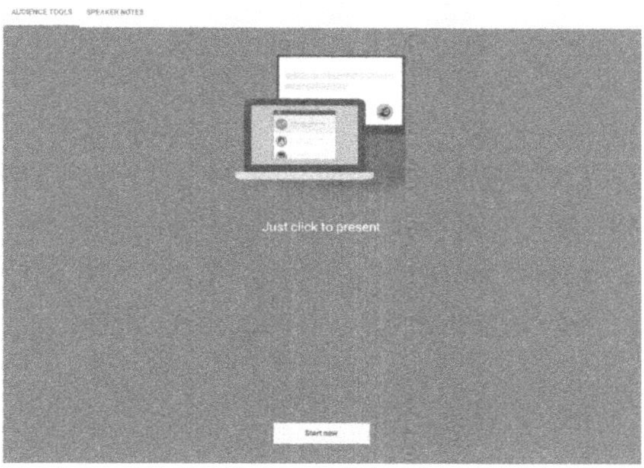


There's a toggle to turn it on and off, and a link to send people.

When the person goes to that link, they are presented with a forum to ask ask their questions. They can either do it as a person or anonymously.

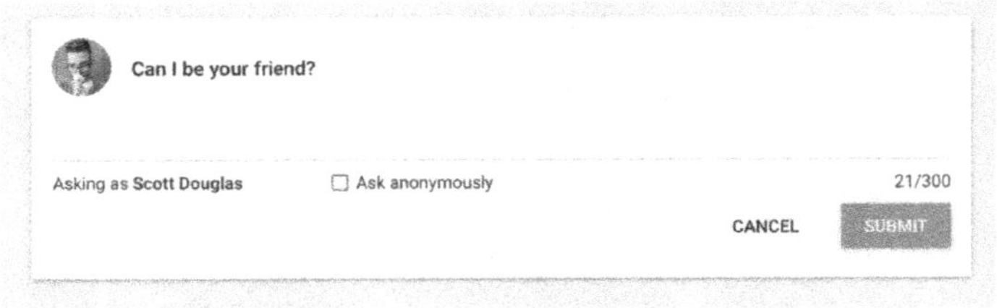


Other people will see it and they can upvote it or downvote it. That helps push up or down questions; a question with a 20 upvotes will be hire in the question que then a question with 2.

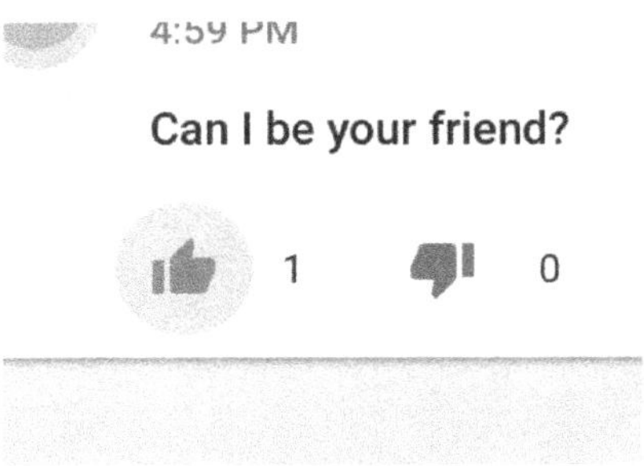


On the presenter version, they will see the question, the number of upvotes, and have an option to present it.

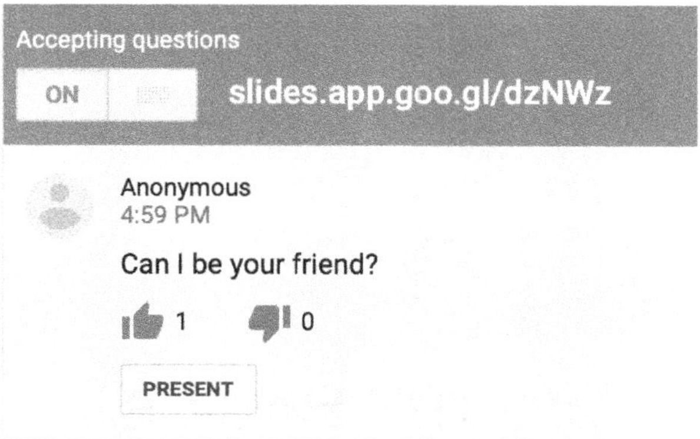


If the presenter hits the Present button, it will replace the presentation with the question.

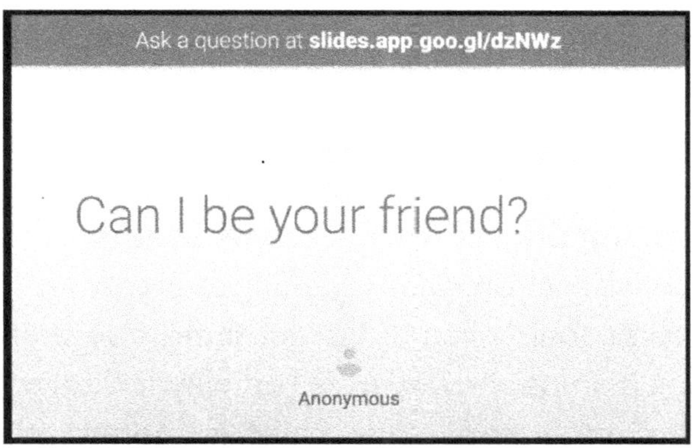


To return to your slide, present the present button below the question again.

# [5]
# BEYOND THE BASICS

This chapter will cover:

- Importing and creating charts
- Creating diagrams
- Adding videos

## Importing Charts from Google Sheets

Collaboration is Google Slides standout feature, as you probably can tell; something else that really makes it shine, however, is the way it interacts with other Google apps. Everything is connected through the cloud, which makes integration a breeze.

To illustrate this point, we are going to import a chart created in Google Sheets into Slides.

Start off by creating a new Slide. I'll make one simple and call it The Friendly Chart.

Now we need are chart. Open up Google Sheets, and create a basic chart. It's simple to do. Just create two columns. One with labels or names and one with data.

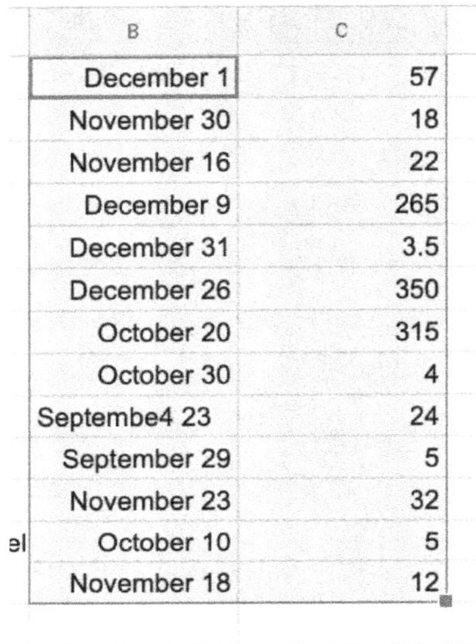

| B | C |
|---|---|
| December 1 | 57 |
| November 30 | 18 |
| November 16 | 22 |
| December 9 | 265 |
| December 31 | 3.5 |
| December 26 | 350 |
| October 20 | 315 |
| October 30 | 4 |
| Septembe4 23 | 24 |
| September 29 | 5 |
| November 23 | 32 |
| October 10 | 5 |
| November 18 | 12 |

Next, highlight the area you are going to make a chart of, and go to Insert > Chart.

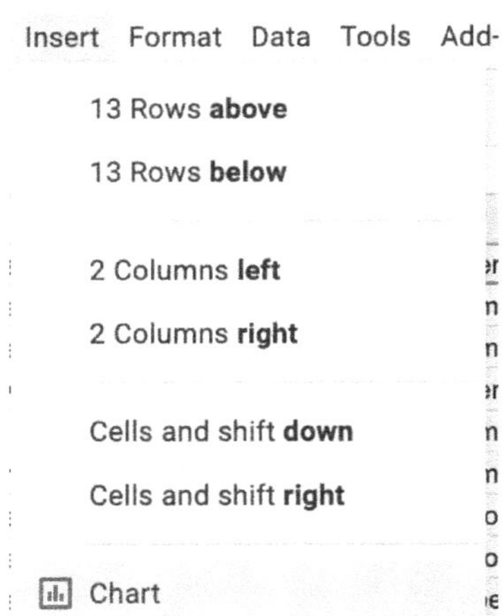

Your chart is added right into your Sheet.

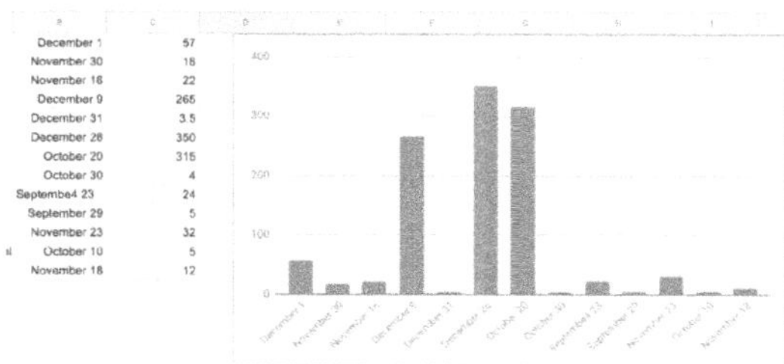

From here, click the chart and do CTRL C, which will copy it. Now go back into Google Slide, select the slide you want to add it to, and on your keyboard, hit CTRL V. This is going to ask you if you want it linked or unlinked.

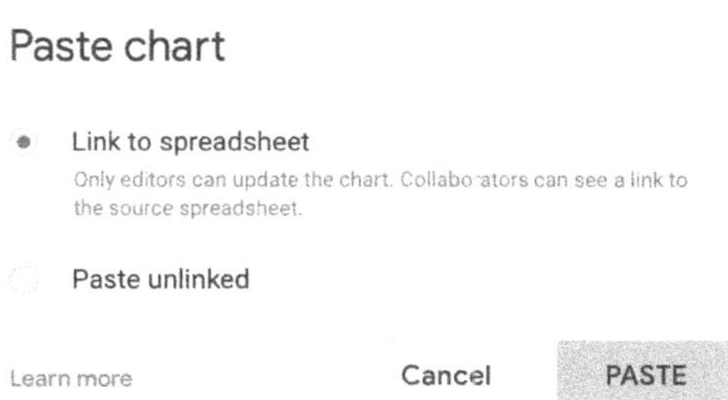


Linked will connect the app to the spreadsheet, so if you update data, it will update here as well; unlinked makes it like a static image that will never change. For this example, we are doing "Link to spreadsheet."

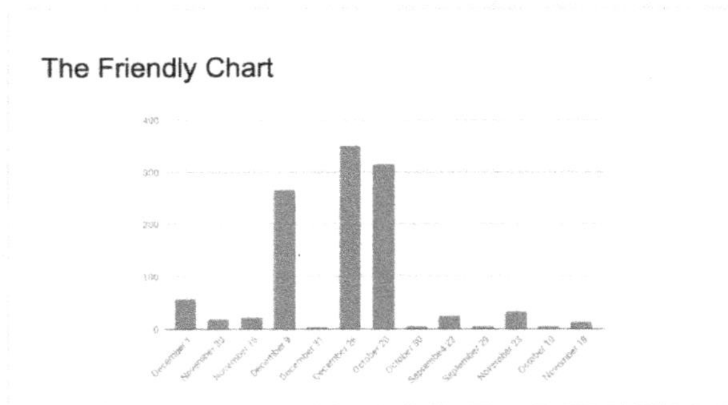


Now that it's added in, you can click on the upper right corner of the chart and have a few options. If you pick Unlink, then you will not be able to link it back, so think carefully here. Open source will let you go back in and edit the data.

When you go back into your spreadsheet and edit the data, it will change the chart in real-time. You don't have to create a new chart.

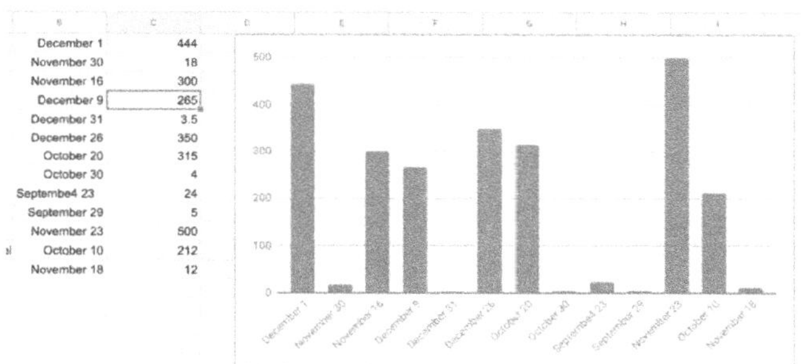


Now that it's changed in the Sheet, it will have a new option when you return to slides. Click the chart in slides. See the Update button?

Click that and it will update the chart to match what's the updated data.

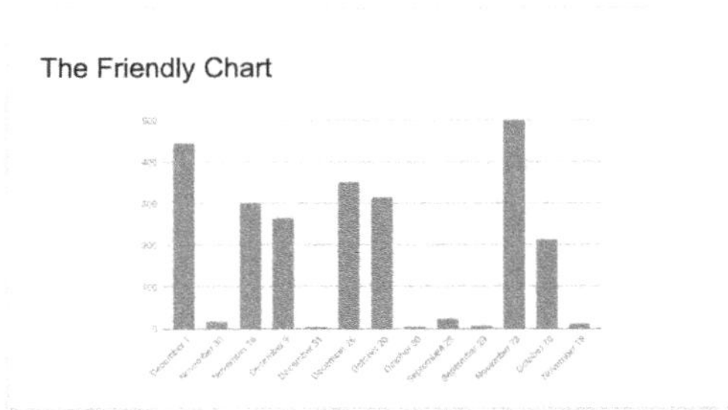


Now that you've entered a caption, go ahead and open up Google Spreadsheets. We're about to do the exact same thing we did when we inserted the chart into our Google Doc. Save the chart as an image on your hard drive, and then upload it into your presentation.

If you don't have a chart and want to do it from scratch, you can also go to Insert > Chart.

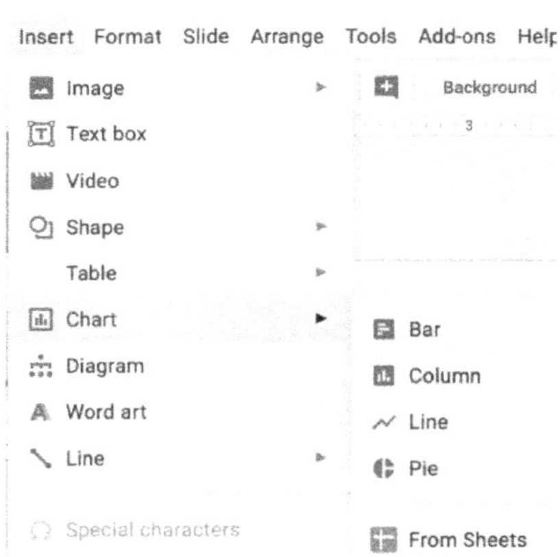

When you insert a chart from here, you will be creating a spreadsheet that's tied to the chart. It's going to add in a dummy chart; from here, you will click the menu button in the upper right corner of the dummy chart, then select "Open source."

## Creating Diagrams

Diagrams aren't as common as charts, but are very resourceful when creating things like pricing tables and timelines.

To get started, create a new slide, and then go to Insert > Timeline.

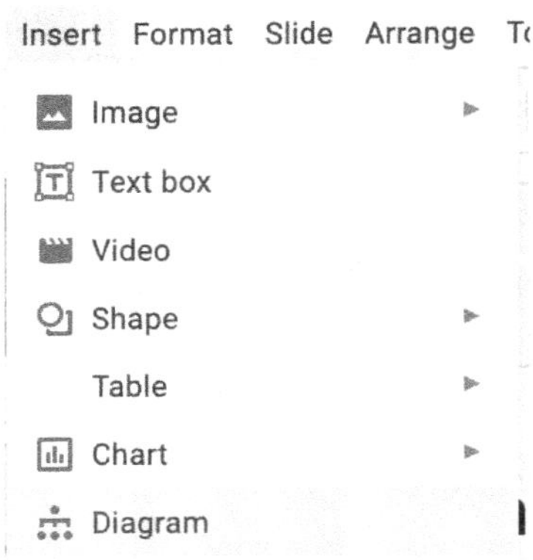


What's nice about diagrams, is the hard part is already done. Google has several prebuilt templates and all you have to do is customize them a little. To start with, you'll see several different types of diagrams you can work with.

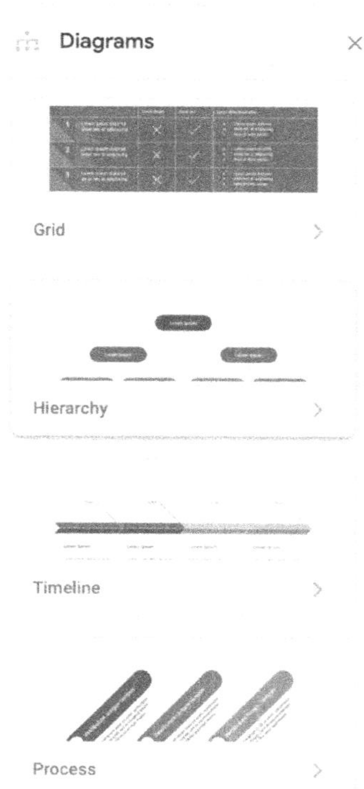


Depending on the type you select, you'll next be able to select how many dates you want to show and the color that will be used. As you update these two fields, you'll notice the preview thumbnails changing in real-time. Once you get this portion customized, select the type of diagram you want to use.

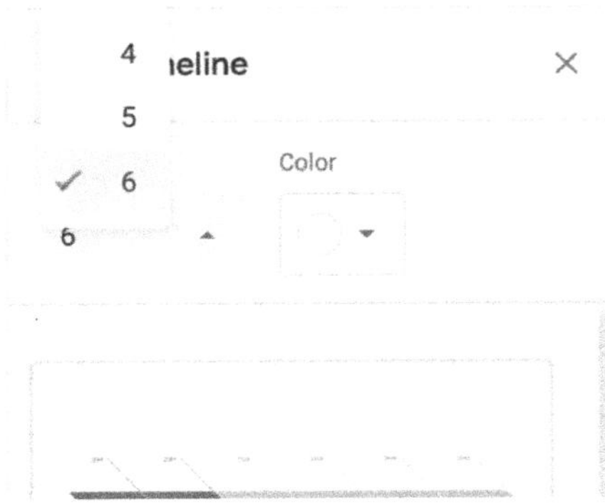


The diagram is added into your slide, and from here you can customize it to whatever suits your needs.

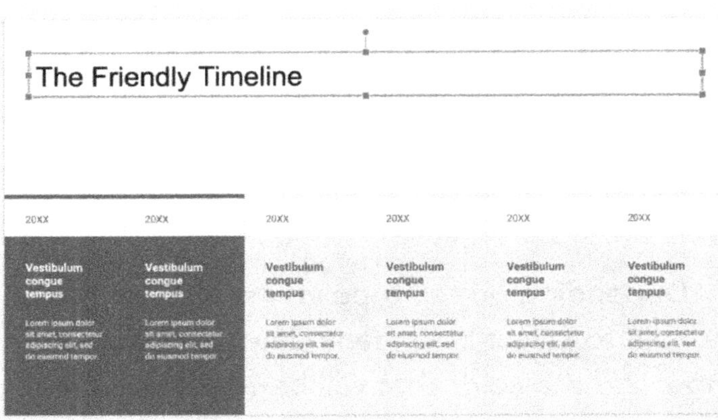


## Adding Video to a Presentation

There's another app integration you can use with Google Slides. Unless you just spent the past ten years living under a rock, you've probably heard of it: YouTube.

When you add a video to Slides, you can either add a YouTube video or add one from your Google Drive. Both are easy to do, but there's a caveat here: both are online. That means if there's no Internet where you are presenting, that videos not going to load.

To get started, add another Slide, and then go to Insert > Video.

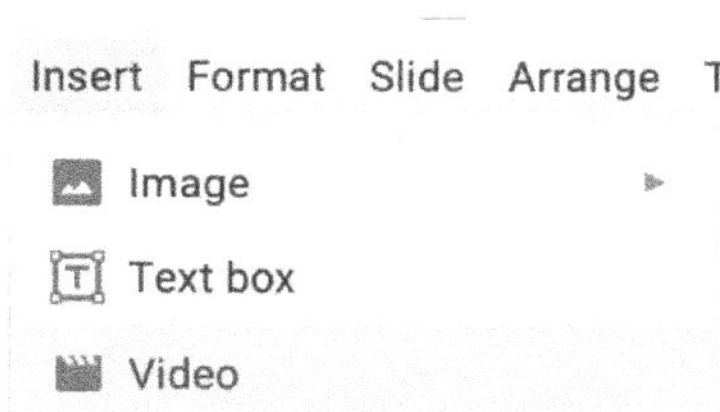


The first thing you'll see is a search bar to find your video on YouTube. That's the easiest option—especially if you don't already have a video and want to use something already created.

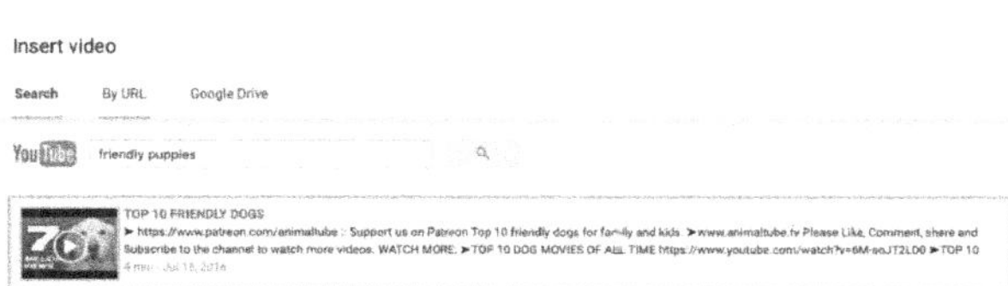

If you have a video on YouTube, then you can use the "By URL" option to copy in the link—this is only YouTube links, so if that video is on something like Vimeo, then you are out of luck. The last option is Google Drive. If you have a video in Google Drive, select this. Unlike photos, where if you don't have it upload it, then you can upload it directly, videos is a bit more cumbersome. You have to upload it to Google Drive, then come back and find it here. It's not complicated, but the extra step makes it a little less user friendly.

Once the video is added, right-click and select video options. This will bring up a menu with several options. The one you'll want to pay the most attention to is Format options. Under format options, you can select when the video will start and end, which is great if you only plan on showing a short clip.

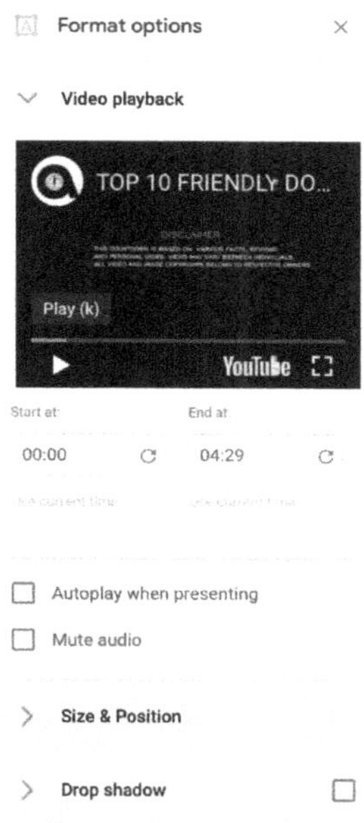


You can also check off autoplay when presenting. When this is selected, the video will start as soon as you get to the slide. It can work for some videos, but if you haven't practiced the timing of your presentation, it could make for an awkward transition. If you don't check it off, then you start the video by pressing the play button.

# [6] This and That

This chapter will cover:

- Overview of Slides menus
- Finding and using templates

The goal of this book is to get you up and running quickly; it's not to give you a comprehensive look at every feature—even the ones you will probably never used.

Before leaving you, however, I'll give you a high-level overview of some of the features not covered. Some are self-explanatory, so I'll move quick.

The view menu is what you see on the screen—do you want to see the presentation? The outline? Speaker notes? This is where you change it.

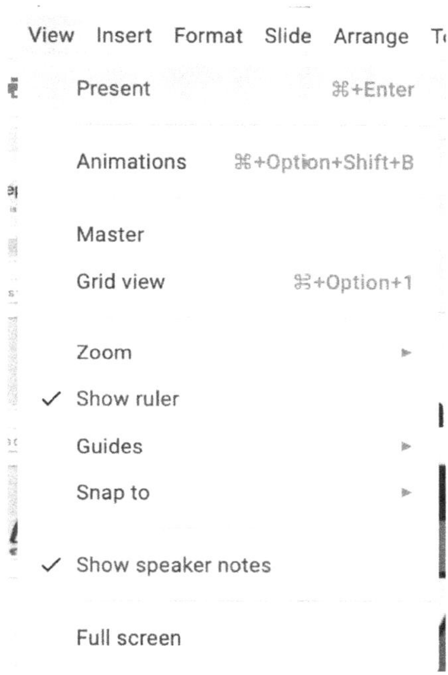


Some of the less obvious views:

Animations – we didn't cover animations in the book. Animations isn't exactly what it sounds. It's not a cartoon dancing across the screen. Think of animations like slide transitions, but for objects. So you can have the slide start, and then say "on click, I want this object to dissolve in." It's a resourceful feature, but too many animations can also make a presentation feel gimmicky, so be careful. If you want to add an animation, right-click on the image or object (object could be text) that you want to animate, and select Animate.

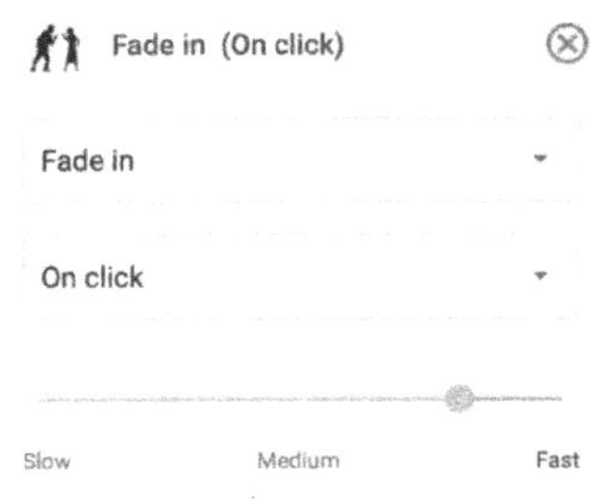


The animate view let's you see all of your animations, and also edit each one.

Grid view simply lays out all of your slides in a grid. It's helpful if you have dozens of slides and need to organize or print them, but not useful for shorter presentations.

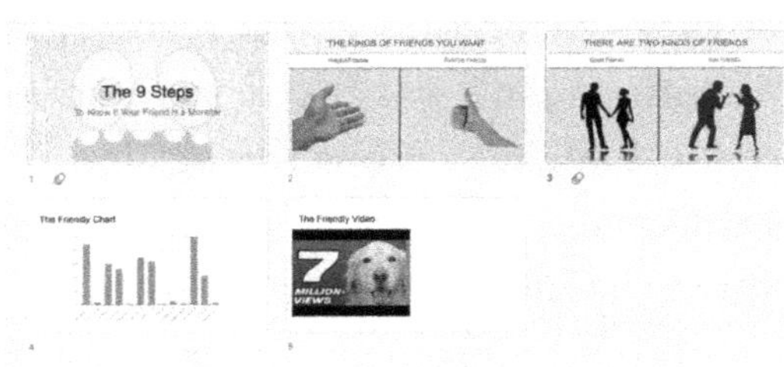


Guides will turn on rulers and is useful if you need to add in something with more precision.

We've covered most of the features in the insert menu.

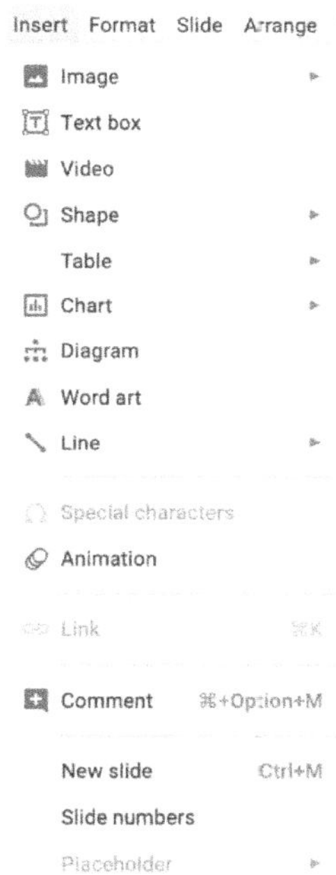


Some of the ones not covered:

- Word Art – If you've used Word, then you might be familiar with this; it makes text pop a little more by giving them a more 3D feel.
- Slide numbers – page numbers, but for slides.

Both the View and Slides menu have something called "master"; in the Slides menu it's "edit master."

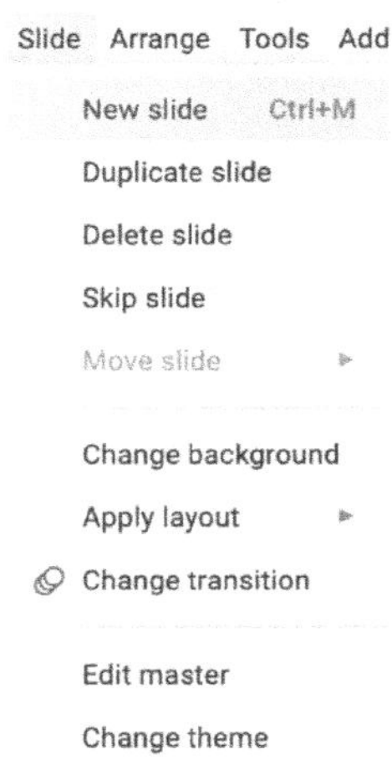


What the heck is master? It's a very technical area of slides that probably 90% of users never step foot in, but it's still good to know. This is where you can change how styles look. For example, you want to say "whenever I use a heading 1, I want it to be 30 in size, not 16." It saves you a lot of time if you are working on several presentations.

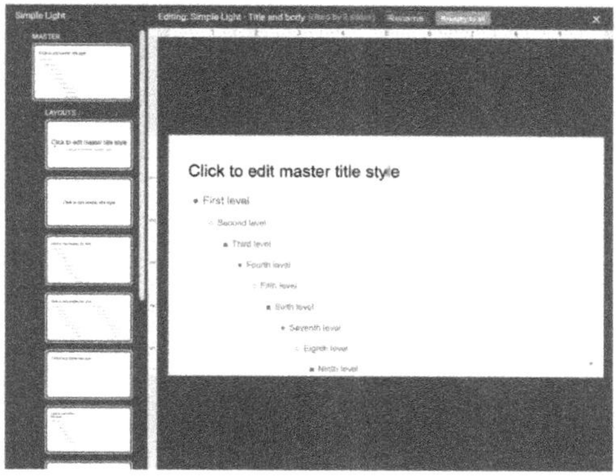


Spell checker and dictionary are found in the tools menu; that's what most people go to that menu for. If you are doing a Q & A, it's helpful to note there is a history option here. If you already gave the presentation, this is where you would go to review all the questions.

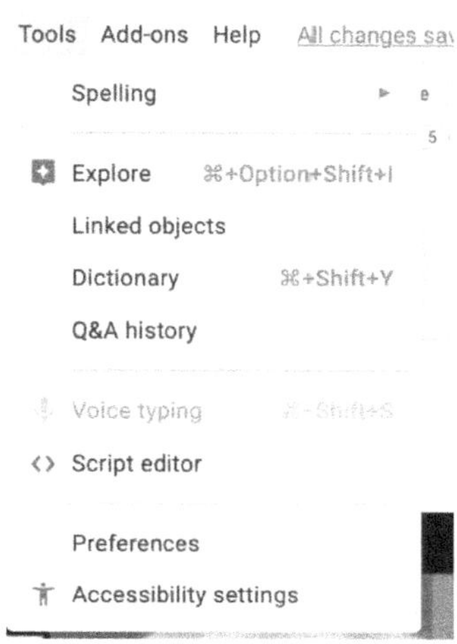

There are a lot of third party apps. This can be found in the "Add-ons menu."

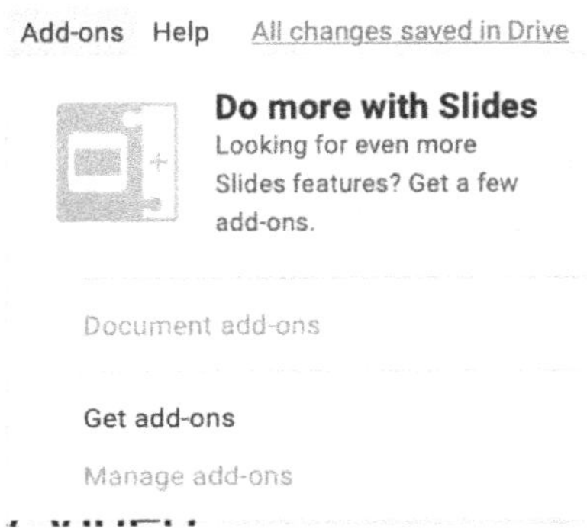


Finally, the help menu is obviously where you go for help, but there's also trainings here. These are free and very useful when you have time to learn more.

## Custom Presentations from Templates

You'll recall when you first started that you could add a blank presentation or start from a template. We did blank to get started. Once you know your way around Slides, adding from a Template could save you a lot of time.

To add a template, go to your Google Drive, and select New > Google Slides > Start from a template.

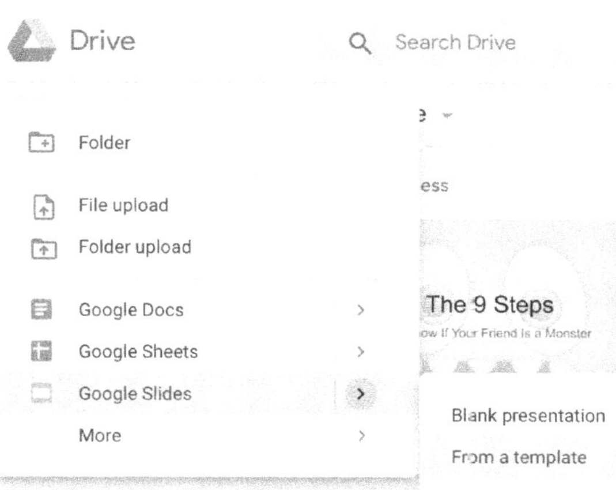


This brings up a template gallery of dozens of different presentations. The idea here is to find a style you like and then add in your own version. Don't let the names fool you. Just because it says it's a wedding template, for example, doesn't mean it's not ideal for business.

Once you select one, you'll notice right away that several slides have already been added in.

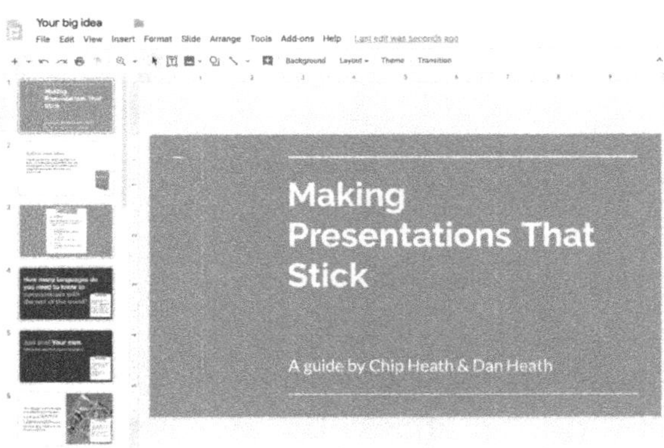


Nothing about these templates are locked in. What do I mean by that? You can change literally everything about them—images, color backgrounds, font sizes, text boxes. Now that you know your way around Slides, you'll have no problem customizing them to fit your needs.

The template gallery is nice. There's a lot there. But it's not comprehensive. I recommend browsing it, but when you are out of ideas, then go to the place with millions of ideas: Google.

Start by Googling "google slides templates."

There are only 55,000,000 results, so you'll have no problem sorting through that in no time!

In all seriousness, I do recommend browsing through some of the top matches, but I also recommend making the search specific to your industry. Such as "google slides templates for education."

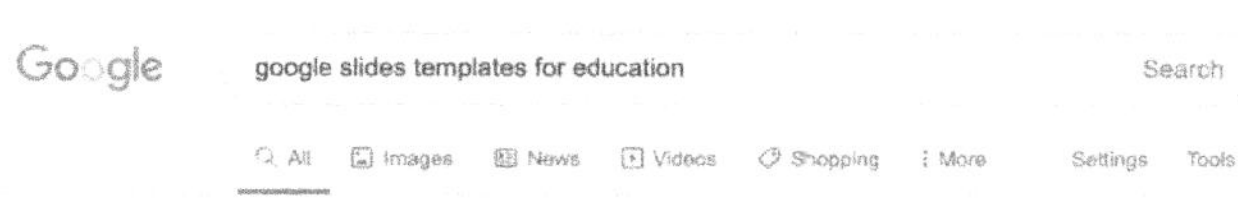

People use slides for more than presentations. You can create books with it, resumes, portfolios—it's a powerful tool, so don't be afraid to think outside the box.

Once you see something you like, then download it, and then upload it to your Google Drive as a file.

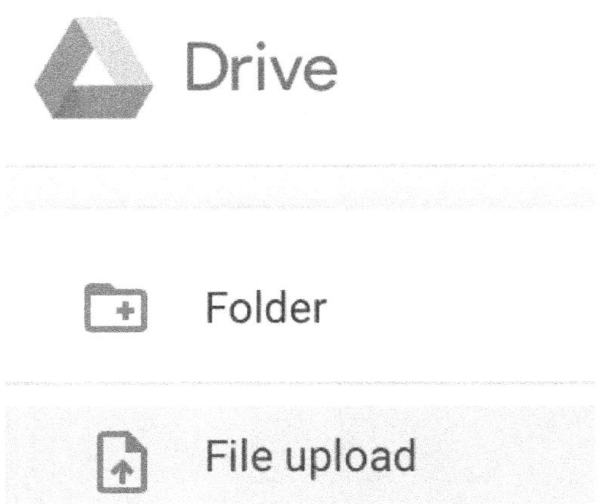


From here just right-click on the file once it's uploaded and open it as a Slide.

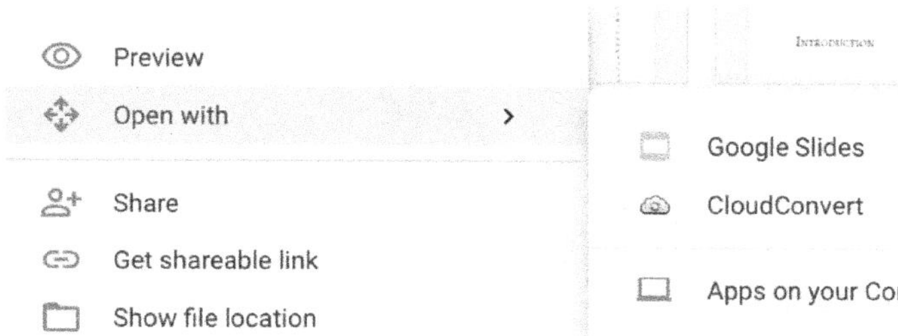
Preview
Open with
Share
Get shareable link
Show file location
Google Slides
CloudConvert
Apps on your Co

# [7] Google Slides Keyboard Shortcuts

You can see all the keyboard shortcuts in Google Slides by selecting Help > Keyboard shortcuts.

For your reference, below are some of the most common ones you'll use.

| **Common actions** | |
|---|---|
| New slide | **Ctrl + m** |
| Duplicate slide | **Ctrl + d** |
| Undo | **Ctrl + z** |
| Redo | **Ctrl + y**<br>**Ctrl + Shift + z** |
| Copy | **Ctrl + c** |
| Cut | **Ctrl + x** |
| Paste | **Ctrl + v** |
| Insert or edit link | **Ctrl + k** |

| Open link | **Alt + Enter** |
|---|---|
| Delete | **Delete** |
| Select all | **Ctrl + a** |
| Find | **Ctrl + f** |
| Find and replace | **Ctrl + h** |
| Open... | **Ctrl + o** |
| Print | **Ctrl + p** |
| Turn on captions while presenting | **Ctrl + Shift + c** |
| **Text** | |
| Bold | **Ctrl + b** |
| Italic | **Ctrl + i** |
| Underline | **Ctrl + u** |
| Subscript | **Ctrl + ,** |
| Superscript | **Ctrl + .** |
| Strikethrough | **Alt + Shift + 5** |
| Clear formatting | **Ctrl + ** |
| | **Ctrl + Space** |
| Left align | **Ctrl + Shift + l** |
| Right align | **Ctrl + Shift + r** |
| Center align | **Ctrl + Shift + e** |
| Justify | **Ctrl + Shift + j** |
| **Presenting** | |
| Stop presenting | **Esc** |
| Next | → |
| Previous | ← |
| Go to specific slide (7 followed by Enter goes to slide 7) | **Number followed by Enter** |
| First slide | **Home** |
| Last slide | **End** |
| Open speaker notes | **s** |
| Open audience tools | **a** |

| | |
|---|---|
| Toggle laser pointer | **l** |
| Print | **Ctrl + p** |
| Toggle captions (English only) | **Ctrl + Shift + c** |
| Toggle full screen | **F11** |
| **Video Player** | |
| Toggle play/pause | **k** |
| Rewind 10 seconds | **u** |
| Fast forward 10 seconds | **o** |

# GOOGLE FORMS

# [1] Google Forms and Lesser Used Google Apps

This chapter will cover:

- Using Google Forms
- Overview of Google Drawing, Google Map, Google Sites, Google Jamboard

**Google Forms**

If you click that "More" option when you are creating a new document, one very handy application you'll see is "Google Forms."

Google Forms lets you create custom surveys. It's very simple and resourceful. Once you click on a blank form to get started, you see a screen like this:

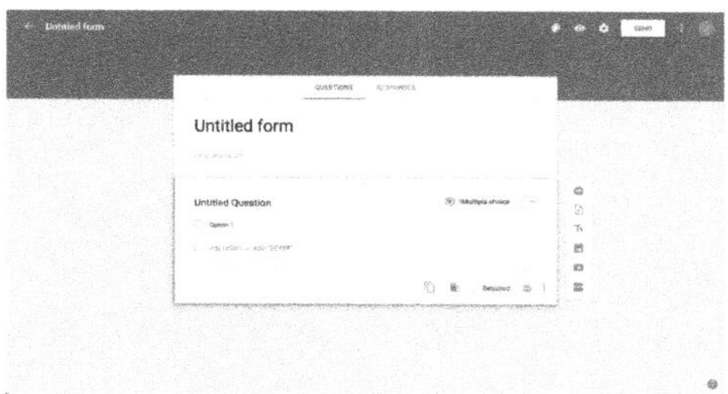


The first question is already there. You just have to name everything—the name of the form, and what the question is. By default, it's multiple choice, but if you click the multiple-choice dropdown, you'll get several other options:

To add a new question, just click the "+" on the side menu:

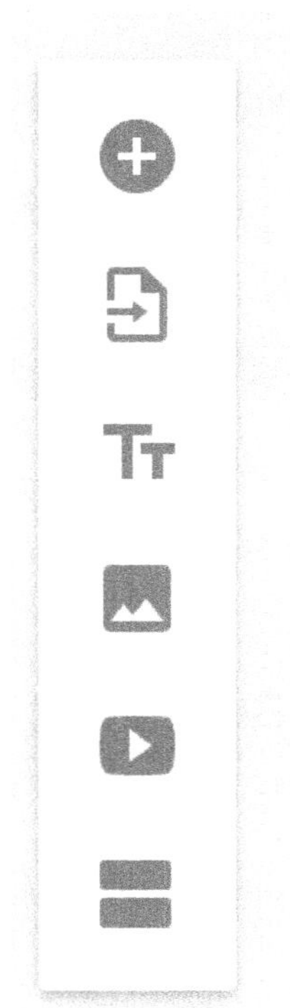

It will add the question under the previous, but you can change its position by clicking the six small boxes to drag it above (or if there's multiple questions, below).



You can also use that side menu, to add links, text, images, YouTube videos, and sections.

When you are done with your form and you want to share it, click the send button:

This will bring up a box that lets you specify how you will share it: by email, link, or embedded on a webpage:

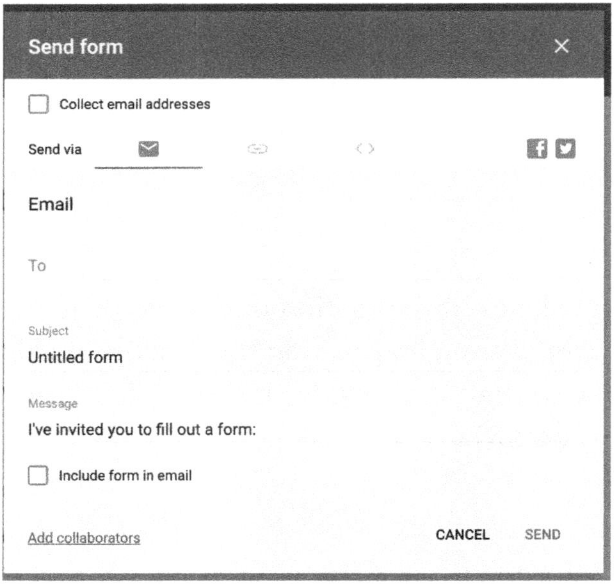


To toggle between each, just click the icon that represents how you want to see it. The middle, for example (seen below), is by link; the < > is to embed in a webpage.

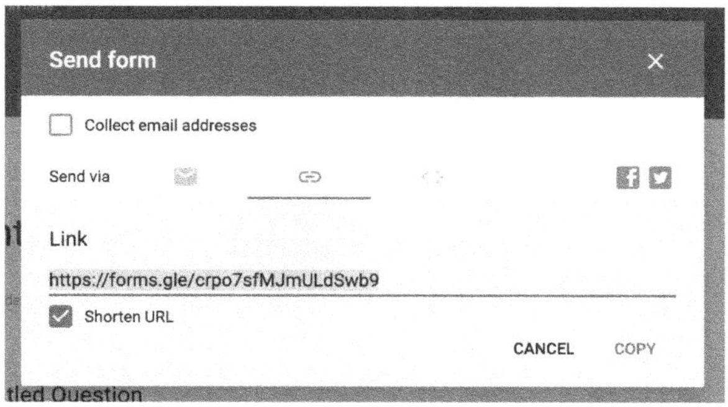


When you embed into a webpage, you'll be able to customize the size:

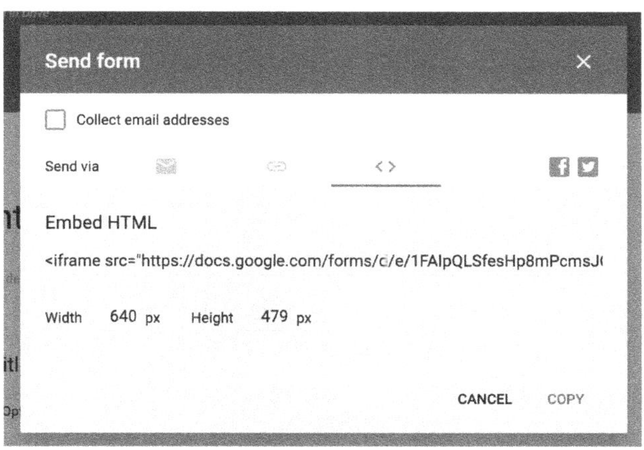

## Other Apps

Google has four other apps bundled in their productivity suite, which won't be covered in detail here, but for your reference, I'll explain what they are. They are not covered because this guide is meant to get you started quickly and only cover commonly used features and apps—these apps are used in some industries, but not widely adopted by most people.

### Google Drawing

The name "Drawing" kind of implies that this app is for all the little artists in the world—an online app to draw to your heart's content.

While you can do drawing on the app, it's not the sort of thing you use to create the next Mona Lisa. Google is collaborative software and there's not really a big market for collaborating on art-work. Instead, Google Drawing is more suited for things like flowcharts, organizational charts, wireframes, diagrams.

## Google Maps

Google Maps, unlike Google Drawing, is exactly what the name implies: a Google Map.

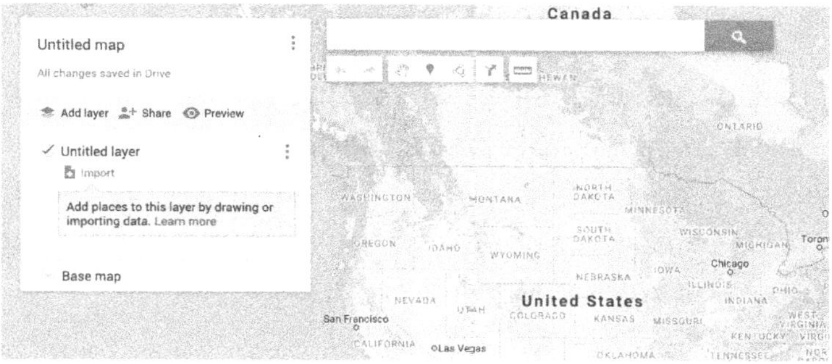


You can use it to add pins and layers.

## Google Sites

Wouldn't you love to create a website with no coding whatsoever? Well, get out from under your rock—there are lots and lots of websites for that: Squarespace, Wix, Weebly, just to name a few.

But for those who require free and ugly, there's Google Sites!

Google Sites isn't for people who want a webpage for their business. It's for people who want a very simple page that they can collaborate with others on. It would be great, for example, if you are making a fan site for your favorite TV show, and you want everyone to be a part of it.

### Google Jamboard

And finally: Jamboard.

Jamboard is basically a digital white board. If you are mounting a giant 4K TV and want to use Google, this is your solution. You can collaborate in real-time; it's perfect for business meetings and drawing cluster maps, but the hardware is too expensive for most consumers.

# PART 3: GOOGLE ANALYTICS

# INTRODUCTION

If you have a website, then you have probably already heard all about rate, exit rate, organic search traffic, and more. They're nice words, but how do you use them to understand your visitors and get more?

Google Analytics is a powerful resource that can tell you the smallest details about your visitor traffic, but if you are asking yourself what it means or why it even matters, then you're like most businesses. Analytics is so data heavy that you can be easily overwhelmed and lost.

If you are new to Analytics, or even have used it a few times, then this guide will help you understand what's in front of your eyes. It won't get into the weeds with professional tips better suited for professional marketers. It also won't go into detail about advanced Analytics elements—the keyword here is Basics! The goal is to get you started quickly.

Analytics will break down the data into simple terms that you can actually understand, so next time you open Analytics, or talk to your marketing team about what they're seeing, you'll be able to ask the right questions.

Ready to get started? Let's go!

# [1]
# Setting Up Shop

This chapter will cover:

- Creating an account
- The terms you should know

The goal of this book is to help you understand what's in Analytics. If you are brand new to Analytics and haven't even set it up, then you might need extra help. I'll walk you through what the steps are here, but getting started from scratch means you need to add a code into your website, and if you don't know how, then you'll probably need to ask your developer or CMS provider (i.e. SquareSpace, Wix, Weebly, etc).

Every platform has different steps for how this action is performed. If you are using a paid platform like SquareSpace to host your website, then they'll have a short tutorial and you can do it in less than five minutes. If someone has created a custom page for you, or you really aren't sure what you have, then you'll need to track down the person who created the page and ask.

## Setting Up Your Account

To get started, head over to analytics.google.com. It's going to quickly explain what you need to do, and then there's a button to sign up. Click that button:

Next it will ask you about your website (or mobile app in the case of an app). Just fill that information out, and then you will get a tracking code to add into your website. That's what you'll want to give your developer, or, copy and paste the code into your web host. It's really nothing technical! It's literally copying and pasting a line of HTML; the most difficult step is knowing where you are supposed to paste it, and that's where you'll need to seek a little help. It will be painless!

Once it's setup, then you'll see your main Analytics dashboard. I'll be using an example website that I have access to in this tutorial, so my data will obviously not match yours. If you are brand new to Analytics and just added the code, then you will show zero data. Just give it time. Google Analytics can only get data from the time you added the code—not from the time you created your website.

## Analytics Glossary

If you are new to Analytics, then bounce, exit new visitor, etc., might be words you've heard, but not necessarily words you understand. Before we jump into where everything is in Analytics, I'll start by going over some of the terms you should know.

There's going to be other terms that come up as we go, but these are the ones you'll hear the most.

- **Page Views/Unique Pageviews** – I'm grouping the first two together because what you really need to know here is not what it is but how it's different. Page views is what it sounds like—how many people view your page. A person may come back to your website or they may refresh their browser and load it again; there are a number of reasons why they might want to see your website more than once. Unique pageviews only counts the first time.

- **Sessions** – Just to throw you off a little more, let's mix Sessions into the views. Sessions sounds like page views, and in some ways it is, but many ways it isn't! Sessions tells you in a period of time (30 minutes) how many pages a user viewed. They might come back later, and this would mean the user has multiple unique Sessions. If you have a low number of Sessions, then that could tell you users aren't too interested in what your page is offering.
- **Avg. Time on Page** – Avg. Time on Page tells you exactly what it sounds like: the average time a viewer spent on a page. What's more important is knowing why that matters. Average Time on Page tells you if your page is working. Let's say you have 1,000 people going to your page that has 2,000 words, and the average time on page is ten seconds. A person will take anywhere from four to sixteen minutes to read something that long, but the average person is only on the page for ten seconds. What does that tell you? It tells you that people are not reading

what's on the page. If the traffic is good but the read time is bad, then the users' expectations are not being met. You need to fix the page.

- **Entrances** – Entrances are the number of times a page was the starting point for your traffic. For many companies, the page with the highest Entrances will be their main landing page; if there's another page with higher Entrances, then it could mean you have a page with higher SEO value, and you should think about how you're positioning that page to get the highest retention to your website.
- **Bounce Rate** – Bounce rate is the number of people who come to one of your webpages and then leave without clicking anything else. The lower the bounce rate the better. A high bounce rate tells you that people don't see value in what you're selling.
- **Exit Rate** – Bounce rate is frequently confused with Exit rate. Bounce rate tells a user the percentage of people who left your website after one session on the page. Exit rate tells you how many people were on this page as their last page. So a person could go to two or more

pages, but when they eventually leave, they leave on that page x% of the time.

- **New User** – A new user is someone who "technically" is new to your website. I say "technically" because Google can't tell if the person has visited your page before from a different location or if they've cleared their cookies (or turned cookies off). It's the best indicator you can get.
- **Organic Traffic** – Organic traffic is gold to a website. Ideally, you want this number as high as possible. It tells you how many people find your website organically—meaning they search for it and find it and you don't pay a dime to get them.
- **Conversion Rate** – Conversion rate is the percentage of users that take an action that you want them too. Let's say your goal is to have users click a Call-to-Action (CTA) (such as a button to sign up for your service). You have ten people come to the page and one person click on the button; that means your conversion rate is 10%. The goal is to get that conversion rate as high as possible.
- **Segment** – Segments is something you can define to help you understand your users. You could segment users

geographically, for example, to see if users in place X are more likely to do what you want the users in place Y. Or you could segment users who click your CTA to see if there's something about this group that you should know. For example, maybe people in this segment are more likely to have a previous action than your general users and to get more conversions, you just need to rethink what you are doing with the general users.

- **Sources** – Sources are where users come from. Do they come from social media (like Twitter or Facebook), referral traffic (someone mentions you on a blog), search engine, paid traffic, etc.

# [1]

# The Analytics Crash Course

This chapter will cover:

- Understanding basic elements of Analytics
- Who is audience?
- What is acquisition?

Now that we know the terms that are going to come up the most, let's look at Analytics from a high level and learn about where everything is and what everything does. Analytics really starts to shine when we start adding goals and running reports, but it's important to know where you can find measures before we get too deep into those things.

First things first, most of these sections will look very similar. As an example, here's the page for Channels in my Analytics:

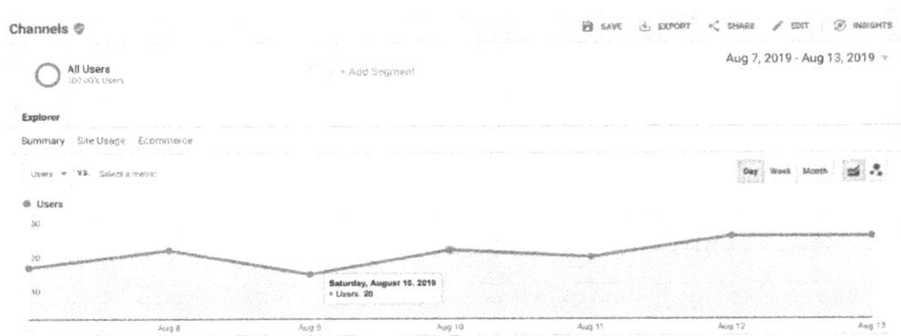


And here, the one for pages:

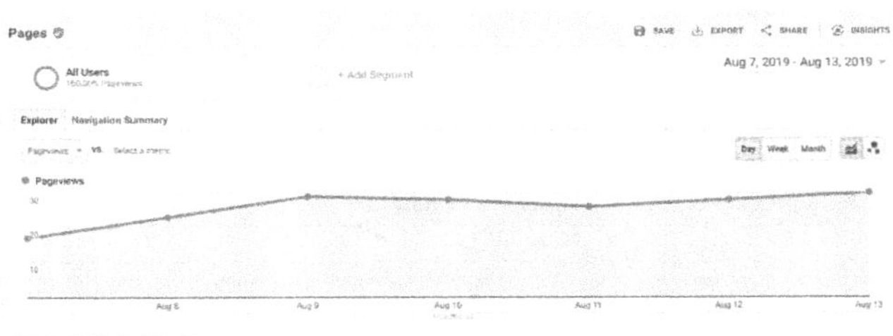


The graphics look different, obviously, but the buttons are pretty much the same. So let's talk about those buttons because once you understand them on one page, you can use them on all pages.

First, All Users and Add Segment. This is where you can change the view based on your predefined user. By default, you are looking at All Users. You can click on All Users and uncheck it, then check something else (or leave it checked and run it along something else)—for example you want to look at All Users and New Users side-by-side. Segments lets you create and save segments—you might create a segment, for example, that's only looking at New Users on Mobile Devices.

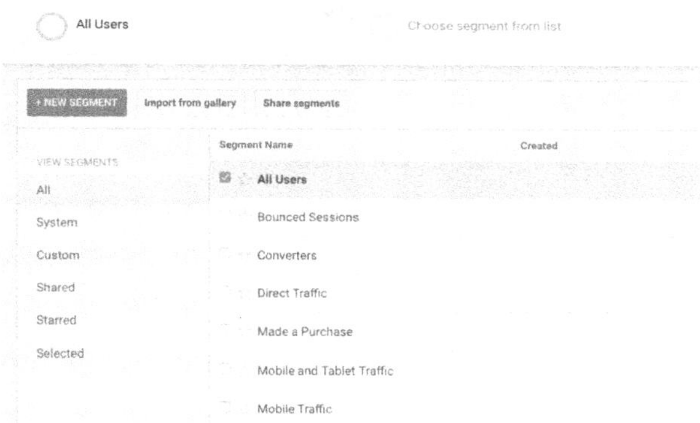


Over to the right side is a date. Date lets you select the period of time you're looking at. You can go back as far as you have had Analytics running. You can also do side-by-side comparisons so you can see where you were at the same period another year. This is helpful because sometimes you'll see a spike in traffic due to seasonality. You can look at that same period to see if there might be some seasonality in that spike:

Above the graph, you will see two tabs: Explorer and Navigation Summary. Explorer is the default graph. Navigation Summary is the report that helps you understand a single page a little deeper. You can use it for all pages, but it's particularly helpful when you are looking only at one page. It shows you the paths people took before and after that page—what page (if any) they were on before they entered this particular page and what page they went to afterwards.

Below these tabs is an option that says Pageviews vs. Select a metric. By default, it's not vs. anything. If you click that you can make it vs. several things—such as average time on page. You can also select Pageviews to change the graph you are seeing, for instance, if you want to see how bounce rate fluctuates month to month. If you've made changes to the page to improve the bounce rate, this is a good way to see if it has improved.

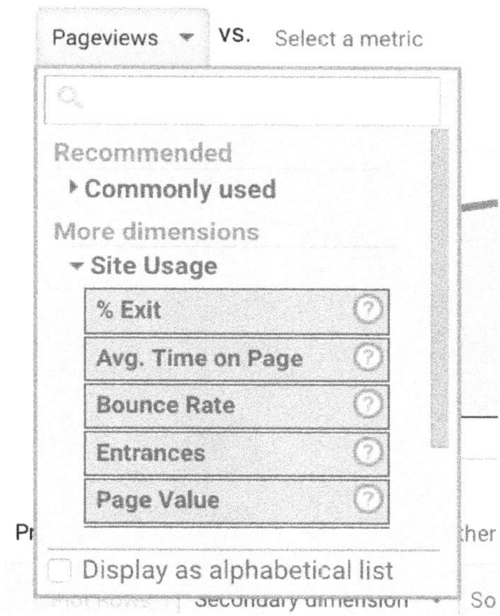


Below the graphic is a drop-down that says Secondary Dimension. This just adds one more column to your report:

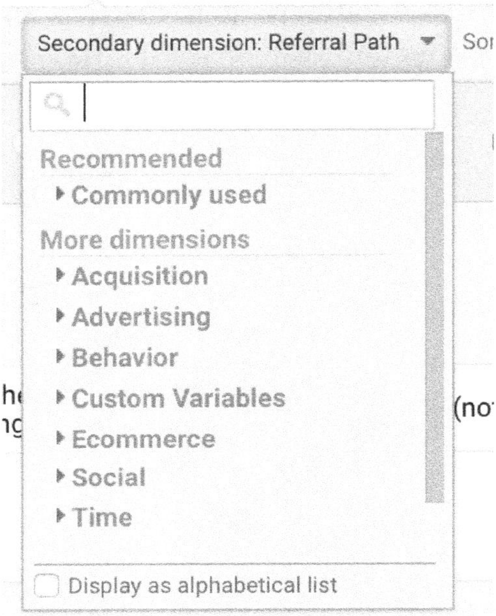


This is not very common, but you can also change the primary dimension just above this (it's a little bit smaller in size):

Let's say you're looking at all your pages and you just want to see how your blog is performing. If you click on advanced, you can run a report that searches for pages only containing a value (such as blog); this brings back only pages matching that criteria.

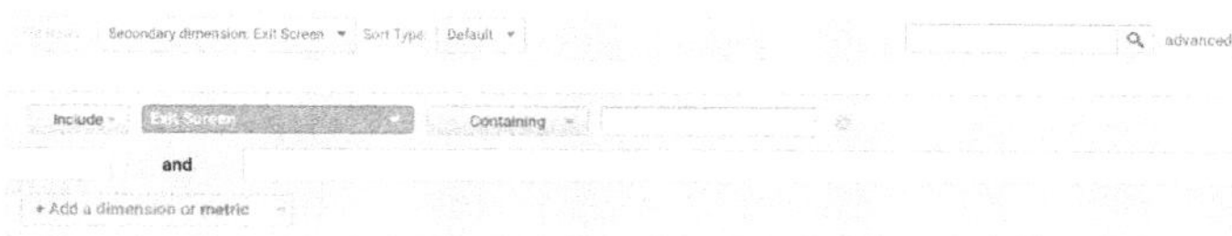


Over on the far right, there's an option to change how the results are displayed. By default, it's a grid; if you want to see any charts, click on any of these buttons to change the view:

Now that we know what some of the buttons do on these common reports, let's look at the different sections of Analytics. Go to the left side to the navigation. We'll look at each, beginning with Realtime. Click that section and it drills down to show you all the possible things you can see.

## Realtime

If your page is new, Realtime won't matter a lot. It shows you what's happening on your page, like, right now. If you have a new page, then there is probably nothing. Overview gives you a broad overview of everything happening. Locations is where visitors are geographically. Traffic sources tells where visitors are coming from. Content tells you what page people are on. Events tells you actions that are happening. Finally, Conversions tells you how many people are achieving a goal (I'll talk about goals a little later).

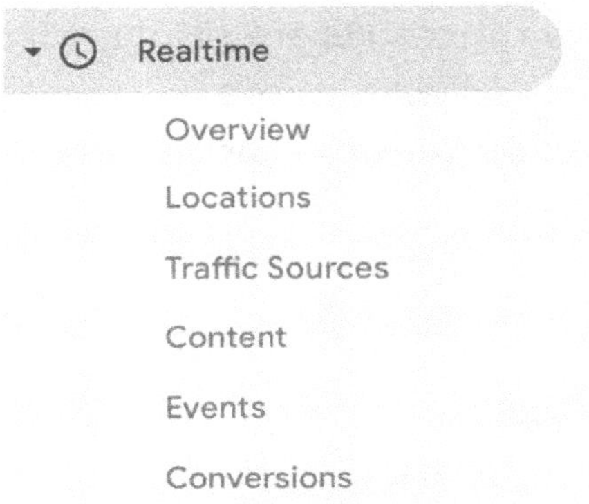


### Audience

Audience tells you about your audience and will help you as you think about segmenting. Most of these terms will be self-explanatory.

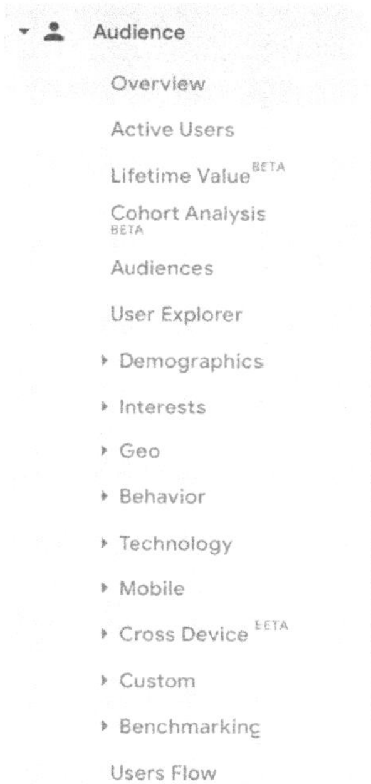


A few that aren't:

**Cohort Analysis**—This is a group of people who share a common characteristic. Think about a group of people at a concert. You can group them based on how many are wearing band t-shirts and how many aren't. Based on this data you can start saying things like "people in group x are more likely to do y than people in group z." It's useful when you are trying to find trends. To update it, use the dimensions. You can update who your "Cohort" is above the chart.

**Cross Device**—Currently in beta (which means this feature could change or completely go away soon), Cross Device helps you understand different behaviors based on the type of device the user is using (phone, tablet, PC, etc); this can help you understand if users start with one device, but don't convert unless they are on something else—and the paths they take to reach that conversion.

**Benchmarking**—Benchmarking lets you compare how your pages are doing against others in your industry.

**User Flows**—User flows helps you understand the pages users view as a whole. So in the example below, it's telling me the majority are starting in the United States and then going to one particular page. From there it shows me the next page they visited. It's helpful in determining where you have drop-off happening. You can also use it to look at specific pages. So let's say, for example, you have a sign-up page with five steps and only 30% of your users make it to the last page. You can use User Flows to see where most people stop the sign-up process and determine if maybe the process needs to be changed—maybe everyone drops off when you ask for a credit card, for example, and you have to reconsider asking for it during the sign-up—it could be a trust issue and people want to use the software before giving you their money.

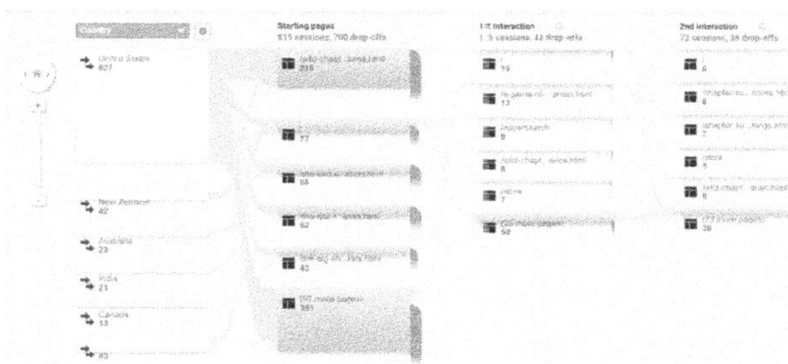

## Acquisition

Acquisition tells you how you are getting your users. If you are running ad campaigns, then it is highly recommended to follow the steps to connect the two so you can use analytics reporting alongside it. This book won't cover that, but there are books and videos on AdWords that will.

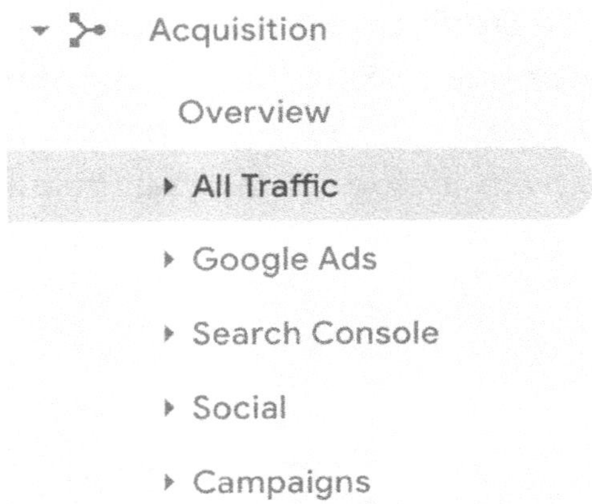


The place you will probably spend the most time in is All Traffic. In this drlil-down menu, you can see Channels (which breaks down organic traffic, referral traffic, etc); Sources (do people come from Yahoo more than Google, for example); and Referrals:

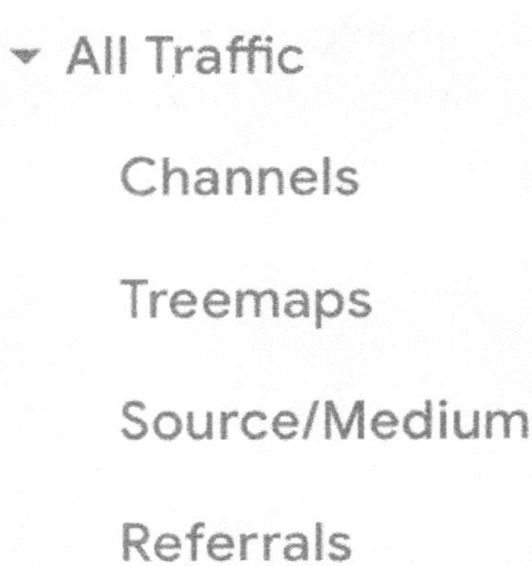

# [2]
# THE BASICS

This chapter will cover:

- Behavior
- Conversions
- Goals

## Behavior

All these segment tools are nice, but what you probably really want to know is how many people are even visiting your page. Behavior is where you will find that:

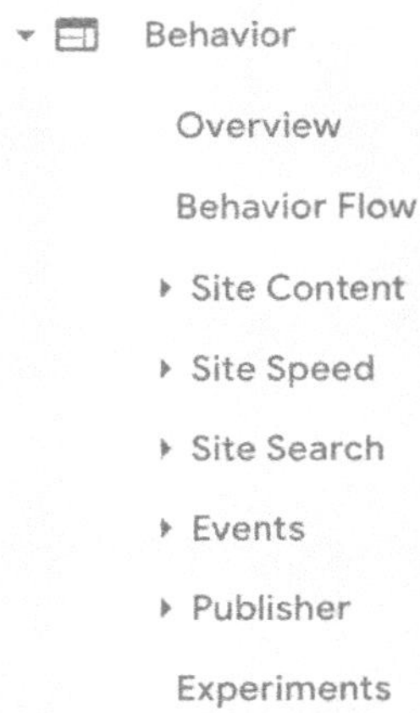


The area you'll probably spend the most time at is Site Content. That's where you can go to see how many people visit each of your pages. You can also break it down to see just your landing pages or exit pages:

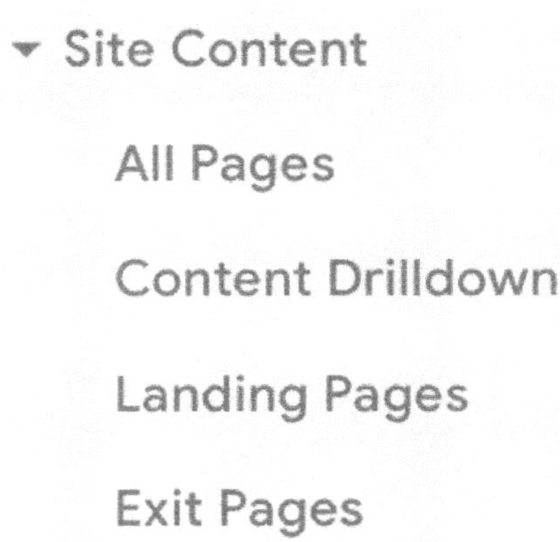

## Conversions

Conversions is one of the single most important areas of Analytics, but if you haven't used it, then it's not helpful at all. Before you can use it, you have to set up goals so it knows what it's measuring:

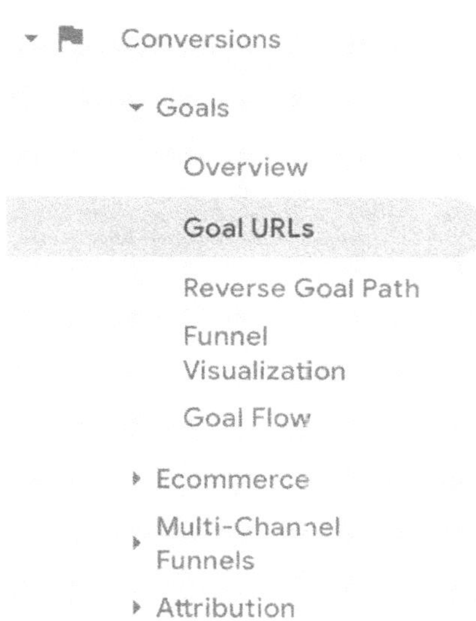


Goals can be anything you define. It can be the number of people who add things to a shopping cart or how many people actually make a purchase.

The area I use the most here is Reverse Goal Path. Reverse Goal Path tells me what people did before they reached their goal—what page they were on, for example.

## Goal!!!

Now that I got you all worked up about goals…how do you add them?

There are several ways—one is by going into your admin panel (from there go to Profile > Goal Tab > + Goal). But let's skip that. Click on Conversions > Overiew. If you don't have any goals, then it will look like this:

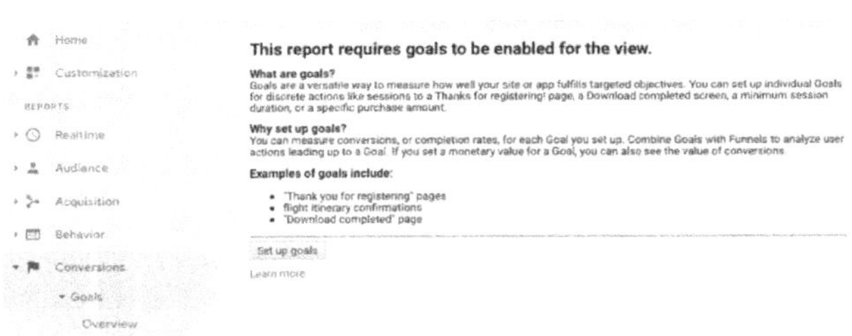


Click on Goals. From this page, click the red + New Goal button:

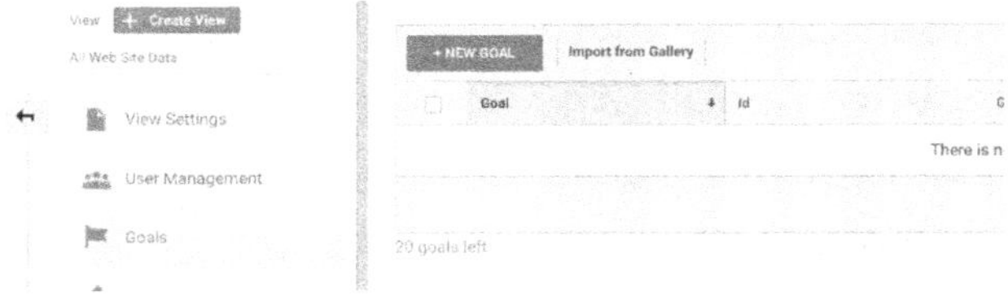

Next you need to set up your goal. It has a template of common goals to get you started:

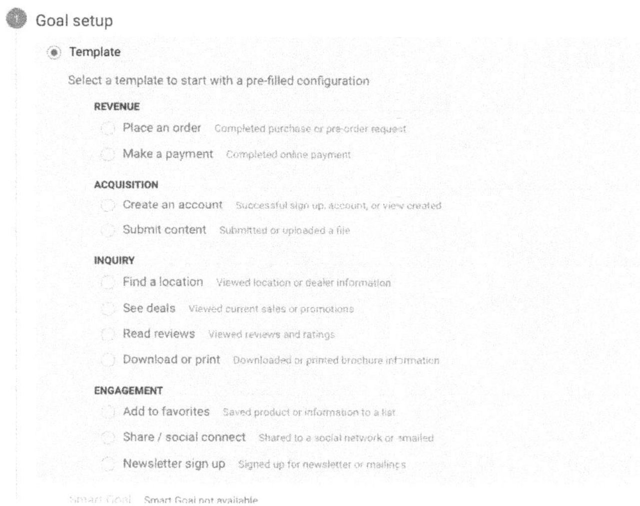


There are four types of templates:

- **Revenue** – a goal you make money from—for example, they buy something.
- **Acquisition** – they sign up for your service.
- **Inquiry** – They give some kind of information.
- **Engagement** – They share a page, sign up for a newsletter, or add the page to their favorites.

If you want to get fancy, then scroll to the bottom and click Custom.

You are currently limited to twenty goals, but if you delete a goal, then you can add a new one.

The next step is to name your goal and tell Analytics what kind of goal it is:

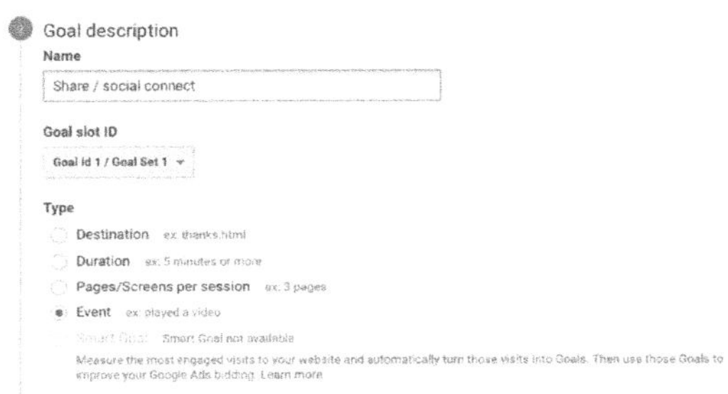


Finally, enter the details for the goal—how the goal is defined:

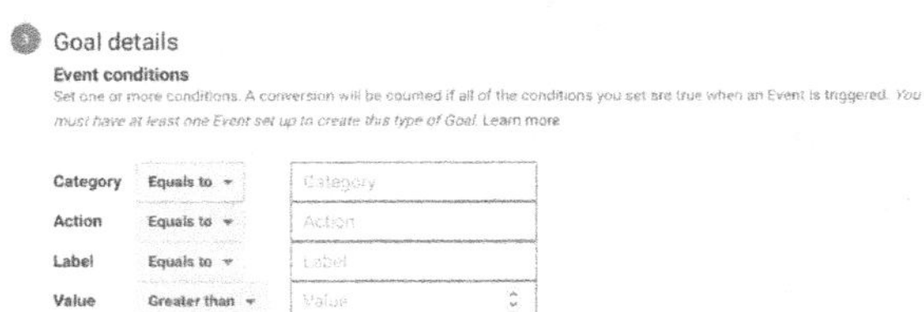

# [3]

# Dashboards and Reports

This chapter will cover:

- Creating custom dashboards
- Running reports

## Dashboards

All this data is nice, but do you really want to keep doing the same thing every single day to get the data you want? That's where Dashboards and Reports come in handy. They let you set pre-defined aspects that you regularly monitor. So you can go in and have the data you want already prepared for you.

Dashboards is a bit high-level; it can show you several data points in one area that's a bit more visual then a report. Reports lets you focus on smaller details.

We'll start with Dashboards. Go to your left menu and click Customization. Next, click Dashboards:

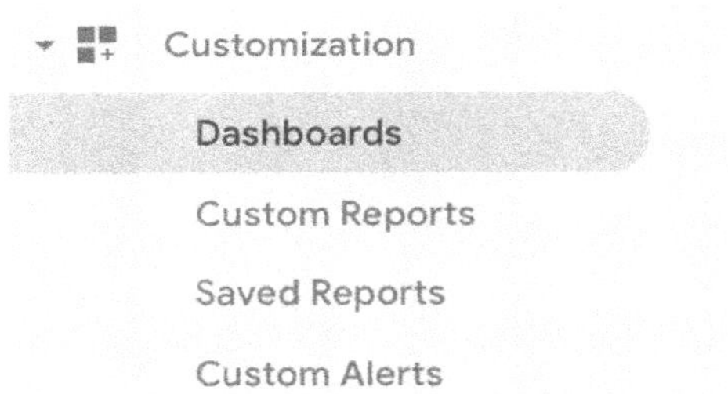


If you already had a Dashboard, then you'd open it from here. Since we haven't created one, then click the red Create button:

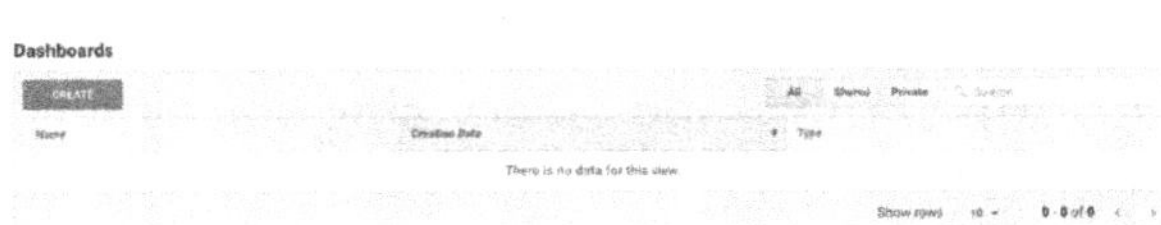

It's going to give you three options. Two on the top (Blank Canvas and Starter Dashboard) and one on the bottom (Import from Gallery):

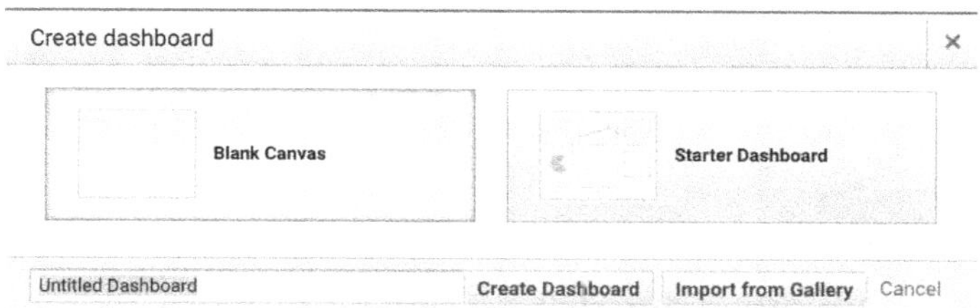


Import from Gallery is a fun place to start. The gallery is where top marketers have shared their dashboards that you can essential clone to fit your own. Personally, I found it helpful when learning about Analytics, but once I knew my way around, I wanted to create custom Dashboards.

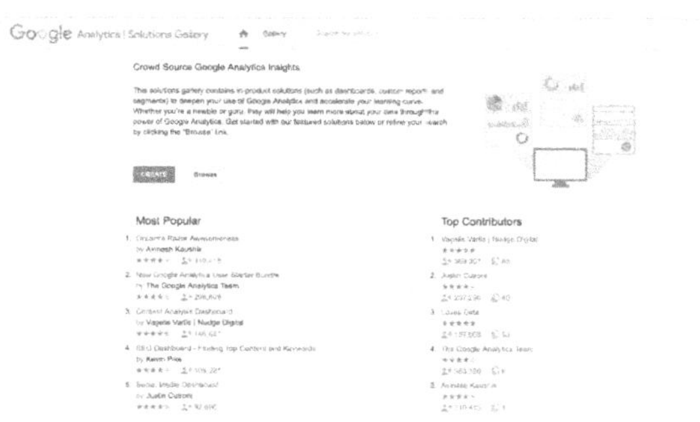


Starter Dashboard is also a helpful Dashboard to start with. It gives you all the Widgets (widgets are what Analytics calls each area of your Dashboard—you can have a widget that's a chart, a number, or several other things), that are commonly used in Dashboards:

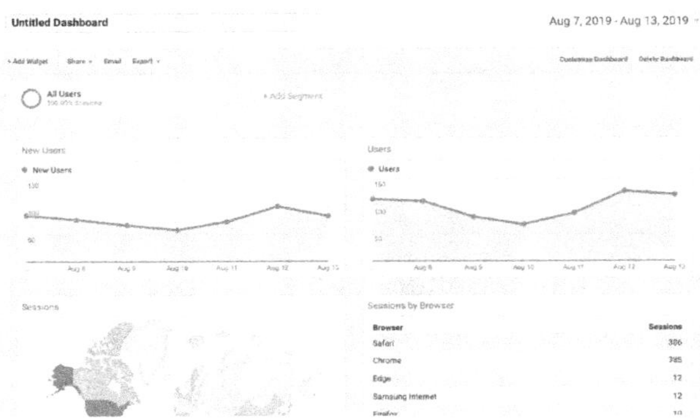


You can customize how it looks by clicking on Customize Dashboard over in the right corner:

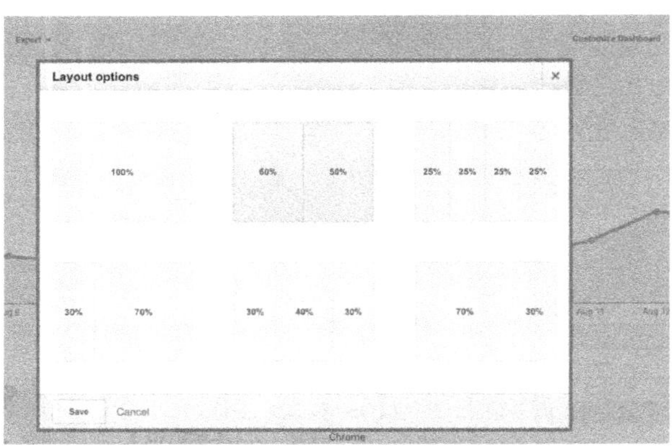

On the top left, you can add a new Widget, share your report with users of your organization, email it to people, or export it:

The last option (Blank Canvas) starts things from scratch, so it will be up to you to define everything. When you select this option, the first thing you'll have to do is add a Widget. I'm going to add a 2.1 (it will make the Widget a number), and make the metric % of New Sessions:

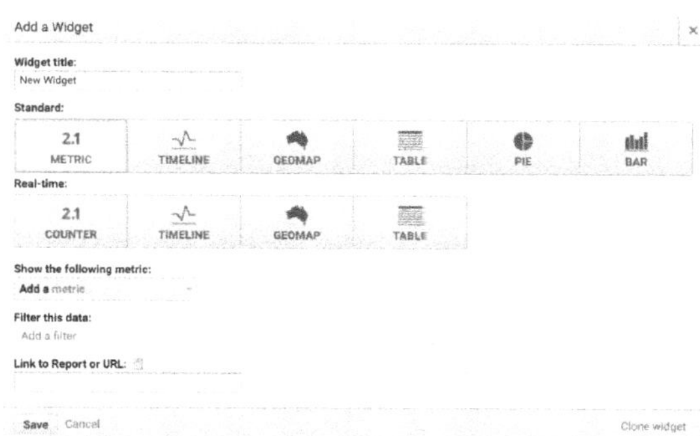


Once I save my Widget, it will appear on the canvas:

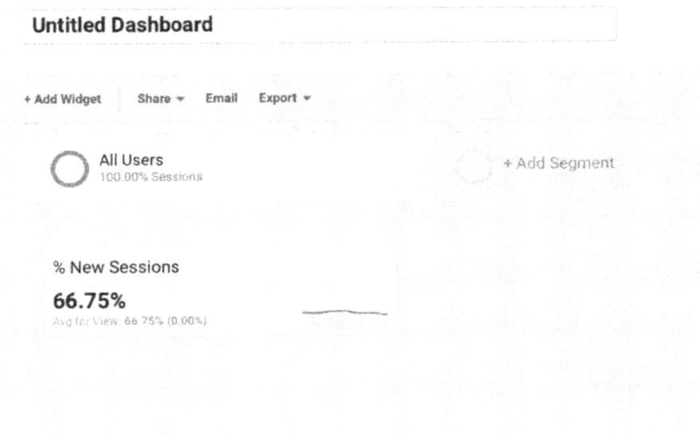


That's a bit lonely. I'm going to select Add Widget and create a timeline widget that compares Exit to New Sessions:

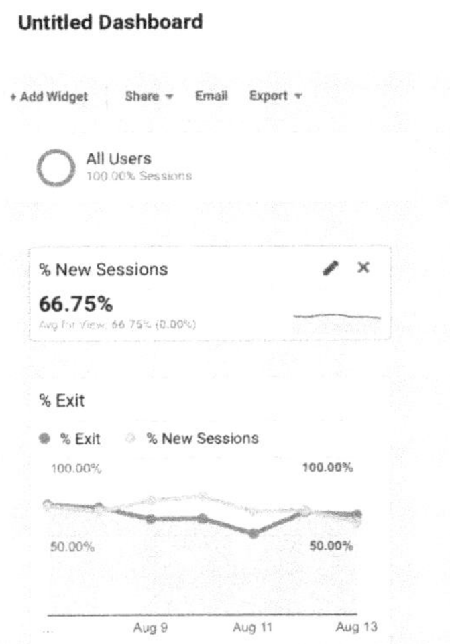

Now that you have more than one Widget, you can click and drag any of the Widgets to move its place on the canvas. As you move it, you'll see areas that turn green; when you see that, you can snap it into the new area:

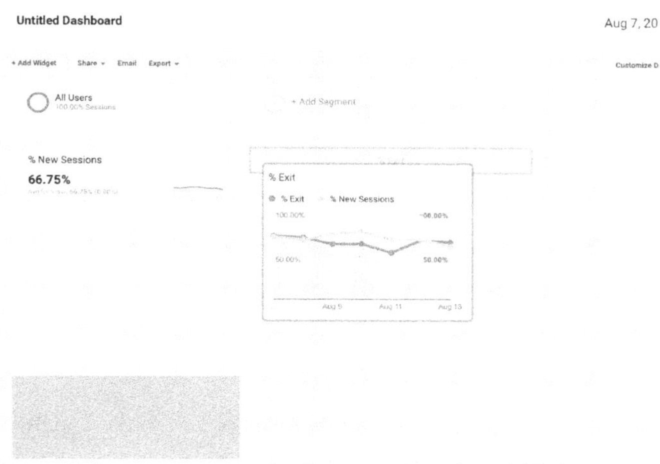


## Reports

Creating reports is similar to Dashboards—the results just look different. Go to the left menu, click Customization, and then Custom Reports. Once you save the report it will show up in the next menu item: Custom Reports:

The report creator asks you what exactly you want to show and how you want to show it—such as a text/column view or graph:

I'll start with something simple: A Flat Table of all my pages with the metric being Sessions:

This presents the results as a table:

Changing the view (but keeping the values the same), I switched to Explorer, and it shows me a graphic (with a data table under it):

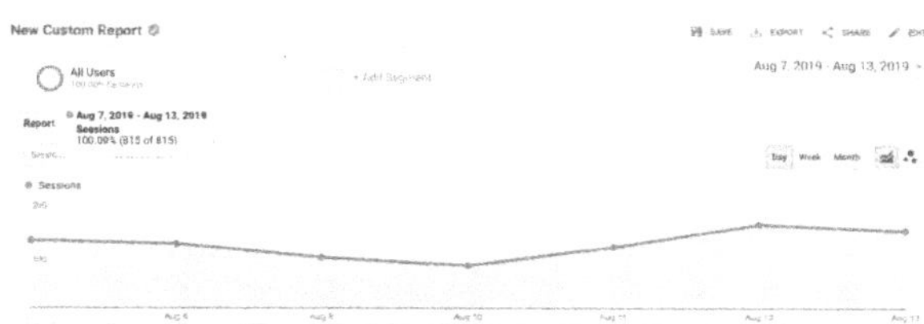


The last report shows me the data as a map of where the sessions are located in the world:

I can edit any of these reports by clicking on the Edit button in the upper right corner:

Just because you have a report doesn't mean it's going to be there when you return. Unlike most things Google does, reports do not save automatically. The reason is you'll probably run a lot of single-use reports. To save it, click the Save button in the upper right corner:

This will ask you to give it a name. Once it's named, you can view the report at any time by going to your left menu then Customization > Saved Reports:

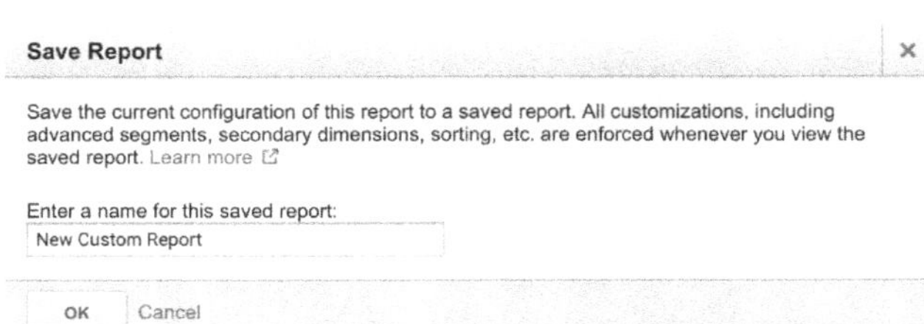

That's a very simple look at Google Analytics. Hopefully, by now you have some questions and more things you want to try. The goal of this book was to get you to a place where you knew the questions to ask and the things to look for, so I hope it accomplished that.

# [4] Google Search Console

This chapter will cover:

- What is Google Search Console?
- How to set up Google Search Console?
- Finding your keywords

One thing it didn't show you: Keywords. You now know how to find where visitors went, who they were, and where they came from. But Google didn't tell you the keywords they used to find it.

To get that, you need another free Google tool: Google Search Console. Go here to get started: https://search.google.com/search-console/

Just like Analytics, there's a lot there. What we are concerned with, however is that keyword/search traffic, so I won't go over other things.

If you've never used Search Console, then you'll have to set it up first—you have to set it up even if you've set up Analytics already; I recommend setting it up together just so you aren't adding codes twice; you can get it done in one shot.

It's going to ask you how you want to set it up: Domain or Prefix:

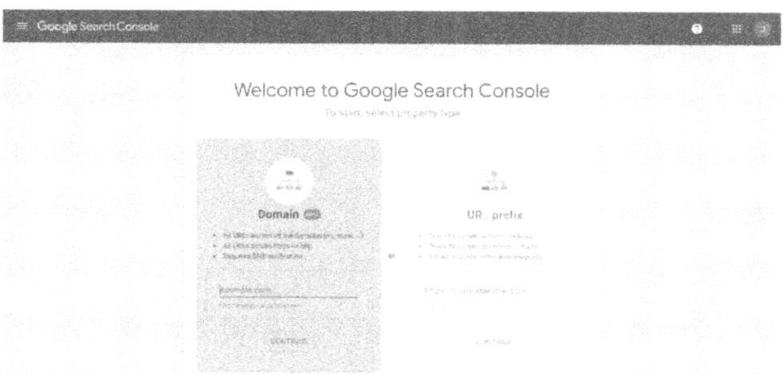


Then it will have you verify it by pasting in the code:

Once it's in, you'll have your main dashboard. Mine has data because it's been running for a while. Just like Analytics, the tracking starts after you add in the code, so it will take a few days—or up to a few weeks—before it shows anything. It's a bit slower in reporting than Analytics, which tracks in realtime.

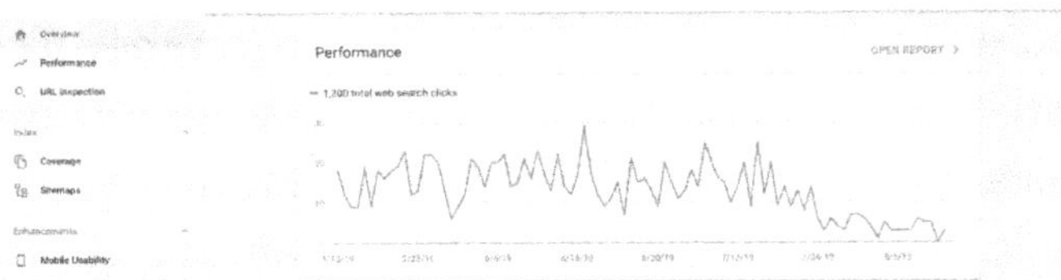


The area we will want is Performance. You can get it on the left menu:

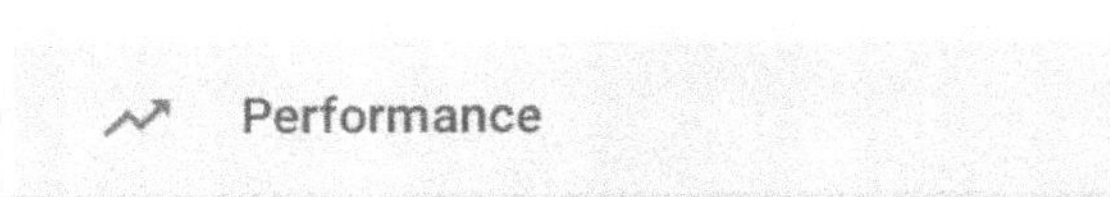


This report tells us overall how the website is doing:

Up on top, you can change the data ranges:

Beneath that, it shows you what the report is showing. The white areas mean it's not showing that in the graph or report. Click the last two so the columns will be added:

Once you click them, they change colors:

Below the graph is your report. You can see the search terms (queries) people are using, pages, countries, devices, and search appearances:

Let's start with Queries. This shows me all the terms people have used to find my website:

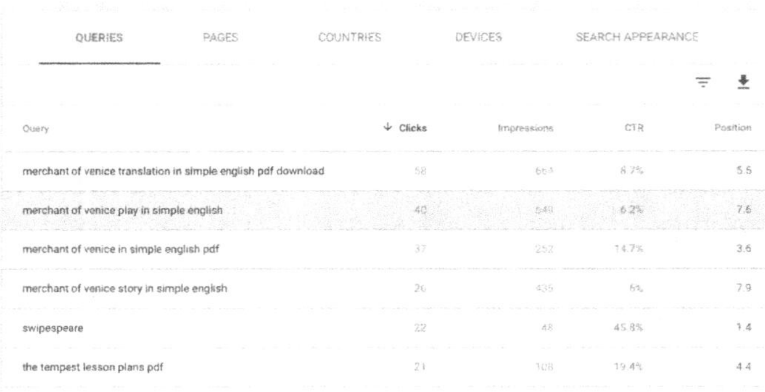


You can sort each column. The first column, Clicks, shows me how many people click on that page after they see it in a search:

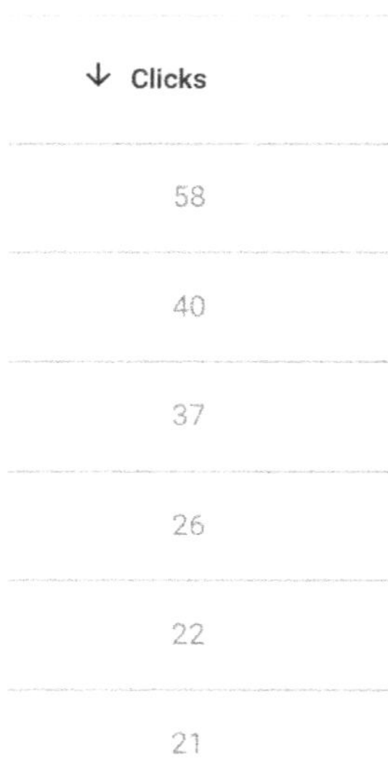

Impressions tells me how many times it's shown up in a search result (regardless of if it's tracked):

| ↓ Impressions |
| --- |
| 1,266 |
| 664 |
| 649 |
| 582 |
| 465 |
| 435 |
| 252 |

CTR is the percentage of people who click on it when they see it in the search results. So let's say the impression is 1,000 and the clicks is 100; that means 10% click it when they see it in the search results.

| ↓ CTR |
| --- |
| 100% |
| 100% |
| 100% |
| 100% |
| 50% |
| 45.8% |
| 34.4% |

Finally, Position tells you the place in the results it is. The lower, the better—everyone wants the coveted #1 place:

Click on any of the search queries and it will show you what page is ranking for that keyword—sometimes you'll have several pages:

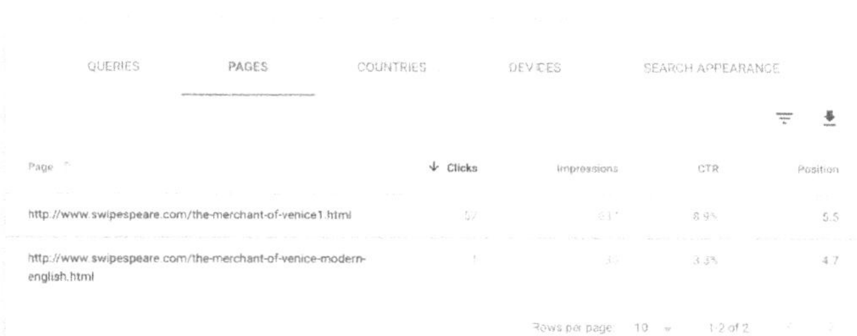

To get back to all queries, go up to the top of the page, and hit the X next to the query name:

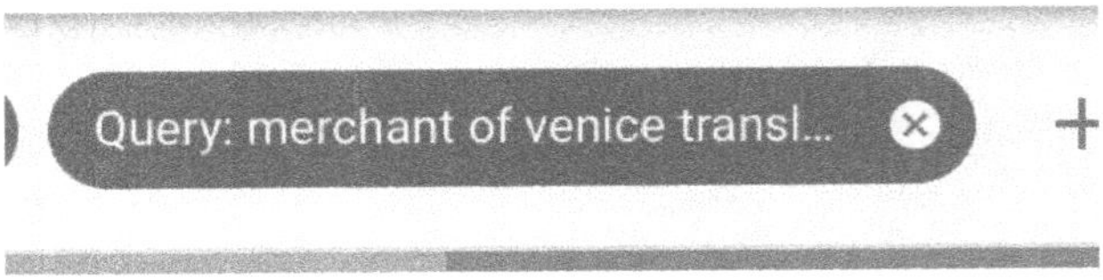


That's it! You now know how to analyze your traffic and how to find the keywords they're coming from.

# About the Author

Scott La Counte is a librarian and writer. His first book, *Queit, Please: Dispatches from a Public Librarian* (Da Capo 2008) was the editor's choice for the Chicago Tribune and a Discovery title for the Los Angeles Times; in 2011, he published the YA book The N00b Warriors, which became a #1 Amazon bestseller; his most recent book is *#OrganicJesus: Finding Your Way to an Unprocessed, GMO-Free Christianity* (Kregel 2016).

He has written dozens of best-selling how-to guides on tech products.

You can connect with him at ScottDouglas.org.

CPSIA information can be obtained
at www.ICGtesting.com
Printed in the USA
LVHW111523061122
732493LV00005B/60

9 781629 178066